From *the*

Grand Canal
to the Dodder

Illustrious Lives

From the Grand Canal to the Dodder

Illustrious Lives

Beatrice M. Doran

The History Press

For my late parents and my sister Madeleine

Cover illustrations: © Patrick Tutty

First published 2020

The History Press
97 St George's Place,
Cheltenham,
Gloucestershire,
GL50 3QB
www.thehistorypress.co.uk

British Library Cataloguing in Publication Data.
A catalogue record for this book is available from the British Library.

ISBN 978 0 7509 9557 3

Typesetting and origination by Typo•glyphix, Burton-on-Trent
Printed and bound by TJ Books Limited

Contents

Acknowledgments 11

Picture Credits 12

Introduction 13

Aikenhead, Mother Mary (1787–1858) Founder, Religious Order 14
    15 Gilford Road, Sandymount, Dublin 4

Armstrong, Harry Reginald (Reg) (1928–1979) 17
    9–19 Ringsend Road, Ringsend, Dublin 4

Ashford, William (1746–1824) Landscape Artist 21
    Sandymount House (Roselyn Park), Sandymount, Dublin 4

Barry, Spranger (1719–1777) Actor 24
    Mespil Road & Merrion Road, Dublin 4

Beatty, Sir Alfred Chester (1875–1968) Mining Engineer and
    Philanthropist 27
    10 Ailesbury Road, Ballsbridge, Dublin 4

Behan, Beatrice (1925–1993) Artist 31
    5 Anglesea Road, Donnybrook, Dublin 4

Behan, Brendan (1923–1964) Writer and Dramatist 34
    5 Anglesea Road, Donnybrook, Dublin 4

Bernelle, Agnes (1923–1999) Cabaret Artist 37
    9 Strand Road, Sandymount, Dublin 4

Best, Richard Irvine (1872–1959) Celtic Scholar and Librarian 40
    57 Upper Leeson Street, Dublin 4

Briscoe, Robert Emmett (1894–1969) Former Lord Mayor and Politician 43
    12 Herbert Park, Ballsbridge, Dublin 4

Bryant, Sophie (1850–1922) Mathematician, Educationist and Suffragette 46
    Sandymount, Dublin 4

Butler, Eleanor (1914–1997) Lady Wicklow, Architect and Politician 49
    73 Ailesbury Road, Donnybrook, Dublin 4

Byrne, Frankie (1922–1993) Broadcaster and Public Relations
  Consultant 52
    Dunbur, Brookvale Road, Donnybrook, Dublin 4

Cameron, Sir Charles Alexander (1830–1921) Physician and City
  Medical Officer for Health 55
    27 Raglan Road, Ballsbridge, Dublin 4

Coghill, Rhoda (1903–2000) Pianist, Composer and Poet 59
    100 Marlborough Road, Donnybrook, Dublin 4

Colles, Abraham (1773–1843) Professor of Surgery and President, RCSI 62
    Donnybrook Cottage, Stillorgan Road, Donnybrook, Dublin 4

Colum, Mary Catherine (1887–1957) Critic and Teacher 65
    2 Belmont Avenue, Donnybrook, Dublin 4

Colum, Padraic (1881–1972) Poet, Novelist and Playwright 68
    2 Belmont Avenue, Donnybrook, Dublin 4

Costello, John Aloysius (1891–1976) Taoiseach and Attorney General 71
    20 Herbert Park, Donnybrook, Dublin 4

De Valera, Éamon (1882–1975) Taoiseach and President of Ireland 75
    33 Morehampton Terrace, Donnybrook, Dublin 4

De Valera, Sinéad (1878–1975) Teacher, Author and Playwright 79
    33 Morehampton Terrace, Donnybrook, Dublin 4

Dunlop, John Boyd (1840–1921) Veterinary Surgeon and Inventor 82
    Leighton, 46 Ailesbury Road, Donnybrook, Dublin 4

FitzGerald, Garret (1926–2011) Politician, Taoiseach and Economist 85
    75 Eglinton Road, Donnybrook, Dublin 4

French, William Percy (1854–1920) Engineer, Writer and Artist   88
    35 Mespil Road, Dublin 4

Fuller, James Franklin (1835–1924) Architect   91
    83 Eglinton Road, Donnybrook, Dublin 4

Goodfellow, Kathleen (1891–1980) Writer, Poet and Translator   94
    4 Morehampton Road, Donnybrook, Dublin 4

Heaney, Seamus (1939–2013) Poet and Translator   97
    Strand Road, Sandymount, Dublin 4

Hearn, Lafcadio (1850–1904) Writer and Translator   101
    73 Upper Leeson Street, Dublin 4

Heath, Lady Mary (1896–1939) Aviator and International Athlete   104
    Pembroke Road, Dublin 4

Hooper, Patrick Joseph (1873–1931) Barrister and Journalist   107
    102 Morehampton Road, Donnybrook, Dublin 4

Humphreys (Ui Dhonnchadha), Sighle (1899–1994) Republican Activist   110
    17 Eglinton Park, Donnybrook, Dublin 4

Jones, Sir Thomas Alfred (1823–1893) Portrait Painter   113
    41 Morehampton Road, Donnybrook, Dublin 4

Kane, Sir Robert (1809–1890) First President of Queen's College, Cork   116
    2 Wellington Road, Ballsbridge, Dublin 4

Kavanagh, Patrick (1904–1967) Poet and Journalist   120
    62 Pembroke Road, Ballsbridge, Dublin 4

Kelleher, Kevin D. (1921–2016) Headmaster   123
    St Conleth's College, Ballsbridge, Dublin 4

Kellett, Iris Patricia (1926–2011) International Showjumper   127
    Mespil Road, Dublin 4

Kettle, Thomas Michael (1880–1916) Parliamentarian, Writer and Soldier   131
    119 Upper Leeson Street, Dublin 4

Kiely, Benedict (1919–2007) Writer and Journalist   134
119 Morehampton Road, Donnybrook, Dublin 4

Larkin, Delia (1878–1949) Trade Unionist and Journalist   137
41 Wellington Road, Ballsbridge, Dublin 4

Laverty, Maura (1907–1966) Writer and Broadcaster   140
25 Pembroke Road, Dublin 4

Lavin, Mary (1912–1996) Short Story Writer and Novelist   143
5 Guilford Place, Sandymount, Dublin 4

May, Frederick (Freddie) (1911–1985) Music Composer   146
38 Marlborough Road, Donnybrook, Dublin 4

McBride, Maud Gonne (1866–1953) Irish Revolutionary   149
Floraville, Eglinton Road, Donnybrook, Dublin 4

McCourt, Kevin (1915–2000) Businessman and Director General
of RTÉ   152
Harmony Cottage, Eglinton Road, Donnybrook, Dublin 4

MacNeill, Eoin (1867–1945) Nationalist and Politician   156
63 Upper Leeson Street, Dublin 4

Mitchell, Susan Langstaff (1866–1926) Writer and Poet   160
21 Wellington Road, Ballsbridge, Dublin 4

Nangle, Edward (1800–1883) Church of Ireland Clergyman   163
23 Morehampton Road, Donnybrook, Dublin 4

O'Connor, Batt (1870–1935) Builder and Politician   167
1 Brendan Road, Donnybrook, Dublin 4

O'Kelly, Seán T. (1882–1966) President of Ireland   170
38 Anglesea Road, Ballsbridge, Dublin 4

O'Rahilly, Michael Joseph (The O'Rahilly) (1875–1916)   173
40 Herbert Park, Ballsbridge, Dublin 4

Pearse, Margaret Mary (1878–1968) Educator and Politician   176
   5 George's Villas, Sandymount, Dublin 4

Pearse, Padraig (1879–1916) Barrister, Writer and Revolutionary   179
   5 George's Villas, Sandymount, Dublin 4

Plunkett, Joseph Mary (1887–1916) Poet and Revolutionary   183
   17 Marlborough Road, Donnybrook, Dublin 4

Purser, Sarah (1848–1943) Portrait Painter and Artist   186
   Mespil House, Mespil Road, Dublin 4

Roe, Alderman George (1796–1863) Distiller and Former Lord Mayor
   of Dublin   189
     Nutley, Priesthouse, Donnybrook, Dublin 4

Salkeld, Blanaid (1880–1959) Poet, Publisher and Actor   193
   43 Morehampton Road, Donnybrook, Dublin 4

Shackleton, Sir Ernest (1874–1922) Antarctic Explorer   196
   35 Marlborough Road, Donnybrook, Dublin 4

Smyllie, Robert M. (1893–1954) Editor of the *Irish Times*   199
   23 Pembroke Park, Donnybrook, Dublin 4

Solomons, Estella Frances (1882–1968) Artist and Portrait Painter   202
   2 Morehampton Road, Donnybrook, Dublin 4

Starkie, Enid Mary (1897–1970) Academic and Writer   206
   Melfort, Shrewsbury Road, Ballsbridge, Dublin 4

Starkie, Walter Fitzwilliam (1894–1976) Hispanic Scholar and
   Travel Writer   209
     Melfort, Shrewsbury Road, Ballsbridge, Dublin 4

Travers, Pamela L. (1889–1996) Writer and Novelist   212
   69 Upper Leeson Street, Dublin 4

Trollope, Anthony (1815–1882) Writer and Novelist   215
   5 Seaview Terrace, Donnybrook, Dublin 4

Whitaker, Thomas Kenneth (Ken) (1916–2017) Economist and Civil
   Servant   219
     148 Stillorgan Road, Donnybrook, Dublin 4

Woods, Mary (Mollie) Flannery (1875–1954) Republican Activist   223
     St Enda's, 131 Morehampton Road, Donnybrook, Dublin 4

Yeats, Jack B. (1871–1957) Artist   227
     61 Marlborough Road, Donnybrook, Dublin 4

Yeats, William Butler (1865–1939) Poet and Nobel Prize Winner   230
     5 Sandymount Avenue, Sandymount, Dublin 4

Select Bibliography   235
Index   241

Acknowledgements

Many people, libraries and archives helped me with my research for this book. I am grateful in particular to the staff of the following institutions:

Ballsbridge, Donnybrook & Sandymount Historical Society, Chester Beatty Library Dublin City Library services – Pembroke Library (Librarians Angela O'Connell and Liz Turley). Staff of the Gilbert Library, Dublin City Libraries, Dublin City Archives (Dr Mary Clark). Dublin Institute for Advanced Studies, Fuigi Merrion (Conor McCarthy), Institute for Advanced Studies, Irish Architectural Archive, National Gallery Photographic Unit. Representative Church Body, National Library of Ireland, Nutley Newsagent, The Library of the Royal Dublin Society (Gerard Whelan). Royal Irish Academy, Royal College of Surgeons in Ireland Library, UCD Libraries, Belfield and Smurfit Business School Library (Blackrock). Model Gallery, Sligo. Mother Superior, Religious Sisters of Charity.

Thank you to: Dr Eileen Campbell (for proof reading). Julie Armstrong Bostock, Michael Brennan, Dr Cliona Buckley, Dr Mary Clark (City Archivist), Enda Cogan, Sheila Cosgrave, Professor Fergus D'Arcy, Patricia Elliott, Gay Fallon, Penelope FitzGerald, Dr Susan Hood, John Gormley, Harry Havelin, Marie Heaney, Peter Hooper, Felicia Hulme-Beaman, Dr Vivien Igoe, Liam Kavanagh, Frances Kiely, Aine Kearney, Will Keating, Peter Kelly, Deirdre Ellis King, Ita Kirwan, Gillian and Denis Leonard, McCourt Family, Kathleen MacMahon, Croine and Manchan Magan, Ciaran McGonagle, Madeleine McKeown, Brian Maye, Bob Montgomery, Sean J. Murphy, Agnes Neligan, Honor O' Brolchain, Brendan O'Connor, Patricia O'Loan, Hilary Pyle, Annette Quigley, Ann Shepherd, Somerville College University of Oxford, Rory Spain, Eileen Spelman, Dr John Taylor, Dr Patricia Taylor, Dr Elizabeth Twohig, Blanaid Behan Walker, Margaret Walsh, Marion Walsh, Gerard Whelan, Brian Whitaker, Nicky Whitsed. Thank you to the staff of The History Press (Nicola Guy, Juanita Hall and Molly Evans) for their help and advice.

Picture Credits

Alex Aixel
Julie Armstrong Bostock
Board of Trinity College
Chester Beatty Library
Dublin City Library & Archives
Contemporary Music Centre of Ireland
Ersas Films
Jim Fitzpatrick
Marie Heaney
History Ireland
Peter Hooper
Irish Labour Party
Patrick Kavanagh Centre
Irish Architectural Archive
Dr Vivien Igoe
Frances Kiely
Gillian & Denis Leonard
Library Ireland
McCourt family
Grandaughter of Mary Lavin
Croine & Manchan Magan
National Gallery of Ireland
National Library of Ireland
Dermot Peavoy

Pearse Museum
Honor O Brolchain
Percy French Society
Religious Sisters of Charity
Royal Hibernian Academy
Royal Holloway
University of London
Royal College of Surgeons in Ireland
RTÉ Archives
St Conleth's College
Trollope Society
University College Cork
Blanaid Behan Walker
Brian Whitaker
Woods family
Fitzgerald family
Fenian Graves
Harry Havelin
Institute of Advanced Studies
Aine Kearney
Lafcadio Hearn Library
University Archives, Hollins University (Virginia)
Brian Whitaker

Introduction

This book is about people who lived in Ballsbridge, Donnybrook, Sandymount Ringsend and Irishtown. Historically most of this area was part of the estate of the Earl of Pembroke. During the nineteenth century, for local government purposes, townships were formed in Dublin, and the area became part of the Pembroke Township, and an urban district in 1899. A Local Government Act of 1930, dissolved Pembroke Urban District, and added it to the City of Dublin.

I hope that readers will rediscover people who who lived in the area and who appear in this book. I sought advice from friends, librarians and archivists in relation to who should be included, but it was not possible to include everyone they suggested. I enjoyed finding family members, who generously gave of their time, and provided me with information and photographs. The select bibliography lists the major sources I used in my research – books, newspaper and journal articles, together with online resources.

The choice of individuals for inclusion in this book is, of necessity, subjective. The earliest biography dates from the eighteenth century and is that of Spranger Barry, an Irish actor who was celebrated on the London stage, and who is buried in Westminster Abbey. The most modern entry was for the late T.K. Whitaker, renowned civil servant and Secretary to the Department of Finance during the 1950s and '60s, who died in 2017. I chose people from the area who, in my view, led interesting and illustrious lives and with who readers might not be familiar.

From the eighteenth century, the aristocratic classes in Dublin society lived on the north side of the River Liffey. However, when James Fitzgerald (1722–1773), Duke of Leinster, built a substantial home on the south side (now Leinster House), far from other aristocratic residences, on the north side, he was soon followed south of the Liffey, just as he had predicted. Many of the wealthy inhabitants of the City of Dublin migrated to the south-side suburbs in the late nineteenth and early twentieth centuries. The professional, business, political and artistic classes built individual villa-style houses, laid out on leafy roads with large gardens. They have continued to live on the tree-lined avenues, characteristic of this elegant area of Dublin.

Dr Beatrice M. Doran
Dublin, 2020

Aikenhead, Mother Mary (1787–1858)
Founder, Religious Order
15 Gilford Road, Sandymount, Dublin 4

Born Mary Aikenhead in Cork in 1787, her parents were Dr David Aikenhead, who owned an apothecary's shop in the city, and his wife Mary (*née* Stackpole), the daughter of a Cork merchant. There were four children in Mary's family, three girls and a boy. Mary's father was a Protestant and her mother a Catholic. Their children were all brought up in the Protestant faith of their father. As a child, Mary was not considered very strong, and as happened so often in those days, she was fostered out to a Mary Rorke, who lived on Eason's Hill, Shandon, Cork. Mary Rorke and her family were Catholics, and as Mary Aikenhead grew up there, she attended Mass every Sunday with the Rorke family, which she loved, and generally partook of their other religious observances. Her father and mother visited her every week. Finally, in 1793 when she was 6 years old, it was decided that she should re-join the family at their home in Daunt's Square in the city of Cork. Her parents employed Mary Rorke as the family nanny, and she moved to the Aikenhead household together with her husband, who became David Aikenhead's coachman.

When Mary's father was dying, he became a Catholic on his deathbed, and later, on 6 June 1802, when she was 15, Mary too was received into the Catholic Church. Her brother and sisters also became Catholics some years later. Mary was greatly influenced by her aunt, Mrs Rebecca Gorman, her mother's sister, who was a Catholic, and she frequently accompanied her to daily Mass. After her father died, Mary helped her mother run the household, and became involved in their financial affairs, which would stand to her later in life, and contribute to her business acumen, as founder of the Religious Sisters of Charity. While still in Cork she and a friend became aware of the extreme poverty in the city, and they collected food and clothes from their friends and redistributed them to the poor. In Cork as a young girl, Mary had a good social life due to her family's standing in society, so she attended balls, concerts etc. with her many friends and family.

Through the influence of her friend Anna Maria O'Brien, with whom she stayed in Dublin, Mary met Dr Daniel Murray, Coadjutor Bishop of Dublin, who went on to become Archbishop of Dublin. This was a period in Irish history when there was growing unemployment and a number of outbreaks of cholera in the city. Dr Murray had a great interest in helping the poor and was keen to establish an order of nuns to visit and look after the poor of Dublin in their own homes. Mary agreed to join such an order if it was to be established in Ireland. Dr Murray had identified Mary as the leader of such a religious order.

Mary and a companion, Alicia Walsh, set off for York in the north of England in 1812, where they entered the novitiate of the Institute of the Blessed Virgin, Bar Convent, York, for a period of three years. They returned to Dublin in 1815, and Mary founded the Congregation of the Irish Sisters of Charity, and at the Archbishop of Dublin's request, they took over an orphanage in North William Street. Mary had taken the name Sister Mary Augustine on her profession, and with the founding of the Irish Sisters of Charity she became Superior General of the Order. She was most impressed with the Rule of St Ignatius, the founder of the Jesuit Order, which was adhered to by the nuns at the Bar convent in York. She decided to adapt that rule for her new religious order in Dublin. As a member of the Irish Sisters of Charity, nuns took the traditional vows of poverty, chastity and obedience, in addition to a vow to devote their lives to the service of the poor.

As more and more young women began joining the Irish Sisters of Charity, they needed to move to larger accommodation and they found such accommodation in Stanhope Street, where they are to be found to this very day. From their foundation, the Irish Sisters of Charity spread to thirteen others during the lifetime of their founder, including one in Australia where the nuns worked among women convicts and their children. As the number of nuns increased, so did the requests for the Sisters to open additional foundations. Mary returned to Cork in 1826 to oversee the setting up of a new convent. Mary's sister, Anne, had joined the Irish Sisters of Charity too, and she became involved in visiting the poor in the North Parish. This was a time in Cork when people were very poor and many caught typhus fever and extreme forms of infection. The many deaths at the time included Anne, who died at the Stanhope Street Convent in 1828.

In 1831, when Mary was 44 years old, she became ill with acute arthritis that left her an invalid for the rest of her life. She also suffered from bouts of acute bronchitis. Besides ensuring that the Irish Sisters of Charity continued to help the poor, Mary also had a great desire to set up a hospital to look after the poor of Dublin. In 1834, with the help of the Archbishop of Dublin, Dr Daniel Murray, St Vincent's Hospital was founded in a house on St Stephen's Green that had belonged to the Earl of Meath. Mary bought it with a £3,000 donation. It is interesting that at that time St Stephen's Green was very much the home of the Dublin elite.

Mother Mary Augustine, as she was known in religion, spent the best part of thirty years as an invalid, and yet she managed to run the Irish Sisters of Charity congregation during that time. The nuns were responsible for the establishment of schools, hospitals and orphanages for people in need. They were involved in visiting the poor and needy, both in their homes and in prisons. Over the years her congregation continued to spread throughout Ireland, England, Scotland, California, Venezuela, Nigeria, Zambia, Malawi and Australia.

On 22 July 1858, Mary died at the Irish Sisters of Charity convent in Harold's Cross. However, her funeral Mass took place at the old chapel in Donnybrook, which at that time was located in the present graveyard in the centre of the village. She is buried in the nuns' graveyard in the grounds of St Mary Magdalen's in Donnybrook. In recognition of the extraordinary work and life of Mary Aikenhead, the Pope declared her Venerable, which is a step on the way to becoming a saint. Archival material relating to the life of Mother Mary Aikenhead is located in the Irish Sisters of Charity Archives in their convent in Sandymount.

Further Reading

Hallack, C., *The Servant of God*, The Anthonian Press, Dublin, 1951.
O'Dea, C., *Our Lady's Handmaid*, Clonmore & Reynolds, Dublin, 1961.
Rynne, C., *Mother Mary Aikenhead, 1787–1858*, Veritas, Dublin, 1980.

Armstrong, Harry Reginald (Reg) (1928–1979)

9–19 Ringsend Road, Ringsend, Dublin 4

Harry Reginald (Reg) Armstrong was born in Dublin to Frederick (Fred) Wrench Armstrong and his wife, Marjorie (*née* Wilson), who were both from Dublin. His parents were living temporarily in Liverpool at the time of his birth. Reg was an only child. The family returned to Ireland in early 1935. His father, Fred, had participated in motor races, trials and hill climbs in the immediate post-war years, and he gave his son every help and encouragement with his motor cycling career, as indeed, did his mother.

On returning to Dublin, the family lived in Rathfarnham Park, and Reg was educated at High School, then located in Harcourt Street. He started riding motorcycles with his cousin, Harry Lindsay, who taught him to ride. He and Harry joined the Irish Defence Forces for a brief period (1944–1945) near the end of the Emergency during the Second World War. They both operated as dispatch riders in the Army Motorcycle Squadron. Their motivation in joining the Defence Forces may have been to get some petrol, which was severely rationed at that time!

Armstrong married his first wife, Rosemary Adams, from Ballymena, Northern Ireland, at Christ Church Rathgar, in December 1955. They had two daughters, Julie and Lynda. Both daughters now live in England. He and his wife Rosemary divorced in the 1970s, and she returned to Northern Ireland. She died in Belfast on 10 November 2007. In 1974, Armstrong married Eileen Robertson (*née* Peters), a popular Isle of Man-born opera singer, who died at the age of 98 in 2017 in Douglas, Isle of Man. She had outlived Armstrong by thirty-eight years. They had no children, but she had children from her previous two marriages.

Armstrong's involvement with motorcycles began at the age of 12, when his father, Fred, gave him £10 to purchase a machine – a 12-year-old JAP-engined Rudge. At first he competed in grass track races and trials in the Dublin area, before making his road race debut in the summer of 1946 at Bangor Castle short circuit meeting in Co. Down. In September 1947, at the age of 19, Armstrong made his Isle of Man debut in the Manx Grand Prix lightweight (250cc) race, in which he finished fifth, riding an Excelsior. The race was marred by the death of fellow Dubliner Benjy Russell, from Kiltiernan, who crashed into a wall near Ramsey while riding a Moto Guzzi entered by Stanley Woods.

Armstrong competed in the Manx Grand Prix again the following year, taking fourth place in the senior race on a Triumph machine. In the junior (350cc) race, his luck ran out 10 miles before the finish, when he had to retire while holding third place. His big break came later, as team managers began to take notice of him, and over the following few years, Armstrong became one of the world's leading motorcycle road racers. During his racing career, which concluded at the end of the 1956 season, Armstrong rode for all the top teams of the time – AJS, Velocette, Norton, MV Augusta, NSU and Gilera.

Armstrong's greatest victory came in the 1952 Isle of Man TT when he won the Blue Riband Senior Race on a Norton at an average speed of 92.97mph. The legendary luck of the Irish was with him that day, for just as he came up to take the chequered flag at the finishing line on Glencrutchery Road, the primary chain on his machine snapped and dropped on to the road. Armstrong competed on all the classic circuits in Europe during his Grand Prix career. He was runner-up in the world Road Racing Championship five times. He won a total of seven Grand Prix events between 1952 and 1956. In Ireland, he had wins in the Ulster Grand Prix, the North-West 200, and six victories in the Leinster 200, which was held on the 8.34-mile Wicklow–Rathnew circuit.

Armstrong announced his retirement from motorcycle racing in November 1956 and indicated his intention to take up car racing, which he did with limited success over the following twelve years. However, his ever increasing business commitments prevented him from racing on a regular basis. From as early as 1953 his company, Reg Armstrong Motorcycles, had been assembling NSU machines in their works at 63 Drury Street, Dublin. Production was later moved to larger premises at Liberty Lane (off Kevin Street). By 1958 all of the NSU motorcycles were being produced at his facility in Halston Street, Dublin. The same year, Armstrong was awarded the contract to assemble the new NSU Prinz cars in Ireland. The company expanded and he purchased a 65,000 sq ft premises on Ringsend Road for £30,000 to deal exclusively with car production.

There were now two separate companies, Reg. Armstrong Motors Ltd and Reg Armstrong Motorcycles Ltd. The latter company won the contract to assemble the new Japanese Honda motorcycles in the early 1960s. In November 1962, Armstrongs were appointed to assemble and distribute German Opel Cars in Ireland, and in 1966 they added the American Pontiac cars to their list. The Honda Company invited Armstrong to take on the role of Honda Racing Team manager for the 1962 season, and he continued in that role in 1963. In 1967 Armstrong's company formed a Northern Ireland subsidiary, Reg Armstrong Motors (Northern Ireland) Limited, in Belfast. This meant that they could distribute Opel cars in Northern Ireland, which it had the licence to assemble and distribute in the Republic of Ireland.

In the mid–1970s, Armstrong's company began assembling the Mini for British Leyland but soon afterward the Irish Government allowed the importation of fully assembled cars. Unfortunately, this led to the loss of many highly skilled jobs at the Ringsend plant. About 130 assembly workers were made redundant and a group of them occupied the plant in protest. Then there was an embargo on imports of Opels by seven unions associated with the motor assembly industry. However, according to a statement by Armstrong, supplies of Opel spare parts were not affected during the closure of the assembly lines, and deliveries of new Opel vehicles continued. In 1973, Reg Armstrong Ltd became the Republic of Ireland's agent for AEG-Telefunken, the German television and washing machine manufacturer. This led to the formation of another subsidiary – Reg Armstrong Electronics Ltd based at Broomhill Road in Tallagh.

Armstrong represented Ireland in the 1978 World Clay Pigeon Shooting Championships in Korea. His other hobbies were fishing and shooting. He bred Charolais cattle, and had a great interest in ancient Egyptian architecture. On

Saturday, 24 November 1979, after a day's pheasant shooting in Co. Wicklow, Armstrong was returning to his home at Inchinappa House, in Ashford, when his Opel Senator car crashed at Kilqueeny, near Avoca. No other vehicle was involved in the accident. He was killed instantly. He was 51 years old. The inquest recorded that he died as a result of cardio-respiratory failure due to a fractured skull. He is buried with his parents in the Church of Ireland graveyard at Enniskerry, Co. Wicklow.

Further Reading

Clifford, P., *The Art and Science of Motorcycle Road Racing*, Hazleton, London, 1985.

Havlin, Harry, *Notes on Reg. Armstrong and his Career*, Dublin, 2019.

Montgomery, Bob, 'Past Imperfect', *Irish Times*, 22 June 2005.

Ashford, William (1746–1824) Landscape Artist

Sandymount House (Roselyn Park), Sandymount, Dublin 4

William Ashford, the distinguished landscape painter, was born in Birmingham in 1746. Very little is known of his early life in England, but he seems to have had some technical and artistic education there. He came to Ireland to take up a position with the Ordnance Survey Office in 1764. His work for the Ordnance Survey necessitated him travelling throughout Ireland carrying out audits of the armaments and munitions in forts and barracks throughout the country. Perhaps these travels resulted in his

interest in landscape painting, at which he came to excel. He was one of the leading landscape painters in Ireland, although his earliest paintings were of flowers and still life. During the eighteenth century the subject matter of painting broadened and landscape paintings, sometimes with classical subject matter, became more common. It appears that topography also became central to the landscape painters of the eighteenth century. Richard, the 7th Viscount Fitzwilliam of Merrion, commissioned William in 1804 to produce six large paintings of his demesne at Mount Merrion. Ashford also completed a folio of twenty-six grey wash drawings of Mount Merrion and Richmond, the English residence of Viscount Fitzwilliam. These are now on display in the Fitzwilliam Museum in Cambridge.

Shortly after he arrived in Ireland, Ashford exhibited at the Society of Artists in William Street. His first landscape was exhibited in 1772 at the Dublin Society and he was awarded a second premium there. His talent was very quickly recognised when in 1773 he exhibited seven paintings at the Society of Arts, where he won first prize. At this time the leading landscape artist in Ireland was Thomas Roberts (1748–1778) but after his death Ashford took his crown. Roberts died in 1777 at the very young age of 28 in Portugal, where he had gone to gain some respite from a galloping consumption. Ashford was elected President of the Irish Society of Artists in 1813 and was then involved in the negotiations that set up the Royal Hibernian Academy (RHA), of which he was a founding member and its first elected president in 1823. He exhibited at the Royal Academy in London from 1775, and with the Society of Artists again in London, from 1777. He also exhibited at the British Institution from 1806. While exhibiting in England, Ashford lived at a number of different addresses in both Dublin and London. Although Ashford did paint some interesting views in, for example, North Wales, the major part of his work was the Irish landscape.

Ashford exhibited at the Royal Academy in London from 1775 and with the Society of Artists again in London from 1777. He also exhibited at the British Institution from 1806 and at various exhibitions held in Dublin between 1800 and 1821. He held an exhibition of his own work, which included his pictures and drawings, in the Dublin Society's House in Hawkins Street. Anne Crookshank has suggested that Ashford's work was influenced by painters such as Claude Lorraine and Richard Wilson. Ashford's output was considerable and many of his works were engraved, in particular Malton's Views. As an artist, Ashford appears to have had a penchant for topographical views – in particular beautiful parks and grounds of county houses or rivers and valleys. In the latter part of his life he seems to have extended his subject matter to include a number of sea views. His many images of country estates were popular with land-owning patrons, and this led him to becoming one of the most successful Irish landscape painters.

It was during the eighteenth century that it became fashionable for city or country gentlemen to commission sets of views of their estates, houses and gardens. Ashford received many commissions from the landed gentry in Ireland such as the 1st Lord Rossmore, the Earl of Drogheda, the Duke of Leinster, the Earl of Charleville, Viscount Fitzwilliam, the Earl of Bessborough, the Earl of Kilmorey, Lord Rockley and the Hon. William Wellesley-Pole to paint their houses and gardens. Ashford obtained a very large commission from the 7th Viscount Fitzwilliam to paint his large estate and house at Mount Merrion. This appears to have been Ashford's last set of commissions. The Fitzwilliam commission included six views and a volume of twenty-four drawings that are dated 1806, and they are preserved in the Fitzwilliam Museum in Cambridge.

While exhibiting in England, Ashford lived at a number of different addresses in both Dublin and London. For many years he lived in College Green. Nicola Figgis has suggested that Ashford was involved in art and property dealing from which he acquired some of his wealth and enabled him to commission James Gandon, the leading Irish architect of the day, to build a house for him in

Sandymount in Dublin known as Sandymount House. He lived here for most of his life. Originally known as Sandymount House, it later became Sandymount Park House, then Park House and now it is known as Roselyn Park. This building survives today and has been beautifully restored. It is interesting that more recently the Irish Department of Education has decided to base two new schools in Roselyn Park.

William Ashford married, although the name of his wife is not certain. He had two sons and one daughter. His son, Daniel, became an artist but was not as well known as his father. Ashford senior also painted many seascapes, perhaps due to the fact that he lived in Sandymount and looked out on Dublin Bay. William Ashford died at his home in Sandymount on 17 April 1824, aged 78. He is buried in Donnybrook graveyard. After his death, an auction in Dublin saw the sale of his pictures, drawings and sketches.

Further Reading

Crookshank, Anne, *A Life Devoted to Landscape Painting: William Ashford (c.1746–1824) Irish Arts Review*, xi (1995), pp.119–31.

Crookshank, Anne, and the Knight of Glin, *Ireland's Painters 1600–1940*, Yale University Press, 2002, pp.150–54.

Figgis, Nicola, and Rooney, Brendan, *Irish Paintings at the National Gallery of Ireland*, National Gallery of Ireland, Dublin, 2001, pp.28–9.

Barry, Spranger (1719–1777) Actor

Mespil Road & Merrion Road, Dublin 4

Spranger Barry was an Irish actor and theatre manager who was born in Skinner's Row in Dublin on 23 November 1719. His father, William Barry, a successful silversmith, was warden to the Dublin Goldsmiths Company in 1715–1718, and master in 1718–1719, 1719–1720, and again in 1733–1734. Spranger was named after his paternal grandmother, and he worked with his father for a number of years and then took over the business. His first wife, Anne, provided him with a dowry with which he set up his own silversmith's business. Unfortunately, throughout his career Barry's skills as a businessman were poor, and he was quite unsuccessful in his various ventures, and this included his father's business. With his first wife he had two sons. In appearance, Barry was quite tall for his time, being almost 6ft. He is also reputed to have a powerful speaking voice – a great attribute for an actor. He seems to have always had an interest in acting and the theatre, and first performed on stage at the Theatre Royal in Dublin in 1744.

Barry moved to London and performed on the London Stage in Drury Lane in 1746. He had moved there at the invitation of David Garrick. In London he turned out to be very talented and in a short time he became a well-known Shakespearean actor, rivalling his famous friend, Garrick. His first role was as the leading role in *Othello* in Drury Lane (1746), which he performed to much acclaim. This was soon followed by *Macbeth* and *Hamlet*, which on occasions he alternated with Garrick. Over the years his strength as an actor grew and it is said that he graced the stage with ease and grace and was skilled at dancing and fencing. He appears to have been famous for his good looks as well.

Barry had a large circle of friends in both London and Dublin, which included artists, writers and actors. It is interesting that he brought a young screen painter to London with him from Dublin called Robert Carver. In London, Barry became a friend of Nathaniel Hone, the painter, and was a patron of Joshua Reynolds. His stage performances led Barry to become a favourite of Frederick, Prince of Wales, who was a keen theatregoer, and it was at his request that he took dancing lessons from the Prince of Wales's family dancing master. His voice was such that he was referred to as the 'silver-toned Barry'. However, despite the softness of his tone, Barry was also capable of expressing great rage in plays such as *Macbeth, Hamlet* and *King Lear*. It seems that his most outstanding performance was that of Othello as well as the aforementioned Shakespearian roles.

Barry was skilled, too, in performing romantic roles such as Romeo, which in 1748 was so popular that it led to a strained relationship with Garrick. Barry then moved to Covent Garden where the two actors' rivalry on the London stage continued. There he played Romeo, King Lear and Richard III. Two productions of *Romeo and Juliet* took place at the same time in London, one in Covent Garden, and the other in Drury Lane. Garrick played Romeo in Drury Lane, and Barry took the same role at Covent Garden! At that time, it was said that the public preferred Barry's performance but in fact, Garrick's production had a longer run. Barry also took part in a number of comedies during his time in London.

He returned to Dublin in October 1758 and opened his Dublin theatre in Crow Street and later a second theatre in Cork called the Theatre Royal. The construction of the Cork theatre began with the assistance of forty subscriptions of £50 each from members of the Cork gentry. The building was completed in 1760 and was modelled on Barry's Dublin theatre. During the first year six Shakespearean plays and nine other classics were staged.

The Crow Street Theatre in Dublin was in existence between 1758 and 1820. It had been built by Barry and another actor, Henry Woodward (1714–1777), who had saved £6,000 and had agreed to participate in the project to build a new theatre on the site of an old music hall. Another Irish actor, Charles Macklin (1690–1797), was involved at an early stage, but later withdrew from the project. Macklin is an interesting actor who came from Donegal and was a regular performer at the Theatre Royal in Drury Lane. He is known to have revolutionised the acting profession in the eighteenth century by introducing what was known as a natural style. Barry's Dublin theatre cost some £22,000 to build and it was considered similar to a contemporary playhouse at Drury Lane in London. Later it became known in Dublin as the Theatre Royal. In Dublin, Barry's theatre struggled from the onset as a rival to the Smock Alley Theatre, which was the second purpose-built venue in Ireland and dated back to 1662. Initially both of Barry's theatres were reasonably successful. However, as he was not a very successful businessman, they failed in the long run and he returned to London. Barry's failure was due in no small part to his taste for high living. He was also an extremely generous man.

It was in the Crow Street Theatre that Barry met Ann Street (1733–1801), who acted under her married name, Mrs Dancer. She and Barry acted in *King Lear* in 1758 – she played Cordelia to his Lear. She and Barry began a relationship as a result, and they married in London the following year after her husband died. Back in London after the failure of his two theatres in Dublin, Barry made a business deal – a profit-sharing agreement with Samuel Foote (1720–1777), whose company occupied the King's Theatre. Sometime later he was recruited by David Garrick in 1767 to act in Drury Lane. After his marriage to Ann, they both had successful careers on the stage in London, where she in particular played in all the well-known tragedies. They had one son, also named Spranger Barry. The Barrys worked for a number of years at Drury Lane until they moved to Covent Garden in 1774.

When Barry died in 1777, Ann remained at Covent Garden and married a younger man called Crawford. It has been suggested that some English drama critics considered her acting to be superior to Mrs Siddons, the well-known English actress. She died in London on 29 November 1801 and was buried in in the north cloister of Westminster Abbey beside her husband.

Further Reading

Morash, Christopher, *A History of the Irish Theatre, 1601–2000,* Cambridge University Press, Cambridge, 2004.

Clark, William Smith, *The Irish Stage in the County Towns, 1720–1800,* Oxford University Press, Oxford, 1965.

Stockwell, La Tourette, *Dublin Theatres and Theatre Customs,* Blom, London, 1968.

Beatty, Sir Alfred Chester (1875–1968)
Mining Engineer and Philanthropist
10 Ailesbury Road, Ballsbridge, Dublin 4

Sir Alfred Chester Beatty was one of the most distinguished men of his generation. He began his career as a mining engineer, became a well-known philanthropist, and went on to be an art collector specialising in oriental manuscripts and rare books. He bequeathed these collections to Ireland. The Chester Beatty Library now housed in the grounds of Dublin Castle stands as a memorial to him.

Beatty was born in New York in 1875, the youngest of three children of John Cumming Beatty, a banker and stockbroker, and his wife, Hetty. His paternal grandparents were Irish and hailed from Co. Armagh and Co. Laois. Chester Beatty was educated at Westminster School in New York and at Columbia University, where he studied to be a mining engineer. After he graduated in 1898, he headed west and worked initially shovelling rock in mines in Denver, Colorado. He very soon became a supervisor of the Kektonga Silver Mine. There he met one of the most respected mining engineers in the American West,

T.A. Rickard, who became his mentor and friend. It was he who introduced him to his wife, Grace Madeleine (*née* Rickard), whom Beatty married in 1900. From working in the mines, Beatty acquired silicosis, an occupational lung disease, which remained with him all of his life. In 1903, he became a member of the management team of the Guggenheim Exploration Company and as a result he became a very wealthy man. He later left this company and set himself up in New York as an independent mining consultant. In 1907, at the age of 32, Beatty was a millionaire, and a director of a number of American mining companies. While in Denver, Beatty had begun collecting stamps, which ultimately became an award-winning collection. He also developed an interest in collecting Chinese snuff bottles and Japanese netsuke.

In 1911, Grace (also known as Ninette) died suddenly of typhoid fever, leaving him with two young children. A year later, he decided to move with his young family to London and he set up his own mining company there called Selection Trust Ltd. Though small at first, it soon became very successful, with interests in many countries including Russia, The Gold Coast and Sierra Leone. However, it was in Northern Rhodesia and the Belgian Congo that he made his fortune while exploring the copper belt. In London, he bought Baroda House in Kensington Palace Gardens, and in the following year he remarried. His new wife was Edith Stone, a divorcee, and a daughter of John Dunne of New York. He and his new wife became avid collectors and they travelled worldwide acquiring new material. He found the climate of Egypt beneficial to his health problems, and he purchased a house in Cairo in 1914, returning every winter until 1939 and the outbreak of the Second World War. It was from there that he began acquiring his marvellous collection of Islamic books and manuscripts. A trip to Japan and China developed his interest in Japanese and Chinese manuscripts and artefacts, and he continued to purchase these throughout his life. He became well known on the international art scene for his purchasing power, and as his reputation grew so did his network of advisors and agents. In 1925, Beatty began a robust partnership with the British Museum, with him and his wife becoming benefactors and trustees and donating nineteen ancient Egyptian papyri.

By 1931, Beatty was recognised as a great collector of books and manuscripts, and about that time he acquired an important collection of biblical manuscripts known now as the Chester Beatty Biblical Papyri. Gradually, his reputation as a collector grew, while his wife established herself as a serious collector in her own right. She focused on buying Impressionist and Post-Impressionist paintings and French furniture. In 1933, Beatty became a naturalised British citizen and became well known as a patron of the arts and a philanthropist. He endowed cancer research and financed a research institute at the Royal Marsden Hospital in London. He became a great benefactor of hospitals and medical research in general. Focusing for most of his life on collecting exceptional Islamic, East Asian and biblical manuscripts, Beatty also acquired outstanding Western printed books, old master prints, and Southeast Asian, Tibetan, Ethiopian and Armenian holdings of great importance.

During the Second World War, Beatty served on a number of committees in Britain and contributed a large amount of raw materials to the Allies, for which he was later knighted. He was shocked at the results of the general election in Britain in 1945, when a Labour Government was returned to power. Changes took place in Britain with rising taxes and the currency restrictions became irritating to him. He also had a great dislike of any form of socialism. His relationship with the British Museum became strained – he had intended giving his entire collection to them, but a new director of the museum insisted on deciding for himself if Beatty's collection could meet its quality standards. He failed to assure Beatty that his collection would remain intact, but instead would be distributed to different museum departments.

Beatty's son bought a home in Co. Kildare in 1948, and this may have caused Beatty to consider Ireland as a home for himself and for his collections. He had visited Dublin in 1937 and had gained a favourable impression of the place. In 1949, he decided to move to the city – he was impressed by Ireland's lower income tax regime and by the enthusiasm of the Irish Government officials he met with in relation to relocating his library and collections. He bought a large house for himself at No. 10 Ailesbury Road and a site for his Library at No. 20 Shrewsbury Road. In moving to Dublin he brought his librarian, publisher, bank managers, book restorer and their families with him. His move to Ireland caused a mini sensation in British financial circles as it was feared that other powerful people might follow him. His estranged wife, Edith, did not move to Dublin but remained in London. Despite his love for Dublin, for the rest of his life Beatty spent only four months there, preferring the south of France for the winters.

In 1950, Beatty presented a bequest of ninety-three French paintings to the National Gallery of Ireland. He also presented a collection of oriental weapons and armoury to the Military Museum in the Curragh Camp. His greatest donation to Ireland was the Chester Beatty Library. Beatty was determined that his library would remain intact after his death. He worked on and was successful in securing exemption from estate duties for his books, manuscripts and other library materials. Today, the Chester Beatty Library has been designated as a National Cultural Institution, and is a public charitable trust under his will. The library is over 80 per cent funded by the Department of Culture Heritage and the Gaeltacht, and it is also a registered public sector body. In Ireland, Beatty continued his philanthropic activities to provide thousands of pounds to hospitals and other medical charities.

Ireland honoured Sir Alfred Chester Beatty with honorary doctorates from Trinity College and the National University of Ireland. He became a Freeman of the City of Dublin in 1956, and he also became the first honorary Irish citizen. After his death in Monte Carlo on 19 January 1968, he was awarded a state funeral by the Government of the day – the first person born outside Ireland to receive this honour. He is buried in Glasnevin Cemetery.

Further Reading

Horton, Charles, *Alfred Chester Beatty: From Miner to Bibliophile*, Town House, Dublin, 2003.

Kennedy, Brian P., *Alfred Chester Beatty and Ireland 1950–68: A Study in Cultural Politics,* Glendale Press, Dublin, 1988.

Wilson, A.J., *The Life and Times of Sir Alfred Chester Beatty,* Little Hampton Books, London, 1985.

Behan, Beatrice (1925–1993) Artist
5 Anglesea Road, Donnybrook, Dublin 4

Beatrice Behan was born in Dublin on 31 December 1925 to Cecil Ffrench Salkeld and Irma Taesler, a native of Berlin. She was educated at Pembroke School, the Loreto Convent on St Stephen's Green and at the National College of Art and Design. She first met Brendan Behan, the well-known writer (whom she later married), when she was a 17-year-old schoolgirl at her home on the Morehampton Road in Donnybrook. Her father, Cecil Salkeld, had met him in a pub and was fascinated by Brendan's knowledge of literature and politics, bringing him home to further their discussions. The young Beatrice was very familiar with the various artists and writers her father would bring home from time to time. The family also had a small house in Glencree, Co. Wicklow, and Beatrice spent time there when she was young. On graduating from the College of Art, Beatrice became a botanical assistant in the National Museum of Ireland, where she worked between 1949 and 1955. She also spent time in Italy, studying in Florence, Siena and Milan. Her paintings were shown at the Royal Hibernian Academy (RHA) annual exhibitions between 1948 and 1950. She also exhibited at the Oireachtas Exhibition of 1957 and 1958 as well as the Irish Living Art Exhibition in 1959 and in New York in 1969 and in 1970.

Over the years, Beatrice met Brendan regularly in her family home on Morehampton Road. Their close relationship dated from the time she attended the premiere of *The Quare Fellow*, Brendan's play, which was produced at the Pike Theatre in November 1954. They soon found out that they had a number of friends in common, and he very quickly asked her out. When she told her family that they were to get married, her father, Cecil, warned her that Behan was a confirmed drinker and pub-goer, who would not change his bad habits after marriage. However, she was prepared to risk it and they were married in the Church of the Sacred Heart Donnybrook on 16 February 1955. The marriage took place at 7.30 a.m. on a Saturday morning. It was an unusual wedding in that none of Brendan's family were present. However, Beatrice's sister, Celia, acted as bridesmaid. After the ceremony, the small party celebrated in about four different pubs in Dublin. The first home for Brendan and Beatrice was a garden flat at 18 Waterloo Road. From there they moved to a ground-floor flat at 15 Herbert Street.

Beatrice Behan had a huge influence on the work and life of her husband. She provided a stable environment for him at their home on Anglesea Road, where they lived for most of their married life. This enabled him to produce his autobiography/memoir *The Borstal Boy* in 1958, and his play *The Hostage* in 1959. In 1963, Beatrice illustrated one of his books, *Hold Your Hour and Have Another*. She later worked with Alan Simpson on the revision of Brendan's unfinished play, *Richard's Cork Leg*. There is some suggestion that in the early days of their relationship, Brendan found her aloof and considered she was a snob. This was untrue, for in fact, she was quite shy. In the early days of her marriage to Brendan, Beatrice worked as a horticultural illustrator for the *Irish Times* in order to supplement their income. Though Anglesea Road was their base in Dublin, Beatrice led quite a nomadic life with Brendan, moving from London to Paris and also to New York, which he loved. This nomadic lifestyle was in part caused by his publicists, who required him to appear at performances of his plays in both Europe and in the United States. It appears he found all the publicity in relation to his writings quite tiring.

Brendan and Beatrice's daughter, Blanaid, was born in 1963, just before Brendan died, so Blanaid grew up not knowing her father. She was called after Beatrice's grandmother, Blanaid Salkeld, who was a well-known poet, dramatist and actress. Blanaid was educated in Ireland but left the country when she was 21 years old, to work in England as a television producer. She worked in television until her two sons were born. Blanaid now helps to run her husband's (Matthew Walker) property company. Both of her sons are now at university, one of whom, Guy, is a student at Trinity College, Dublin.

Brendan's drinking was the bane of Beatrice's life, but she appears to have been extremely tolerant of this and his other outlandish behaviour. She was always there for him, living in his shadow for all their married life. According to her book *My Life with Brendan* (1973), she regarded him as 'a great loveable genius'. After Brendan's death, she devoted herself to bringing up Blanaid. However, there were major financial problems for her after Brendan died as the Government sent her a very hefty tax bill. This she managed to pay by letting out half of their house in Anglesea Road. As a widow, she enjoyed socialising with people interested in talking to her about Brendan. Her final relationship was with Cathal Goulding (1923–1998), who was Chief of Staff of the IRA and the Official IRA. With him she had a son, Paudge Behan, who in later life became a successful actor. The Behan home in Anglesea Road was a redbrick, semi-detached late Victorian house, which Brendan had bought for her in 1959 for £1,400 Irish. Beatrice Behan died in this house on 9 March 1993. She is buried in Glasnevin Cemetery along with Brendan.

Further Reading

Behan, Beatrice, *My Life with Brendan,* Nash Publishing, Los Angeles, 1973.

Behan, Brendan, *Hold Your Hour and Have Another*, Hutchinson, London, 1963.

Lynch, Brendan, *Prodigals and Geniuses*, Liffey Press, Dublin, 2011.

Behan, Brendan (1923–1964)
Writer and Dramatist
5 Anglesea Road, Donnybrook, Dublin 4

Brendan Behan was born in Dublin on 9 February 1923 into a Republican family. He was educated at North Brunswick Street Christian School until he was 14 years old. Then he left school to train as a house painter like his father, Stephen. His father Stephen and mother, Kathleen, were interested in Irish history and Irish music and culture, as well as reading the classics aloud to their children. Brendan and all their children were steeped in Irish literature and in Irish music and ballads. Kathleen was politically active all her life and was a friend of Michael Collins. Her brother was Peadar Kearney, who wrote the Irish National Anthem. In later life, Kathleen became known as a folk singer and at 92 made a long-playing record. She was also interviewed on both Irish and British television and proved to be quite a character. One of Brendan's brothers, Dominic, became a playwright and songwriter. It is interesting that he too had trained as a housepainter before turning to writing. Later, another of Kathleen and Stephen's sons, Brian, wrote his mother's biography, *Mother of All the Behans*. Brian was a political activist and noted actor, author and playwright.

Brendan became a member of the IRA, like other members of his family, and was arrested for IRA activities in Liverpool in 1939. He was sentenced to three years in Borstal (a youth prison) for having explosives in his possession. He remained in Borstal until the end of 1941, when he returned to Dublin. Within a few months of his return to Dublin, he was arrested again in April 1942 for attempting to shoot a policeman. This time his sentence was fourteen years' penal servitude. However, he served less than five years, being released under a general amnesty in 1946. His prison years were spent in Mountjoy Gaol, Arbour Hill Prison and the Curragh Prison, where he learned Irish from other political prisoners. There he became a great reader and started writing.

On release from prison, Brendan tried to establish himself as a writer. He moved to Paris for a period, where his problems with excessive drinking were unacceptable to his Parisian friends. He was a great man for socialising and drinking! His early writing consisted of a number of poems in the Irish language. He also contributed a series of articles and stories to Radio Éireann, to the *Irish Times* and to the *Irish Press*. A significant moment in Brendan's life was when he met and married Beatrice Salkeld, a daughter of the well-known Irish painter Cecil Salkeld. She provided him with a happy home and a certain amount of stability during their nine years of marriage. It was an unlikely match, as she was a shy quiet artist in comparison to Brendan, who was always the life and soul of the party! They had one daughter, Blanaid, who was born in 1963.

Due to his drinking and his raconteur abilities, Brendan became well known and notorious as part of the Baggotonia set, a literary group who frequented pubs in Baggot Street and Merrion Row, Dublin, and included writers such as Patrick Kavanagh, Flann O'Brien, Frank O'Connor, J.P. Donleavy and Elizabeth Bowen. There he entertained the masses with his fine collection of songs, parodies and incidents from the lives of well-known Irish men and women.

Brendan made great use of his prison experiences in his writing career. While in Mountjoy Gaol he wrote his first play, called *The Landlady*, and there too he began to write short stories. His first play, *The Quare Fellow*, was produced by Alan Simpson in the Pike Theatre in 1954. Two years later it was produced by Joan Littlewood at the Stratford Theatre in London, where it was a huge success. As a result, Brendan became well known internationally. Other works he produced at this time included *An Giall*, an Irish play for Gael Linn, and translated into English as *The Hostage*, and an autobiography called *Borstal Boy*. To quote Dr Colbert Kearney, an authority on Brendan who is also related to him: 'Behan exploited his incomparable command of the oral style of Dublin city to produce a dramatic portrait of the artist as a prisoner of national prejudice, in the process creating some of the greatest comic scenes in modern literature.'

During his life, Brendan was interviewed a number of times on television in both Ireland and in the United Kingdom. He generated a great deal of publicity in England for *The Quare Fellow* as a result of appearing drunk on the Malcolm Muggeridge show. He also spent time in New York, Paris and Berlin for productions of the play. His later books were *Brendan Behan's Island*, *Brendan Behan's New York*, *Confessions of an Irish Rebel* and *Richard's Cork Leg*. Brendan loved New York and spent increasing amounts of time there in the 1960s.

Unfortunately, Brendan had difficulty in coping with money and success. His drinking became a major problem in his life, which was compounded by the fact that he suffered from diabetes. Despite his international success, Brendan suffered a lack of confidence in himself and in his writing. He was frequently hospitalised for his drinking and diabetes, but inevitably discharged himself without permission to return to Baggotonia and his former friends. His alcoholism became worse and he was not as welcome in the local pubs there as he would have been in former times. He died on 20 March 1964 in the Meath Hospital at the age of 41. His funeral was one of the largest ever seen in Dublin and took place with full IRA honours. It was attended by the Lord Mayor of Dublin, the Tanaiste Seán McEntee and a number of well-known members of the Baggotonia set including Harry Kernoff, John B. Kean, Frank Norman, Joan Littlewood and Carolyn Simpson; all artists, writers and theatre directors. Brendan and Beatrice Behan are both buried in Glasnevin Cemetery in the French–Salkeld grave.

Further Reading

Behan, Beatrice, *My Life with Brendan*, London, Leslie Frewin, 1973.

Kearney, Colbert, 'Brendan Francis Behan', in *Dictionary of Irish Biography*, edited by James McGuire and James Quinn, Cambridge University Press, Cambridge.

O'Connor, Ulick, *Brendan Behan*, Abacus, London, 2014.

Bernelle, Agnes (1923–1999) Cabaret Artist
97 Strand Road, Sandymount, Dublin 4

Agnes Bernelle, or Agnes Elizabeth Bernauer, was born in Berlin, the daughter of Rudolph Bernauer (1880–1953), who was a Hungarian Jewish actor and playwright, and his second wife, who was a Protestant. Later, both Agnes and her father became Catholics. Rudolph was involved in theatre management in Germany until the mid-1920s, so Agnes grew up in a theatrical household. Due to the outbreak of war in 1936, she moved to London with her father – her mother following a year later. She attended a school in north London for a brief period and, as she states in her autobiography, *The Fun Palace*, that though her formal education was not great, she had a lifetime interest in the world of the theatre, music, opera and literature. On leaving school she worked for a time in a secretarial capacity and then began working as an actress in some of the London theatres and also with repertory companies throughout England.

During the war years in London, Agnes joined the Free German League of Culture, a refugee organisation, and she took part in their satirical revues. From the early 1940s, Agnes became an American intelligence agent, a secret broadcaster for the forerunner of the CIA called the OSS. The radio station was known as Radio Atlantik, a shortwave station masquerading as an underground radio station supposedly broadcasting from inside Germany. Her code name was Vicky and in this capacity she sent coded messages to the Allied troops and passed on misinformation to the German forces, the aim of which was to confuse and lower their morale. About this time too she began to work in cabaret, for which she became famous later in life, and she took the stage name of Agnes Bernelle.

During her time in London, Agnes met Desmond Leslie, an RAF pilot who was the youngest child of Sir Shane Leslie, an Irish peer who was also a first cousin of Sir Winston Churchill. The Leslies were wealthy Anglo–Irish landowners and Sir Shane's mother was Leonie Jerome, a sister of Churchill's mother, Jennie. The Leslies were of English, Irish and Scottish descent. Their home was Castle Leslie, which is a large Victorian country house on the outskirts of the village of Glasnough, Co. Monaghan, and is now a luxury hotel.

In later life Leslie became a filmmaker, sound engineer, writer and musician, and he was one of the first pioneers of electronic music. During his lifetime he was notorious for punching Bernard Levin, the well-known theatre critic, who wrote a poor review of his then wife Agnes Bernelle's show, *Savagery and Delight*, in the *Evening Standard* in 1963. It happened during an episode of Levin's satirical TV show *That Was the Week that Was*. Agnes's show was modelled on the Weimer-type Berlin cabaret. Most early cabarets took place in restaurants or nightclubs where the audience sat at tables and were entertained by a number of singers and dancers, and sometimes by comedians. The concept of a cabaret goes back to its invention in France during the 1880s.

Desmond and Agnes spent ten years in London after the war where Agnes developed her career as a singer and actress, together with raising three children. She acted regularly in the West End Theatre in London and was renowned for her performance of *Salome* by Oscar Wilde, and her dance of the seven veils, which she performed in the nude! She was also on the radio regularly, in series such as *The Adventures of Harry Lime* with Orson Welles. An all-round actress, Agnes also appeared in pantomime at the London Palladium and later at the Gaiety Theatre in Dublin.

During her early 40s, Agnes became interested in the music and work of Bertolt Brecht (1898–1956) and Kurt Weil (1900–1950), for which, as a performer, she became famous. Weil, the German composer, was perhaps best known for his collaboration with Berthold Brecht and *The Threepenny Opera* that includes the famous song 'Mac the Knife'. Later she went on to work with the German composer Michael Dress (1935–1975). She translated into English the poems and songs of Joachim Ringelnatz (1883–1932), a German author and painter also known as Hans Bötticher, which she performed on stage.

As a couple, Agnes and Desmond had an open and often stormy relationship. In 1963, Desmond decided to return to Ireland with their two boys, Seán and Marc. Agnes followed him the following year with her infant daughter, Antonia. Arriving at Castle Leslie, Agnes found Desmond engrossed in endeavouring to make the estate financially viable. She assisted in the opening of a disco in the hunting lodge belonging to the estate, and also developed a cottage knitwear industry by employing local women. One of the fashion models for her crochet brochure who later became her friend was Mary Bourke, later Mary Robinson, President of Ireland. The marriage between Desmond and Agnes became very strained due to his numerous affairs. It finally broke down in 1969 when, returning from a holiday with her children, she found that Desmond had changed the locks on the house, obtained a Mexican divorce and had married another woman – Helen Strong, who had been a friend of Agnes.

In 1969, Agnes moved to Dublin and there she initially managed a clothes boutique and resurrected her acting and stage career. There too she met Dr Maurice Craig, an eminent architectural historian, with whom she lived for the rest of her life. A legal settlement in 1971 saw Desmond purchase a house for Agnes at 97 Strand Road, Sandymount.

Agnes appears to have thrived in Dublin, where she recorded three albums and performed in theatre festivals and underground theatres. She worked in radio, film, and television and, of course, in theatre and cabaret. She became active in the National Women's Council and was a founding member of the Women in Media and Entertainments Group. She was a strong supporter of the Campaign for Nuclear Disarmament and was a supporter of refugees seeking asylum. In Dublin she recorded with artists such as Tom Waits, Elvis Costello, Marianne Faithful (a close friend), Gavin Friday, Guggi and Marc Almond were her protégées, and she seems to have been very proud of them. Over the years Agnes was a generous mentor to many to young musicians and actors, including Camille O'Sullivan and Gavin Friday.

Besides being an actress and cabaret singer, Agnes was also a social activist and a creative director of the Project Arts Centre. Her autobiography, *The Fun Palace*, was published in 1995. She was diagnosed with lung cancer in 1999. Her last role was in a film called *Still Life*, in which she played a dying woman. This film won a jury citation at the Palm Springs short film festival.

Agnes died on 15 February 1999 at Our Lady's Hospice, Harold's Cross. Her funeral has been described as a rock and roll concert with performers including Mary Coughlan singing 'Non, Je Ne Regrette Rien'. Gavin Friday and Anne Bushnell also sang. Very highly thought of as an actress and singer, it was not surprising to find among the distinguished attendees at her funeral the aides de camp of the Taoiseach and the President of Ireland, Ruairi Quinn TD and Senator David Norris, together with her many fellow actors, and a selection of well-known academics and writers.

Further Reading

Bernelle, Agnes, *The Fun Palace*, Lilliput Press, Dublin, 1997.

Bernelle, Agnes, *Decantations: A Tribute to Maurice Craig*, Lilliput Press, Dublin, 1992.

Hewitt, Michael, *Agnes Bernelle obituary*. *The Guardian*, 3 March 1999.

Best, Richard Irvine (1872–1959)
Celtic Scholar and Librarian
57 Upper Leeson Street, Dublin 4

Richard Best was born in Northern Ireland – in Derry to be precise in 1872. His parents were Henry Best, an excise officer, and his wife, Margaret (*née* Irvine). He went to school at Foyle College in Derry, a well-known grammar school, which celebrated its 400th anniversary in 2017. After leaving school, he worked for a few years in a bank and while there he received an inheritance, which enabled him to travel. He spent time in London and then proceeded to Paris, where he became interested in the study of Old Irish. He attended the lectures of Henri d'Arbois de Jubainville, an authority on Celtic languages, literature and law at the Collège de France, and it was from him that he acquired a great interest in palaeography. In Paris he became part of an Irish literary group that included John Millington Synge and Kuno Meyer.

When he returned to Ireland, Best translated and annotated de Jubainville's *Le Cycle Mythologique Irlandais et la Mythologie Celtique* (1884). In 1904 he joined the staff of the National Library of Ireland and went on to become Assistant Director there. In 1924 he was appointed Chief Librarian of the National Library, and director from 1929 until his retirement in 1940. Throughout his life, Best developed a profound bibliographical knowledge base and was well known to international scholars in the world of Celtic studies as a serious academic librarian. While working in the National Library he produced in 1913 the early volumes of his *Bibliography of Irish Philology and Irish Printed Literature (1913)* and later his *Bibliography of Irish Philology and Manuscript literature (1913–1941)*, both indispensable tools for Celtic scholars. The Royal Prussian Academy awarded Best the Leibniz Medal in 1914 in recognition of this great scholarship. Recognition of his scholarship came, too, from the National University of Ireland, when he was awarded an Honorary D.Litt. degree in 1920, and in 1923 he received a similar degree

from Trinity College Dublin. A series of lectures called the R.I. Best Memorial
Lectures were established in his honour by the National Library of Ireland and
these continue to this day.

On his return to Ireland, Best became Honorary Secretary to the School
of Irish Learning, which was founded in 1903. It was incorporated into the
Royal Irish Academy in 1926. By 1911, Best began using palaeographical
evidence in studying the dating of early Irish texts. His work on *Lebor na
Huidre* was described as 'of the greatest significance, not only with regard
to the manuscript itself but for the whole history of the ancient sagas'. In
conjunction with Osbert Bergin, he carried out a complete transcription of the
manuscript where they identified different hands that were distinguished by
changes of type. Best became joint editor of *Ériu*, to which he also contributed
on a regular basis. He contributed academic articles to a number of different
journals of Celtic Studies, such as *Zeitschrift für Celtische Philologie, Revue
Celtique, Études Celtiques Hermathena, The Dublin Magazine* and, of course,
to the *Proceedings of the Royal Irish Academy*. Among his other publications
were *The Irish Mythological Cycle and Celtic Mythology (1903)*. He edited
The Martyrology of Tallagh (1931) and was co-editor of *The Book of Leinster*
with Bergin.

In 1940, Best was made a Senior Professor of Celtic Studies at the Dublin
Institute for Advanced Studies. At this time too, he became an Honorary Fellow
of the Bibliographical Society of Ireland. Best was honoured again in 1943,
when he was elected President of the Royal Irish Academy, a post he held until
1946. There he involved himself in promoting the Academy's work in Irish
studies and served on its Irish Manuscripts and later Irish Studies Committees.

Dr Best was associated with the Irish Manuscripts Commission from 1928,
when he became a member. When he retired from the Institute of Advanced
Studies in 1947 he took over the Chairmanship of the Irish Manuscripts
Commission in succession to Professor Eóin MacNeill. Best continued to
be active in the field of Celtic studies while Chair of the Irish Manuscripts
Commission and was involved in many of the Commission's publications
including *The Oldest Fragments of the Sanchas Már* in collaboration with
Professor Thurneysen. He was involved in numerous other publications of the
Commission, to which he contributed not only his editorial skills but also
his large knowledge of palaeography. As Chairman of the Irish Manuscripts
Commission, Dr Best initiated an examination of the Bodleian archives for
documents of importance not in the Irish Language. Results of this work was
published by Dr Charles McNeill's Reports in *Analecta Hibernica* (1–4). He
also proposed checking on historical documents at the Lambeth Archiepiscopal
Libraries, the British Museum and the London Record Office. Throughout
his life, Best was acknowledged as an outstanding Celtic scholar and he was

consulted by a wide variety of scholars in the field of Celtic studies from all over the world.

Richard I. Best was very much part of Dublin's literary circle during the 1940s and '50s. He knew J.M. Synge and James Joyce, for example, and is featured in James Joyce's *Ulysses* as one of the characters in the National Library scene – a portrait he did not like. He was a close friend of George Moore, who portrayed him in his novel *Hail and Farewell*. When Moore died, Best read the funeral address, which had been written by AE (George Russell). His ashes were scattered on Castle Island on Carra Lake in Co. Kerry. *Binchy Bergin and Best* is a poem by Flann O'Brien that satirised the distinguished scholars Daniel Binchy, Osborn Bergin and Richard Best. It was first published in Flann O'Brien's 'Cruiskeen Lawn' column in the *Irish Times*.

Music was very much a part of Best's life, particularly from the time he met Edith Oldham (1865–1950), a distinguished pianist whom he married. She was a founding member of the Feis Ceoil and undertook major responsibility for its organisation. It was under her leadership that it became an annual event. She pre-deceased her husband in 1950 and he died nine years later on 25 September 1959 at their home in Upper Leeson Street. They are both buried in Deansgrange Cemetery.

Further Reading

Binchy Bergin & Best, http://celtologica.eu/zcp

E[leanor] K[nott], *Richard Irvine Best, 1872–1959*, Ériu, xix, 1962, pp.123–5.

Thom's Irish Who's Who, Thom's, Dublin, 1923.

Woods, C.J., 'Best, Richard Irvine', in *Dictionary of Irish Biography*, edited by James McGuire and James Quinn, Cambridge University Press, Cambridge.

Briscoe, Robert Emmett (1894–1969)
Former Lord Mayor and Politician
12 Herbert Park, Ballsbridge, Dublin 4

Robert Emmett Briscoe was born on 25 September 1894 in Ranelagh to Abraham William Briscoe, a Lithuanian Jew who had fled that country due to anti-Semitic pogroms, and his wife Ida Briscoe (*née* Yoedicke), who was also from Lithuania. Briscoe's father owned a leading furniture store on Ormond Quay in Dublin called Lawlor Briscoe, which was a substantial import–export business. Abraham Briscoe and his wife had seven children – four sons and three daughters – whom they brought up in the orthodox Jewish tradition. One of his daughters, Miriam, became a Catholic during a year-long stay with her sister in Canada. On her return to Dublin, she entered the Carmelite Order of Nuns in Roebuck, Clonskeagh, Dublin 14.

Briscoe was always a great friend of the Irish President Éamon de Valera, and among those attending the profession of his daughter, Sister Miriam Teresa, were the President and his wife. Only two of Briscoe's sons remained in Dublin. His son, Ben, like his father, became Lord Mayor of Dublin in 1998, only the second Jew to hold that office. Joseph joined the Irish Army and retired with the rank of commandant.

For a time, the Briscoe family lived in Upper Leeson Street, and Robert attended Strand School, the Kildare Street Schools and St Andrews College. He was also educated in England for a short time at the exclusive Jewish public school in Ramsgate, Kent. On finishing school, Robert spent time in Berlin, where he worked with an import–export firm. He studied business practice and electrical engineering there too, along with studying Hebrew.

With the possible introduction of conscription to Ireland, Briscoe's father was afraid that Robert would be conscripted into the British Army, so he sent him to New York, where he worked for an import company as well as joining a small manufacturing company as a partner. During his time in the USA, Briscoe became involved in the broad Irish-American Republican movement.

The Easter Rising in Ireland of 1916 made a great impression on the young Robert. On his return home in 1917, Briscoe joined Fianna Éireann, an Irish nationalist youth organisation, founded in 1909 by Bulmer Hobson and Constance Markievicz. Back in Dublin, Briscoe established a clothing business that ultimately became a front for his gun-running activities on behalf of Michael Collins. Briscoe was a member of Collins's personal staff with the designated title of arms procurement officer. Germany was awash with arms after its defeat in the First World War. Briscoe was sent to Berlin (where his fluency in German was useful) to acquire arms for the IRA, and he met with some success. Arms from Germany were successfully smuggled into Dublin on the tugboat *Frieda,* and on the *City of Dortmund.*

During the negotiations in London for the Anglo–Irish Agreement, Briscoe acted as a courier between the Cabinet in Dublin and the group in London led by Michael Collins. However, Briscoe disagreed with Collins in relation to the Anglo–Irish Treaty of December 1921 that led to the partition of Ireland. This Treaty enabled six of the northern counties in Ireland to remain in the United Kingdom. Briscoe henceforth took the anti-treaty side. He joined the Fianna Fáil party and he became a member of Dail Éireann in 1927 until 1965.

During the Civil War that followed the signing of the Anglo–Irish Agreement, Briscoe became a great friend and supporter of Éamon de Valera. This friendship lasted his entire lifetime. He represented Dublin South in the Dail from 1927 to 1948, and Dublin South West from 1948 to 1965. Briscoe became one of the first Fianna Fáil Aldermen and served as a City Councillor from 1950 to 1967. He therefore had an unbroken political career lasting thirty-eight years. Briscoe spearheaded a significant piece of legislation in the Dail in relation to a law limiting the amount of interest a moneylender could charge on a loan. This was The Moneylenders Act of 1933. It was of great significance to the poor, who suffered from very high interest rates charged by Dublin moneylenders.

During the 1930s in Ireland there was a degree of anti-Semitism within the Irish Republican movement. Briscoe suffered from it, especially from pro-treaty people in Dublin. On one occasion in 1917, an unmarked car drew alongside him and fired shots. During the 1930s, with the activities of the Nazi party in Germany, Briscoe was labelled as a Zionist Jew.

He was anxious that Ireland would give asylum to Jewish people fleeing from Nazi Germany. In 1938 he received a visit from Vladimir Jabotinsky, the founder of the Zionist right-wing Revisionist Party, and from his experiences in the War of Independence, Briscoe was able to advise on the training strategy and tactics of guerrilla warfare. During Jabotinsky's visit to Ireland, Briscoe also introduced him to Éamon de Valera. Always supportive of a Jewish state in Palestine, Briscoe went on fund-raising tours of the United States, South Africa and Rhodesia.

In 1945, Briscoe toured the Middle East on a trade mission to promote Irish manufactured goods. Over the years he also made a number of official visits and trade missions to the USA as well as carrying out speaking tours to Jewish Americans. While out of office in 1950, de Valera went on a visit to Israel with Briscoe. There they dined with Ben Gurion, the first Prime Minister of Israel, at Chief Rabbi Herzog's home. Herzog had been the Chief Rabbi in Ireland some years before and he and de Valera were good friends. Briscoe was always a very loyal friend to de Valera and the latter often rewarded him for his fidelity.

During the 1950s, Briscoe's popularity in the political polls soared. He topped the poll frequently and was twice elected on the first count. He became Lord Mayor of Dublin on two occasions – 1956–1957 and 1961–1962. He was the first Jewish Lord Mayor of Dublin, though not the first Jewish Lord Mayor in Ireland. Youghal had the first Jewish Lord Mayor in Ireland in 1555 when William Moses Annyas Eames was appointed. Throughout his political career, though a close friend of de Valera, Robert Briscoe never held a ministerial or secretarial rank in Fianna Fáil. However, de Valera did appoint him to the Council of State in 1965.

Briscoe wrote his autobiography, *For the Life of Me*, in conjunction with Alden Hatch in 1959. Briscoe had a most interesting life and career and was heavily involved in both Irish and Jewish nationalism. *The Fabulous Irishman* was a television film of his life, and it was circulated in both the USA and Ireland. He was also commemorated in a special award called The Robert Briscoe Award, which honours Jews who helped Ireland or Irish immigrants to the United States. A biography of Robert Briscoe published in 2015 by Kevin McCarthy describes Briscoe as a 'Sinn Fein Revolutionary, Fianna Fáil Nationalist, and Revisionist Zionist', which summarised his life succinctly. Briscoe died at his home, No. 12 Herbert Park, Donnybrook, on 29 May 1969. He is buried in the Orthodox Jewish Cemetery in Dublin's Dolphin's Barn.

Further Reading

Briscoe, Robert, with Hatch, Alden, *For the Life of Me*, Little Brown, Boston, 1958.

Keogh, Dermot, *Jews in Twentieth-Century Ireland*, Cork University Press, Cork, 1988.

McCarthy, Kevin, *Robert Briscoe: Sinn Fein Revolutionary, Fianna Fáil Nationalist, and Revisionist Zionist*, Little Brown, Boston, 2015.

Bryant, Sophie (1850–1922) Mathematician, Educationist and Suffragette
Sandymount, Dublin 4

Sophie Bryant (*née* Willock), born in Sandymount, became a very well-known educationist, mathematician and Celtic scholar as well as being active in the Suffragette movement. Sophie was born the third in a family of six children. Her father was Rev. Dr William Willock DD, a Fellow and Tutor in Mathematics at Trinity College Dublin, and her mother was Sophie Morris. The family moved from Sandymount to live in Cork and later to near Enniskillen in Co. Fermanagh, where her father held posts as a clergyman. She was educated mostly at home by her father and by a series of French and German governesses. As a result, Sophie became a fluent French and German speaker.

When Sophie was 13, the family moved to London, where her father was appointed to the Chair in Geometry at the University of London. She grew up with a great love of mathematics and the great outdoors. In London, she continued to be educated by governesses but in 1866 she won a scholarship to Bedford College, the first third-level College for women only. From the 1860s Bedford College became co-educational, and in 1885 it merged with Royal Holloway College, a constituent College of the University of London. In 1857, the Cambridge Local examination became available to girls. Sophie sat for this examination and she obtained a first in mathematics.

Sophie Wilcox married a Dr William Hicks Bryant in 1869 a surgeon, who was ten years older than her, but a year later he died. She never remarried. Instead she became a teacher and joined the staff of the North London Collegiate School founded by Frances Mary Buss, an outstanding educationist. In fact, in 1895 she eventually succeeded Miss Buss as headmistress and remained there until 1918, when she retired. Sophie taught mathematics and, for a period of time, German. She was considered an outstanding teacher, and many of her students went on to study mathematics at Girton College in Cambridge.

During this period Bryant continued with her own studies and, when in 1878 the University of London began admitting women to its degree courses, she became a part-time student, and graduated in 1881 with a BSc in Mathematics and Mental and Moral Science. In 1882, Bryant was elected to the London Mathematical Society, only its third female member. In 1884, she became the first woman to be awarded a DSc in England. She was the first woman, too, to have a research paper published in the *Proceedings of the London Mathematical Society*, a very prestigious publication. An outstanding scholar, in 1898 Bryant was the first woman to be elected by Convocation of London University to the Senate of the University. During all this time, she wrote numerous books, pamphlets and articles on educational topics that were published in well-known educational and philosophical journals of the period. In her work in Mathematics, where she wrote on symbolic language and mathematics, she drew on the work of George Boole, the first Professor of Mathematics at University College Cork.

Bryant became very well known in educational circles and was a member of London County Council's technical education board. She was also a member of the Bryce Commission on Secondary Education in England. Bryant campaigned for women's rights and suffrage, and became President of the local Suffrage Society in Hampstead. She was a leader on the 1908 march organised by the National Union of Suffrage Societies. Bryant went on to become the Chair of the Teachers Training Council and was instrumental in setting up the Cambridge Training College for women, now Hughes Hall, Cambridge. She was also President of the Association of Headmistresses.

Bryant always retained a great interest and love of Ireland, where she had been born. She became active in an Irish campaign to secure higher education for women and was a supporter of Alice Oldham (1850–1907), a leader in the campaign. Bryant also lobbied convent schools to gain support among Catholic educators for their campaign. She was recognised for her work in education when she received an Honorary Doctorate from Trinity College Dublin when it opened its doors to degrees for women.

In Ireland, Bryant became active in the campaign to abolish the old Royal University of Ireland, and her pamphlet, *A Possible Solution of the Irish University Question*, promoted the idea of higher education being available to all on an equal footing regardless of religion. With her continued interest and love of Ireland, it is not surprising that Bryant was interested in Irish politics and was an active supporter of William Gladstone, and the English Prime Minister's policy of Home Rule for Ireland. She was a regular visitor to Ireland and was a frequent speaker at Home Rule rallies in both Ireland

and England. She wrote on the nationalist question in both English and Irish publications. Bryant became a member of London's Irish Literary Society and a Vice President in 1912. She was a pioneer in promoting an understanding of early Irish society in particular. Her love of Ireland also found deep expression in her writings on Irish history. Her three books on Ireland were *Celtic Ireland* (1889), *The Genius of the Gael* (1913) and *Liberty Order and Law Under Native Irish Rule,* which was published posthumously in 1923.

Bryant was not a traditional 'blue stocking'; she was someone who loved the great outdoors. She was a keen cyclist, and she cycled every day from her home in Hampstead to the school in Camden. She loved rowing and was an experienced mountain climber. She frequently led mountaineering trips to the Welsh mountains and was a keen climber of the major peaks in the Alps, including the Matterhorn, which she climbed twice. She retired as headmistress of the North London Collegiate School in 1918 and disappeared on a climbing holiday near Chamonix in 1922. Her body was found two weeks later, with the cause of death assumed to have been an accident. She was 72 years of age. Her place of burial is unknown. Her obituary in the journal *Nature,* described her as 'a teacher and pioneer in education, a mathematician, philosopher, an Irish patriot, and suffragette. She was a great personality, and a splendid friend, a perpetual source of inspiration and joy to those who knew her.'

Further Reading

Beresford, Peter, 'Sophie Bryant 1 & 2', *Irish Democrat*, 10 December 2008.

Glenday, Nonita, and Price, Mary, *Reluctant Revolutionaries: A Century of Headmistresses 1874–1974*, Pitman Publishing, London, 1974.

Obituary, *Times*, 29 August 1922.

Scrimgeour, R.M., *The North London Collegiate School 1850–1950*, Oxford University Press, Oxford, 1950.

Butler, Eleanor (1914–1997)
Lady Wicklow, Architect and Politician
73 Ailesbury Road, Donnybrook, Dublin 4

Eleanor Grace Butler (later Lady Wicklow) was the daughter of Rudolf Maximillian Butler, 1st Professor of Architecture at University College Dublin, and Anne Butler (*née* Gibson). She was born in Dublin on 7 September 1914. Her father was a Protestant and half German and her mother a Catholic from the West of Ireland She was one of five children who grew up at the family home at 73 Ailesbury Road, Donnybrook, which had been designed by her father. Along with her siblings, Eleanor was brought up a Catholic. As a child she contacted polio and walked with a limp for the rest of her life. She attended Alexandra

College Dublin and spent a year studying at the University of Poitiers before proceeding to University College Dublin, where she studied architecture, receiving her BArch degree in 1938. Shortly after her graduation, Eleanor suffered a severe riding accident and spent a year in hospital. While there she decided she would devote herself to improving social injustice in Ireland, which she continued to do all her life. On graduating with a first-class honours degree, Butler joined her father's architectural practice and worked there for a number of years along with her brother, John Geoffrey Butler. On the death of their father in 1943, the two siblings took over his practice. Eleanor became the first woman Fellow of the Royal Institute of Architects in Ireland.

While working as an architect, Butler had a great interest in the architecture of Georgian Dublin and went on to become the honorary secretary of the Irish Architectural Records Society. Over the years she also wrote articles on Irish Architecture for *Country Life,* the well-known British magazine. While active in architecture, she gave a paper in 1947 at the annual architects' conference in

Dublin on the city's architecture. Despite her architectural qualifications, this did not take up a great deal of her time in later life.

Butler joined the Labour Party and became active in the trade union movement. She remained friends with Denis Larkin all their lives. Butler was also a member of Dublin Corporation. She stood for the Dail in 1948 and was defeated by the late Dr Noel Browne and 400 votes. It was he who is credited with eliminating tuberculosis, which had decimated generations of the youth of Ireland. As a nominee of John A. Costello's Inter-Party Government of 1948, she acquired experience of Europe's early Coal and Steel Community. She was also a member of the Irish delegation that helped to draft the statute of the Council of Europe. She served as a member of the Senate until 1951. Later she spent time in India studying political developments. While a member of the Senate, she travelled throughout the world promoting the campaign for Moral Rearmament, 'a modern, non-denominational revivalist movement' founded by American churchman Frank N.D. Buchman (1878–1961). It sought to deepen the spiritual life of individuals and encouraged participants to continue as members of their own churches.

Butler met the 8th Earl of Wicklow (1902–1978), William Howard in 1946. He was an Anglo–Irish peer and the only child of Ralph Howard the 7th Earl of Wicklow and his wife the Countess of Wicklow, formerly Lady Gladys Mary Hamilton. Educated at Eton, Magdalen College Oxford, and St Stephen's House, he was ordained as a Church of England minister. In the 1930s he was an ardent Anglo–Catholic, converted to Catholicism in 1932 and lived after that as a layman. The Earl of Wicklow was a well-known figure in literary and ecclesiastical circles as a writer, editor and publisher of *The Dublin Review*. He founded the firm of Clonmore and Reynolds, a well-known publishing house. In the 1950s he wrote on religious subjects and was also active as a translator. After a courtship of thirteen years, Billy Wicklow and Eleanor Butler married quietly in Glasthule Catholic Church in 1959. Both she and her husband proved to have a great social conscience, which led them to become involved in a number of different good causes that included adult education, the Cheshire Homes, travellers, work with the aged and the Society of St Vincent de Paul.

In the 1970s and '80s the Countess of Wicklow was involved in movements directed at reconciliation in Northern Ireland. The outbreak of violence there led to her becoming involved in helping Catholic refugees. Later she came to realise that reconciliation between Unionists and nationalists was essential to the future of peace in that part of Ireland. She became a founder member of the Centre for Peace and Reconciliation at Glencree and was the architect of their headquarters. She was also a Board member of Co-operation North, which focused primarily on the business sector. All these activities created a momentum that eventually led to the development of such bodies as the Southern Movement for Peace, Co-operation North and the Ireland Fund of America.

As an architect, Butler became home planning advisor and housing consultant to the *Irish Countrywomen's Association*. She travelled all over the country on behalf of the Association carrying out surveys of farming communities and rural housing. In the 1970s, the Countess of Wicklow was involved in setting up an Association of Women's Voluntary Groups, which was formed under her chairmanship. It included twenty women's organisations, including the Irish Countrywomen's Association and the Irish Housewives Association. All her life, the Countess of Wicklow had great energy. She was on the boards of numerous Dublin hospitals and it was she who persuaded Leonard Cheshire to found a Cheshire Home in Ireland. She also worked on behalf of Irish itinerants and their resettlement.

The Countess of Wicklow suffered from ill health in her later years and lived in a nursing home in Co. Dublin. She died on 21 February 1997 and is buried with her husband in Kilbride Churchyard, Arklow, Co. Wicklow. The Earl and Countess of Wicklow had no children, so with the death of her husband in 1978 the title became extinct.

Further Reading

Butler, Eleanor, Oireachtas Members Database. Retrieved January 2020.

Dictionary of Irish Architects, 'Eleanor Grace Butler', Irish Architectural Archive, Dublin.

Butler, Eleanor, Countess of Wicklow, obituary, *Irish Times*, 12 March 1997.

Byrne, Frankie (1922–1993)
Broadcaster and Public Relations Consultant
Dunbur, Brookvale Road, Donnybrook, Dublin 4

Frankie or Frances Byrne was born in Dublin in 1921. Her parents were Michael (Sport) Byrne, a journalist, and Frances McDonald. At the time of Frankie's birth, the family lived at 2 Florence Terrace, Leeson Park. When Frankie was young they moved to the North Circular Road. Her parents led a hectic social life, mixing with the racing fraternity and the leading social classes of the day. The children did not see a lot of their parents, and as a result maids brought them up. There were five children in the family and Frankie was the middle child, being the second daughter among three girls and two brothers. She became a boarder at the Loreto Abbey in Rathfarnham from the age of 8 and remained there until she was 18. Frankie's sister, Olive, worked at the Brazilian consulate in Dublin and when she left to get married, Frankie replaced her. Byrne worked there for a number of years before she left to join McConnell's advertising agency. The job in the embassy came with living quarters at its premises in O'Connell Street as well as a car.

All of this provided Byrne with access to the cream of Dublin's social life. Her wide-ranging contacts proved invaluable to her later when she moved to the advertising agency. She became a real pioneer of the public relations industry and eventually, in 1963, she set up her own agency, Frankie Byrne Public Relations Ltd – the first woman to set up a PR agency in Ireland. She celebrated the launch of her new business with a big party at Jury's Hotel attended by the Lord Mayor of Dublin and 200 guests. Her first major public relations job was to handle the publicity for the visit of President John F. Kennedy to Ireland that same year, which was quite a coup.

Byrne's next big contract was with Jacob's biscuit factory and she began hosting a daily lunchtime programme on Radio Éireann sponsored by the company. Initially the programme was to be about matters of domestic science, with which Frankie was not too familiar, so she suggested it would be a good idea to change the format to a sort of agony aunt slot. Her programme, *Dear Frankie*, ran on Radio Éireann from 1963 to 1985. Every day she responded to letters she had received regarding listeners' personal problems, their relationships and other aspects of their lives. Byrne's programme played a very important part in the lives of Irish women from all over the country. It was a time without the availability of self-help books both in book shops and in public libraries. Her programme always opened with 'Welcome to Woman's Page, brought to you by Jacob's, the people who make better biscuits better, every day; a programme for and maybe about you.' Another of her catchphrases was, 'It may not be your problem today, but it could be someday!'

For more than twenty years Frankie Byrne solved many of the relationship problems of the Irish nation. During this time, she answered more than 5,000 letters and an entire generation of young people were raised listening to her solving Ireland's personal problems in between Frank Sinatra songs and advertisements for Jacob's biscuits. She received anything up to 100 letters every week and over the period of time the programme was on the air, more than 1,000 programmes were broadcast. Her advice was of the no-nonsense variety, and she gave it with sympathy, humour and sensitivity. She told a *Sunday Independent* reporter later in life that she was always interested in people's problems because she was always interested in people, and therefore treated the letters she received with compassion and understanding. Certain topics were taboo on Radio Éireann for most of the time her programmes were on the air, such as domestic violence, sexual dysfunction or child abuse. However, by the 1980s it was possible to discuss adultery, non-marital cohabitation and contraception on *Dear Frankie*.

Byrne will always be remembered for the annual prestigious Jacob's TV and Radio Awards for broadcasting, in which she played a key role in their promotion. She was always very friendly with Jacob's chairman Gordon Lambert. Byrne initiated the awards in 1962 and her role appears to have been crucial to their success. The winners were presented with their award by a member of the Irish Government and sometimes by the Taoiseach of the day. Unfortunately, no further award ceremonies took place after Byrne's death in December 1993.

Byrne also wrote a column for the *Evening Press* during the 1980s in a similar vein to her *Dear Frankie* programmes. However, behind the façade she presented to the public, Byrne had a sad personal life herself. She never married but for thirty years had a relationship with a married man, a well-known RTÉ journalist and broadcaster. In 1956, Byrne had a daughter as a result of this relationship, and the baby was given up for adoption. Byrne suffered greatly as a result and this may have contributed to her addiction to alcohol and the prescription drug valium in later life. Her daughter, Valerie McLoughlin, found her birth mother in 1983 and they were reunited.

A documentary on Byrne was aired on RTÉ in 2005 in which they explored her life following the show, and included interviews with her family and friends, including her daughter. Byrne lived with her sister, Esther (who worked in production in RTÉ Television) in Brookvale Road, Donnybrook, in a bungalow called Dunbur. When the two sisters died, their home was demolished and replaced by an apartment block now called by the same name, Dunbur. Despite her public persona, Byrne suffered from self-doubt and feelings of inferiority. For many years before her death she suffered from alcoholism and latterly from Alzheimer's disease. She died at St Vincent's Hospital Dublin on 14 December 1993, aged 71, and is buried in St Fintan's Cemetery, Sutton, Co. Dublin.

Further Reading

White, L.W., 'Byrne, Frankie (Frances)', in *Dictionary of Irish Biography,* edited by James McGuire and James Quinn, Cambridge University Press, Cambridge.

O'Dea, Patrick (ed.), *Dear Frankie*, Mentor Books, Dublin, 1998.

Dear Frankie, Mint Productions television documentary for RTÉ, 2006.

Cameron, Sir Charles Alexander (1830–1921)
Physician and City Medical Officer for Health
27 Raglan Road, Ballsbridge, Dublin 4

Charles Alexander Cameron was born in Dublin to Captain Ewen Cameron, a Scottish soldier, and his Cavan wife, Belinda (*née* Smith). There were three children in the family. He was educated in Dublin at Mr Halahan's School on York Street, and in Guernsey where the family lived for two years.

Back in Dublin, Charles became apprenticed to Bewley & Evans, apothecaries. He went on to study Chemistry in Germany, where he graduated with a PhD in 1856. In Dublin he attended the Apothecaries Hall, a well-known medical school, as well as studying at the Dublin School of Medicine, and the Ledwich Medical School. He was awarded an MD from Trinity College Dublin in 1865. In 1868 he obtained the Licentiate of the Royal College of Physicians of Ireland and was made a Fellow of this College in 1893. Prior to this in 1874, he had become a Fellow of the Royal College of Surgeons in Ireland in 1874. He also held a Diploma in Public Health from Cambridge University, and received an honorary MD from the Royal University of Ireland in 1896.

From a young age, Cameron took a great interest in Chemistry, and though still a student, he was elected 'Professor of Chemistry' by members of the Dublin Chemical Society. He was only 22 years old. He received great publicity from the local press for his lectures and practical demonstrations at that time. He became a well-known lecturer subsequently and lectured in places such as the Dr Stevens's Hospital Medical School (formerly the Dublin School of Medicine) and at the Agricultural Institution in Glasnevin. In 1868 he obtained the Chair of Chemistry and Hygiene at the Royal College of Surgeons in Ireland (RCSI). For fifty-five years Cameron was a professor on the staff of the RCSI, and finally in 1886 he became President of the college.

In 1862, Cameron married Lucie Frances MacNamara, daughter of a well-known solicitor, John MacNamara. The marriage took place at St Mary's Church, Anglesea Road. They had six sons and two daughters. Unfortunately, three of their sons died tragically. Their two daughters married, one to a Resident Magistrate in Cavan, and their younger one to a Professor of Physics and Electrical Engineering in Belfast. Charles's wife, Lucie, died, from heart disease in 1883, much to his sorrow, and he shunned society for a period of two years afterwards. During that time, he wrote a history of the Royal College of Surgeons in Ireland. A second edition was published in 1916. It contains an incredible amount of information on old Dublin, doctors, surgeons and the various private medical schools then in existence. Cameron was a prolific writer and he published at least twelve medical books. He was also an editor and part owner of *The Agricultural Review* and *The Country Gentleman's Newspaper*. Cameron always had an interest in the theatre and knew a number of well-known Irish and international actresses whom he would have met at various dinner parties for celebrities visiting Dublin. He was an enthusiastic theatregoer and became a noted drama critic.

Cameron was a leading member of the ecumenical movement in Ireland during the late nineteenth and early twentieth centuries. He was a Protestant, and a strong Unionist, and although not a teetotaller himself, Cameron became one of the Hon. Secretaries of the Fund subscribed to erect a statue to Fr Matthew, the Apostle of Temperance in Sackville Street in Dublin. He was also involved in the erection of a statue to Lord Ardilaun in St Stephen's Green.

It was as a Public Health Medical Officer that Cameron carried out his most important work. He was Medical Officer for Health for the City of Dublin for more than fifty years until his death in 1921. During his medical career he was responsible for improving the living conditions of the poor of Dublin. He also received a number of personal honours, including a Knighthood, and in 1911 he was made an Honorary Freeman of the City of Dublin. During his career, he persuaded the Lord Lieutenant to ask the Prince of Wales during a visit to Dublin in 1885 to visit the slums of Dublin to allow him to see the conditions the poor lived in. The Prince agreed after the visit that the houses and tenements should be condemned. Some twenty-five years later when King Edward VII (formerly the Prince of Wales) visited Dublin again, Cameron brought him to see the new houses that had been built and other tenements he was trying to have demolished.

In his work as City Medical Officer for Health, Cameron was responsible for working closely with the poor of Dublin trying to improve their living conditions. After the exodus of the gentry from Dublin subsequent to the Act of Union, their former homes were transformed into the equivalent of death traps for the poor, with anything up to ten families living in one unfurnished house or tenement with little or no facilities and killer diseases rampant among them.

Dublin Corporation eventually assumed responsibility for the poor of Dublin, and it was only then that the poor health, hygiene and housing conditions began to be investigated. Cameron was a ceaseless campaigner for proper housing for the poor. Until then, the high mortality rates, hygiene and housing problems had been almost ignored. Due to his great work, hundreds of decaying tenement houses, with their lack of proper water closets, running water etc., were cleared. 'Build houses for the poor' became his war cry. He continued in his endeavour to persuade Dublin Corporation of the importance of providing public housing for the poor, who so desperately needed them.

Cameron took on the most senior posts in the Corporation of Dublin, assuming the roles of City Analyst, Superintendent Medical Officer of Health and Executive Sanitary Officer of the City of Dublin. Food inspection became a focus of Charles Cameron's work. He became aware by the 1870s that diseased cattle could pass their diseases to humans through their meat. Cameron also investigated the passage of human and animal diseases to other humans through the medium of milk. He may also be one of the first to highlight the role of shellfish in transmitting typhoid. His work and research was a major contributor to discussions on germs and their role in diseases in the late nineteenth century in Ireland.

Over the years, while in the posts he held, Cameron's opinion was sought by public bodies in other countries as well as in Ireland. Because of his work as a sanitary scientist, he was known throughout Europe. He received honorary membership of a number of foreign learned societies, including the Swedish Academy of Medicine and the Hygienic Associations of Paris and Bordeaux.

Cameron has also been given credit for discovering kaolin on the estate of a Mr J.C. Bloomfield at Caldwell Castle on Lough Erne, Co. Fermanagh. He spotted a white patch of clay and on tasting it recognised it was porcelain clay. This discovery in 1857 led to the establishment of the well-known Belleek porcelain factory.

Cameron became a Freemason in 1859. The Freemasons initiated a Lodge called the Charles A. Cameron Lodge 72 in Dublin, which was named in his honour. He became Deputy Grand Master of the Great Priory of Ireland and was ultimately elected deputy grand master of the Grand Lodge of Ireland between 1911 and 1920.

He was a very sociable gentleman and loved dinner parties in particular. He was a well-known member of different gentlemen's clubs. In 1899 he founded and became President of one of the very fashionable Dublin clubs, called The Corinthian Club. In 1920 he published his autobiography called *Autobiography of Sir Charles A. Cameron*.

Cameron died on 27 February 1921 at his home, No. 27 Raglan Road, and he is buried in Mount Jerome Cemetery.

Further Reading

Cameron, Sir Charles A., *Autobiography of Sir Charles A. Cameron*, Hodges Figgis, Dublin, 1921.

Lyons, J.B., 'The Royal College of Surgeons in Ireland and its Worthies', *Dublin Historical Record*, xlviii (1), 1955, pp.52-.

Mac Thomáis, Éamonn, 'Sir Charles A. Cameron', *Dublin Historical Record*, XXII (2), 1968, pp.214–224.

Coghill, Rhoda (1903–2000)
Pianist, Composer and Poet
100 Marlborough Road, Donnybrook, Dublin 4

Rhoda Coghill was born in Dublin and lived most of her life in the family home at 100 Marlborough Road in Donnybrook. Her parents were Alexander Sinclair Coghill from Thurso in Scotland and his wife, Rhoda Ann Sinclair (*née* Baily). The young Rhoda was born into a middle class family of nine children living in Donnybrook. She was educated at Alexandra College. Her musical education began with piano lessons from her mother and she then proceeded to the Leinster School of Music, where she studied with Patricia Read, a well-known piano teacher. At the age of 15 she was billed as 'the child pianist', a star attraction at Dublin's Theatre Royal. On leaving Alexandra College she went on to attend Trinity College Dublin and graduated with a BMus degree in 1922. In 1923 she made her London debut as a pianist at the Steinway Hall to great acclaim. On the advice of Colonel Fritz Brase, Director of the Irish Army School of Music, she spent time (1927–1928) studying piano with Artur Schnabel in Berlin. Coghill was a winner of all the major piano competitions in the Feis Ceoil – piano solo, piano accompaniment and piano duet in and around 1923, for composition. In 1928 she was appointed official Feis Ceoil accompanist.

During her career Coghill taught at the Read Piano School for a number of years. With the establishment of the Dublin Philharmonic Society Orchestra in 1927, she was a piano soloist with the orchestra and also played the double bass. During her time, she was also involved with the managing committee of the Society. She later played with the Radio Éireann Symphony Orchestra under a number of different conductors. In 1939, Coghill became a member of the staff of RTÉ as official accompanist in succession to Kitty O'Callaghan. Her salary was £4 per week. In her role Coghill worked with a variety of Irish and international performers and remained with the station until her retirement in 1968. However, she was retained as an accompanist by RTÉ for almost ten years after retirement. She had remarkable sight reading skills, a wonderful ear and had a great facility to transpose material for any performer. International artists found her to be a marvellous accompanist.

During her career Coghill had a string of solo concerto performances to her credit and has been described as one of the finest Irish musicians of the twentieth century. Besides being an outstanding musician and performer, she was also a composer of some significance. In 1923, while still a student, she composed the rhapsody 'Out of the Cradle Endlessly Rocking' from a text by Walt Whitman for tenor solo, chorus and orchestra. This is one of the few significant musical works by an Irish composer before the Second World War. The first performance of this important work did not take place until the mid-1950s, when it was performed with a small orchestra and a vocal quartet replacing the chorus. It is perhaps unusual that until then Coghill had never heard an orchestra in action but knew about orchestral music from working on scores. 'Out of the Cradle Endlessly Rocking' did not have its full premier until 1990, which was attended by the composer at the age of 87! The work was also revived at the National Concert Hall's 2016 Composing the Island Festival, when it was performed on 25 September 2016 with both the National Symphony Orchestra and the RTÉ Philharmonic Choir.

In the 1930s, Coghill was very involved in Ireland's major emerging musical infrastructure. She was a member of its major orchestra, was a member of staff of Radio Éireann and was very involved in the Feis Ceoil. This organisation was founded in 1897 with the aim of promoting music in Ireland through concerts, performances and composition competitions. For a number of years Coghill continued with her solo career but continued to be in great demand as an accompanist. It is interesting to recall that, like many other organisations, Radio Éireann discriminated against female musicians by paying them a rate that was only 80 per cent of that earned by their male colleagues. However, orchestral leaders and accompanists were paid at a slightly higher rate, which benefited Coghill. During her time there too, women had to retire on marriage, which was similar to the Civil Service ban on employing married women. While working in Radio Éireann, Coghill also performed in public such concerti as Beethoven's Emperor (1944), Schumann's Piano Concerto (1956), Beethoven's Piano Concerto No. 4 (1946), and Rachmaninov's Second Piano Concerto (1948).

In comparison with other Irish composers such as Ina Boyle, her original compositions were quite small. With the exception of her orchestral rhapsody, the majority of Coghill's compositions are songs she composed between 1923 and 1941. Her *Gaelic Fantasy* (1939) was published by An Gum. Some of her songs had words by Padraic Colum and AE. It seems she gave up composing during the early 1940s. During this period Irish composers in general had great difficulty in getting their work published, so perhaps that is why she turned to poetry. There are a number of unpublished music works by Coghill archived in the Library of Trinity College Dublin. As Laura Watson has so clearly pointed out, Coghill was at her most prolific in the 1920s and early '30s with 'a burst of activity again in the early 1940s before going silent'. It should also be pointed out that many of her original songs and arrangements were associated with the Irish Literary Revival. It is interesting to note that parallel with her compositions, Coghill was also an arranger of Irish folk music.

From the early 1940s, Coghill turned her attention to poetry. She had poems published in *The Dublin Magazine*, *The Bell*, the *Irish Press* and the *Irish Times*. Her first collection of poetry, *The Bright Hillside*, appeared in 1946 and was published by Hodges Figgis in Dublin. The introduction was written by Seamus O'Sullivan, editor of *The Dublin Magazine*. She was also said to be admired by another distinguished Irish poet, Austin Clarke. There was one more collection of her poetry, *Time is a Squirrel* (1956), which was 'printed for the author at the Dolmen Press'. Coghill also appeared in the first *Field Day Anthology of Irish Women Writers* published in 2002. She was a member of the Society of Friends (Quakers) and her interest in nature is exemplified in her poetry.

Coghill was a highly successful pianist and accompanist, teacher, broadcaster and poet. From 1982, she lived in Westfield House, a retirement home run by the Quakers, on Bloomfield Avenue, Donnybrook. She died aged 96 in February 2000 and is buried in the Friends Burial Ground at Temple Hill, Blackrock, Co. Dublin.

Further Reading

Klein, Axel, 'Coghill, Rhoda', in *Dictionary of Irish Biography*, edited by James McGuire and James Quinn, Cambridge University Press, Cambridge.

Bourke, Angela *et al* (eds), *The Field Day Anthology of Irish Writing*, vol. iv: *Irish Women's Writing and Traditions*, Cork University Press, Cork, 2002.

Sadie, Julie Anne; Samuel, Rhian, *The Norton/Grove Dictionary of Women Composers* (digitised online by Google Books), 1994, retrieved 9 February 2019.

Colles, Abraham (1773–1843)
Professor of Surgery and President, RCSI
Donnybrook Cottage, Stillorgan Road, Donnybrook, Dublin 4

Abraham Colles was born into a wealthy Anglo–Irish family at Millmount near Kilkenny on 23 July 1773. The family became wealthy through their business quarrying the famous black Kilkenny marble. His father was William Colles and his mother was Mary Anne Bates from Co. Wexford. Abraham's father died when he was only 6, leaving his mother with three sons and one daughter. His mother took over the running of the quarry, which allowed her to provide her family with a good education. Colles attended a local school and then attended the Kilkenny Endowed School (Kilkenny College). In 1807 he married Sophie Cope, daughter of the Rev. Jonathan Cope, Rector of Ahascraghin, Co. Galway. They had a large family of six sons and five daughters, one of whom a boy, died young and is buried in Donnybrook graveyard. In 1841 Colles' son, William (1809–1892), succeeded him as surgeon to Dr Steevens' Hospital in Dublin. In 1863 he became Regius Professor of Surgery at Trinity College and President of the RCSI in 1863. He was also surgeon to the Queen in Ireland.

From an early age, Colles had an interest in surgery, probably brought about by him acquiring an anatomy book given to him by a local doctor. His great grandfather, William Colles (1648–1719) of Kilkenny, had been a famous surgeon there, so there was a tradition of medicine in the family. He entered Trinity College Dublin on 4 September 1790 and received the Licentiate Diploma of the Royal College of Surgeons in 1795. While studying at Trinity he was apprenticed to Surgeon Philip Woodroffe at Dr Steevens Hospital and he eventually went on to succeed him in this post.

At this time Edinburgh was considered a great centre of excellence for medical education and Colles continued his study of medicine at the Medical School of Edinburgh University. He graduated there with an MD in 1797. After graduation, Colles headed for London and it is said that he walked the entire 400 miles there from Edinburgh! In London, Colles worked with the distinguished surgeon Ashley Cooper dissecting the inguinal region of the body. When he returned to Dublin, Colles took a house in Chatham Street and he rented rooms at the back of South King Street, where he taught anatomy and surgery. He attended the Foundling Hospital and the House of Industry Hospital, more familiar to us as Jervis Street Hospital. He was appointed to the Dispensary for the Sick Poor in Meath Street, which was a charity established by the Society of Friends (Quakers). He also became involved with the Sick and Indigent Roomkeepers' Society, where he worked with the poor and for whom he later developed a great sympathy.

After returning to Dublin, Colles applied for the Chair of Anatomy and Surgery at his alma mater, Trinity College, but was unsuccessful. Instead he turned his attention to the Royal College of Surgeons in Ireland, of which he had become a member (equivalent to a modern Fellow) in 1799. The name Abraham Colles continues to be closely associated with this College today, where he became President of the RCSI in 1802 at the young age of 29. He also served a second term as President in 1830. He held the Professorship of Surgery in the Royal College of Surgeons from 1804 to 1836 and was Professor of Anatomy and Physiology in the College. Colles was in no small way responsible for raising the reputation of the College as a teaching institution so that by 1836 the student numbers had risen to a thousand. About this time too, Colles joined the Medico-Chirurgical Society dating from 1837, of which he later became President.

Colles is well known in medical circles for his contribution to clinical anatomy. His was the first definitive description of what today is known as a Colles fracture – a fracture of the wrist that will be forever associated with him. It is usually caused by a fall on the palm of one's hand. He published his first paper on the topic entitled 'On the fracture of the Carpal extremity of the Radius' in the *Edinburgh Medical & Surgical Journal* of 1814. In this article, Colles provided a detail description of this type of fracture. It is interesting to note that this is almost eighty years before the development of radiology. Colles always had an interest in the process of teaching anatomy. He is credited with introducing a topographical-based teaching method where emphasis is placed on 'the practical application of anatomical researches to surgical uses'.

Colles contributed greatly to Ireland's role as a leader in world medicine during the early nineteenth century. This indeed was the golden age of Irish medicine when the Meath Hospital was recognised as a famous training and research centre. Abraham Colles will be forever associated with the study of anatomy, especially through the various eponyms including his discovery and description of Colles' fascia (1811), Colles' ligament (1811) and Colles law (1837). Perhaps not so well known is his interest in and observations on treatments for syphilis. While working at Dr Steevens' Hospital as resident surgeon (for a modest salary of £178 4s 5d), Colles became interested in venereal diseases and published a book titled *Practical Observations on the Venereal Disease and on the use of Mercury in its Treatment.* In treating deformities caused by syphilis he recommended reducing the dosage of mercury, which at that time was commonly used to treat the infection. Presumably he recognised the dangerous nature of using the element. He is also credited in performing the first surgery for axillary artery aneurysm.

Among his numerous appointments was that of surgeon in 1803 to the Dublin Fever Hospital. Resigning from other positions, Colles remained working at Dr Steevens Hospital until 1841, two years before his death. Colles continued to publish in his retirement, and his final work was his *Lectures on The Theory and Practice of Surgery*, which was published posthumously in 1845. In his later years, Colles suffered from chronic respiratory disease, gout, and heart disease. Unusually, he arranged for his own post mortem on his death, stating 'it may be of some benefit not only to my own family, but to society at large, to ascertain by examination the exact seat and nature of my last disease'. Abraham died in Dublin on 1 December 1843 and he received a public funeral on the day of his burial in Mount Jerome Cemetery.

Further Reading

Andrews, H., 'Colles, Abraham', in *Dictionary of Irish Biography,* edited by James McGuire and James Quinn, Cambridge University Press, Cambridge.

Fallon, M., *Abraham Colles 1773–1843, Surgeon of Ireland*, Heinemann Medical, London, 1972.

Lyons, J.B., *Brief Lives of Irish Doctors*, Blackwater, Dublin, 1978.

Colum, Mary Catherine (1887–1957)
Critic and Teacher

2 Belmont Avenue, Donnybrook, Dublin 4

Mary Catherine (Molly) Colum was born in Collooney, Co. Sligo, in 1886 to Charles Maguire from Co. Fermanagh and his wife, Maria Maguire (*née* Gunning). Her father was a member of the Royal Constabulary, while her mother was related to the mid-eighteenth-century Gunning sisters, who married into the British aristocracy. When her parents died young, Molly was brought up by her maternal grandmother and on her death was sent as a boarder to St Louis Convent in Monaghan. On finishing school, she was sent to Germany to a convent school to learn the language, and then went on to University College Dublin, where she studied Modern Languages and Literature.

During her period at University College Dublin, the Irish Literary Revival was in full swing. It emphasised the revival of Ireland's Gaelic heritage and was in many ways responsible for the growth of Irish nationalism. While a student at UCD from 1900, Colum and a group of her friends started a small society known as the Twilight Literary Society. The title came from Yeats's *Celtic Twilight*, a volume of essays published in 1893. This society became very active in Dublin's literary and artistic circles and parties of the period, attending all the Abbey plays, the major exhibitions, and the various antiquarian and historical societies. As a result, Molly met all the major figures of the Literary Revival such as W.B. Yeats James Joyce, AE, J.M. Synge and Lady Gregory. Yeats became a great influence on Molly, and it was he who encouraged her to abandon her intention of writing fiction and advised her instead to concentrate on criticism. There does not appear to be any evidence that Molly took easily to the idea of being a critic and while working as one she continued to publish short stories.

Besides being active in the Twilight Literary Society, Molly also campaigned for Irish women's suffrage. She joined Inghinidhe na hÉireann, which became a branch of Cumann na mBan, which dates from 1914, and became a member of its Executive. When she graduated, Molly joined the staff of St Ita's, a girls' school founded by Padraig Pearse. She was involved with fellow teachers Thomas

MacDonagh, Padraic Colum and David Houston in founding the *Irish Review* in 1911. She was the only woman among the male founders of this magazine, which closed in 1915. It was a monthly publication devoted to Irish literature, art and science, and together with Padraic Colum, she edited it. It was in the *Irish Review* that Molly published her first review of the collected works of John Millington Synge. As a result of this review, Molly became in fact, critic in chief for the *Irish Review*, writing numerous book reviews, full-length essays and a short story.

In 1912, Molly married Padraic Colum and they set up house on Belmont Avenue in Donnybrook. Well known as an Irish nationalist, poet, playwright, author and folklorist, Padraic Colum was an ideal husband for Molly since they had so much in common. In 1914, Padraic's aunt offered them a passage to America and their plan was to remain there only for a few months, so he could give some lectures. On their arrival in the United States, Padraic and Molly were introduced to the leading Irish nationalists, academics and Irish literary figures. At that time, they met John Devoy, the editor of the *Gaelic American* newspaper, and they also met Roger Casement, who was in the USA on a fund-raising tour for the Irish Volunteers.

Except for various visits to Europe and a three-year stay in France, Padraic and Molly spent the rest of their lives in the United States of America. They lived predominately in New York at No. 415 Central Park West and they both taught at Columbia University until 1956. They travelled widely in Europe as well as spending summers in New Hampshire and in Massachusetts. They also spent time in Miami at Miami University and carried out lecture tours in the Midwest.

Over the years Colum published in the major American literary journals of the day such as *Scribner's*, *The Dial*, *The New Republic*, *The Saturday Review of Literature*, and *The New York Times Book Review*. The 1930s seem to have been the most prolific period of her publishing in various journals. In 1933 she wrote a series of articles on contemporary literature that became her longest-running column, 'Life and Literature', published in *Forum and Century* (1933–1940). This provided her with a regular platform where she had an appreciative audience. All her life Colum's articles consisted of the book review, the literary history, various editorials and essays. Her writings were pitched towards the intellectual but non-academic audience. When this journal closed in the 1940s, she went on to publish articles in *American Mercury* and wrote a weekly page for poetry in *The New York Times Book Review*. During her career she wrote more than 160 articles for a variety of publications. She became an authority on literary criticism and wrote essays on many of her friends from Ireland and elsewhere, including W.B. Yeats, James Joyce, T.S. Eliot, D.H. Lawrence, Rebecca West, Ernest Hemingway and Virginia Woolf.

As a result of her first Guggenheim fellowship (she received two), in 1930 Colum and her husband spent three years in France, where she worked on a comparative study of the continental and English origins of literary modernism. Her subsequent book, *From These Roots*, was published in 1937 and for it she received an award for criticism from the American Academy.

Molly and Padraic Colum were very friendly with James Joyce and his wife, Nora. Molly wrote an article for an American journal called *The Freeman* entitled 'The confessions of James Joyce', which was published in 1922. This was one of the first reviews of *Ulysses* and was the first article published in the USA that did not condemn the book. Joyce was pleased with the review as he felt it represented his book accurately. She defined *Ulysses* as 'an epic of Dublin. Never was a city so involved in the workings of any writer's mind as Dublin is in Joyce's; he can think only in terms of it.' During their three years in Paris, the Colums spent quite a lot of time with Joyce and his family. Both the Colums played an integral role in the production of *Finnegans Wake* and they became its first readers. Molly was extremely kind to Lucia Joyce, daughter of James and Nora, who had severe mental health problems. So, when Colum discusses Joyce in her autobiography and criticism she writes as someone who knew him well and had an excellent understanding of his life and work.

Perhaps Colum's outstanding contribution to English literature was her autobiography *Life and the Dream*, which was published ten years before she died in 1947. It covers the period of her life from boarding school in Monaghan to her return from living in Europe in 1938. The majority of the book has been described as accurate, especially the writings on her friends and acquaintances. In particular, the portraits of the Irish literary personalities and of literary society in New York and elsewhere in the USA were well described. The book was a great success and went into five editions. Colum was elected to the National Institute of Arts and Letters in 1953 and from 1952 until she died she was a guest professor of Comparative Literature at Columbia University.

In the latter part of her life, Colum suffered from extreme arthritis and neuralgia, and at the time of her death in 1957 she was working on a book with Padraic called *Our Friend James Joyce*, which was published posthumously in 1958. She died in New York on 22 October 1957 and is buried in St Fintan's Cemetery, Sutton, along with Padraic.

Further Reading

Colum, Mary, *Life and The Dream*, The Dolmen Press, Dublin, revised ed., 1966.

Kain, Richard M., 'Mary Colum', in Hogan, R., *Dictionary of Irish Literature*, 1979.

Mary Maguire Colum, *Biography. marycolum.com*

Murphy, Maureen, 'Colum, Mary Catherine (Molly)', in *Dictionary of Irish Biography*, edited by James McGuire and James Quinn, Cambridge University Press, Cambridge, in progress.

Colum, Padraic (1881–1972)
Poet, Novelist and Playwright
2 Belmont Avenue, Donnybrook, Dublin 4

Born Padraic Collumb, to Patrick and Susan Collumb (*née* McCormack) on 8 December 1881 in Longford, where his father was master of the local workhouse, he was the eldest of eight children. In 1889, his father emigrated to the United States to join the gold rush but returned empty handed in 1892. The family then moved to Dublin, where Patrick became the stationmaster at Sandycove railway station. On the death of his mother in 1897, the family was split up, with Padraic and one of his brothers remaining in Dublin, while his father and the other children returned to Longford. Colum therefore grew up in Dublin and was educated at the local national school in Glasthule. At the age of 17, he obtained a post of clerk by competitive examination in the Irish Railway Clearing House. There he began writing and was fortunate enough to secure a four-year scholarship in 1904 from a wealthy American, Thomas Hughes Kelly, which allowed him to study and write at University College Dublin.

Colum joined the Gaelic League in 1901 and also the Irish Republican Army. He then changed his name to the Irish form – Colum. He became a friend of many famous writers and artists over the years, including W.B. Yeats, Arthur Griffith and James Joyce. In 1902, Colum's early poems were to be found in *The Irish Independent* and *The United Irishmen*. Included were two of his best-known poems, 'An Old Woman of the Roads' and 'The Drover'. His first two plays. *The Saxon Shilling* and *Broken Soil* (later rewritten as *The Fiddler's House*), were staged in 1902. At this time, too, he became active in the National Theatre Society and was involved in the founding of the Abbey Theatre. His second play at the Abbey, *The Land*, was produced in 1905 and was a great success.

Padraic Colum's first volume of poetry, *Wild Earth*, was published in 1907 and was dedicated to George Russell, AE. This volume also contained 'An Old Woman of the Roads' and 'A Poor Scholar of the Forties', both now well known to Irish children from their primary school days. Another poem from this collection, 'She Moved Through the Fair', became a well-loved ballad and is still popular today. In 1911, Colum, together with David Houston, Thomas MacDonagh and Mary Maguire, established a literary magazine called the *Irish Review*, which published poems, plays, criticisms and reviews. Colum was a close friend of MacDonagh and became a militant nationalist. He was involved in the Howth gun running (1914) and was part of a group of Irish Volunteers who were fired on by British soldiers at Bachelor's Walk in 1913.

The marriage of Padraic Colum and Mary Maguire (1887–1957), friends from their *Irish Review* days, took place in 1912. They became a very well-known literary couple, but they had no family. For two years, they lived at No. 2 Belmont Avenue in Donnybrook before they moved to New York, where they were to spend the rest of their lives apart from three years that they spent in France. Their Tuesday soirees at Belmont Avenue saw them entertain the literati of the day. In New York there were great opportunities for a young literary couple and both Padraic and Molly (as she was known) Colum lectured at Columbia University for many years. While living there, Padraic wrote poetry and books of Irish folk tales. The publication of his popular *The Adventure of Odysseus* and *The Children of Odin* were responsible for introducing children to classical literature. He also wrote *A Boy in Eirinn* (1913) and *The King of Ireland's Son* (1916).

In New York, Padraic received a commission from the Hawaiian Legislature (via Macmillan Publishers) to write children's stories based on Hawaiian myths and legends. Between 1925 and 1937 he published three volumes of *Tales and Legends of Hawaii*. He loved Ireland, its history, legends and stories. His first novel, *Castle Conquer*, was published in 1923. He published a second book about Ireland called *The Road Around Ireland* in 1926, and a volume of poems called *Creatures* in 1927.

The Colums lived in France from 1930 to 1933, where Padraic renewed his friendship with James Joyce. He helped Joyce in the preparation of manuscripts for publication and wrote a preface for the American edition of *Anna Livia Plurabelle* (1929). The Colums and the Joyce family became firm friends and holidayed together in Nice in the south of France. Padraic Colum worked closely with Joyce typing his manuscripts, and reading to him, as Joyce was almost blind. Once back in America, the two Colums continued to lecture at Columbia University while writing books and plays. Colum published more than sixty books during his lifetime and was involved in a number of different literary projects up until he died in 1972. He continued to write poetry and published a number of books of poetry such as *The Big Tree* (1935), *The Story of Lowry Maen* (1937) and *Flower Pieces* (1938). The *Collected Poems of Padraic Colum* was published in 1953 and *The Poet's Circuits: Collected Poems of Ireland* appeared in 1960. He wrote two significant biographies of two of his close friends: *Our Friend James Joyce* (1958), which he wrote with his wife before she died, and *Ourselves Alone: The Story of Arthur Griffith and the Origin of the Irish Free State*, which was published in 1959.

Colum's five Noh plays written between 1961 and 1966, were a homage to W.B. Yeats. Based on the Japanese tradition, they are a five-play cycle of both poetry and prose. These plays are entitled *Moytura, Glendalough, Cloughoughter, Monasterboice and Kilmore*, and were devoted to the memories of William Wilde, Charles Stuart Parnell, Roger Casement, James Joyce and Henry Joy McCracken.

During the course of his life, Colum was honoured by a number of American and Irish universities, receiving doctorates in 1958 from University College Dublin (his alma mater) and Columbia University. In 1957, after Molly died in New York, Colum divided his time between New York and Dublin, where he stayed with his sister at No. 11 Edenvale Road, Ranelagh. He died on 11 January 1972 in Enfield, Connecticut. His body was returned to Ireland and he is buried with his wife in St Fintan's Cemetery, Sutton, Co. Dublin.

Further Reading

Denson, Alan, 'Padraic Colum: An Appreciation, with a Check-list of his Publications', *Dublin Magazine* VI (1), 1967, pp.50–678.

Bowen, Zack, *Padraic Colum: A Biographical Introduction*, Southern Illinois University Press, Carbondale, 1970.

Sternlicht, Sanford, *Padraic Colum*, Twayne Publications, Boston, 1987.

Costello, John Aloysius (1891–1976)
Taoiseach and Attorney General
20 Herbert Park, Ballsbridge, Dublin 4

John A. Costello was born in Dublin on 20 June 1891 in Cabra and was the younger son of John Costello, a civil servant, and his wife, Rose Callaghan from Westmeath. His father was a staff officer in the Registry of Deeds and, when he retired, he became a member of Dublin City Council. John A. Costello was educated by the Christian Brothers, first at St Joseph's in Fairview, and then at O'Connell Schools, where he completed his secondary education. Costello was a bright student and won a scholarship for the sons of civil servants, which allowed him to study at University College Dublin, where his brother Thomas was already a medical student. In 1911, Costello graduated from the university with a degree in Modern Languages (including Irish) and Law. As a student he was a regular attender at the Literary and Historical Society (L & H) but was not a prize winner and was defeated twice for its auditorship.

On graduation, Costello studied at the King's Inns. He was called to the Irish Bar in 1914 and worked full time as a barrister for a number of years. He joined the Munster circuit initially and received many of his briefs from Co. Clare solicitors. In 1919, he married Ida Mary O'Malley (1891–1956), a doctor's daughter from Galway who was a teacher at the Dominican Convent, Eccles Street. They had three sons: Wilfred, Declan and John, and two daughters; Grace and Eavan. Costello became a member of the staff of the Attorney General in 1922, and three years later, in 1925, he received a call to the Inner Bar. The Irish Free State came into being in 1922 and Costello became assistant to the Attorney General, Hugh Kennedy, who had been his former master. In 1926, he succeeded Kennedy as Attorney General of Ireland, with the formation of the Cumann na nGael Government, under the leadership of W.T. Cosgrave. He gave up private practice at this point in time. As Attorney General, he represented the Irish Free State at Imperial conferences and at the League of Nations. When Fianna Fáil came into power in 1932, Costello lost his position and he then returned to practising at the Bar.

Éamon de Valera, who became the new President of the Executive Council in 1933, called a snap election in which Fianna Fáil won an overall majority. There was a vacancy in an eight-seater Dublin County constituency and Costello applied and was elected to Dail Éireann as a Cumann na nGael TD. This party soon merged with others to become Fine Gael. Later he represented the Dublin Townships and, later still, the Dublin South-East Constituency. Throughout his career, Costello was a prominent spokesman in the Dail on behalf of Fine Gael. He continued to represent his constituency between 1937 and 1948, except for a break between 1943 and the 1944 general elections.

In 1948, an inter-party Government was formed, and Costello, being a member of the front bench, was the most acceptable candidate to the other parties as Taoiseach. His term of office began well with the negotiation of a trade agreement with the British Government in 1948, to improve access for Irish agricultural exports. While on a visit to Canada in September 1948, Costello announced he intended to repeal the External Relations Act of 1935 under which the King signed the credentials of Irish ambassadors. The Republic of Ireland Act repealed the External Relations Act of 1936 and thus ended Ireland's membership of the Commonwealth. This alienated the British Government because it was done without their prior knowledge or consultation. Negotiations between the two countries resulted in a continuation of existing trade, nationality and immigration arrangements. In retaliation, the British Government enacted without prior consultation the Ireland Act 1949, which recognised the Republic of Ireland, and included a declaration that Northern Ireland would not cease to be part of the United Kingdom without the approval of its parliament. It also gave full rights to any Irish citizens living in the United Kingdom. The 1950s saw the Government establish the Industrial Development Authority and the export organisation Córas Tráchtála, which indicated a move away from the economic policies of self-sufficiency common up to then.

One of the big issues in Ireland during Costello's time as Taoiseach was the controversy over the Health Bill and the Mother and Child Scheme introduced by Dr Noel Browne, then Minister for Health. Costello came from a very Catholic background and the Mother and Child Scheme was opposed by doctors, who feared a loss of income, and by the Irish Bishops, who were afraid it would lead to birth control and abortion. In Dublin in particular, the scheme was vigorously opposed by the Archbishop of Dublin, Dr John Charles

McQuaid. Costello supported the Bishops and forced Browne's resignation. The 1950s, too, saw a resumption of IRA activity in Northern Ireland and this became a problem for the Irish Government. Costello deployed the army to the border and availed of the Offences Against the State Act of 1939 when dealing with IRA members. Partition unfortunately remained a problem, which would break out with terrible violence twenty years later.

Achievements of the Costello-led Government included the Anglo–Irish Trade Agreement of 1948, which provided some favourable terms for Irish agricultural exports to Britain. Housing and hospital services were also improved. Costello called an election in June 1951 and Fianna Fáil was returned to power. During this time, Costello continued to be parliamentary leader of the party, with Richard Mulcahy, the leader of the Fine Gael party.

Fine Gael returned to power at the general election of 1954, and Costello once again became Taoiseach. Under this Government, Ireland became a member of the United Nations in 1955. He had a successful visit to the United States the following year, visiting the White House on St Patrick's Day, a tradition that has been followed by all Taoisigh to this very day.

A vote of no confidence in the Government by the Fianna Fáil party in 1957 saw Costello ask the President, Seán T. O'Kelly, to dissolve the Oireachtas. The 1957 Election saw Fianna Fáil return to power with an overall majority, and they went on to serve as the Government of the country for the next sixteen years. As the opposition party in the Dail, Fine Gael fought vigorously a proposal in a referendum to abolish proportional representation, and they were successful. Costello supported policies led by his son, Declan, who wanted to make Fine Gael a natural ally for the Labour party. This led to the emergence of the famous 'Just Society' document, a policy statement adopted by Fine Gael in the 1960s based on the principles of social justice and equality.

In 1966, Costello was canvassed as a possible Fine Gael candidate for the Presidency of Ireland in opposition to Éamon de Valera, who at the age of 83 was running for a second term of office. However, in the event Costello did not run and de Valera was re-elected for a second term. Costello continued as a TD until the 1969 general election, when he stood down in Dublin South-East in favour of Garret FitzGerald. His main contribution to Fine Gael had been to revive the party by moderating its conservative and less nationalistic image.

Of the various legal cases that Costello was involved with, one of the most momentous was when he was part of the legal team in 1934, that represented General Eóin O'Duffy, following his arrest in Westport. Another one was his defence of *The Leader* newspaper in the libel action by Patrick Kavanagh. *The Leader* had published an anonymous profile of Kavanagh that incensed him, but he failed to find out who was the author. Kavanagh had hoped for an out-of-court settlement but in the event the case came before the High Court in

February 1954. Costello was the leading defence barrister and for two days he cross-examined Kavanagh, managing to undermine his credibility as a witness, and *The Leader* won the case.

After ceasing to be Taoiseach in 1957, Costello returned to his legal practice as a barrister. He continued to work well into his 70s and 80s. Over the years, he received a number of honours, including several doctorates from universities in the United States of America, and he received the Freedom of the City of Dublin in 1975.

By 1975, Costello had been diagnosed with cancer and he died at his home in Herbert Park on 5 January 1976. His family declined to have a state funeral for him, and he was buried in Deansgrange Cemetery after Requiem Mass at the Church of the Sacred Heart, Donnybrook.

Further Reading

Jordan, Anthony, *John A. Costello, 1891–1976: Compromise Taoiseach*, Westport Books, Dublin, 2007.

Lysaght, Charles, 'Costello, John Aloysius', in *Dictionary of Irish Biography*, edited by James McGuire and James Quinn, Cambridge University Press, Cambridge.

McCullagh, David, *The Reluctant Taoiseach*, Gill & Macmillan, Dublin, 2011.

De Valera, Éamon (1882–1975)
Taoiseach and President of Ireland
33 Morehampton Terrace, Donnybrook, Dublin 4

Éamon de Valera was born on 14 October 1882 in New York. His father was Juan Vivion de Valera and his mother was Catherine Coll (1856–1932), who came from Bruree, Co. Limerick. It is claimed that they were married in 1881, and the following year their son, Edward, was born. Vivion de Valera was Spanish. He suffered from chest disease and in 1884, in search of a milder climate, he moved to Denver, where he died in November of that year.

De Valera was separated from his mother aged 2 when he was brought back to Bruree, Co. Limerick, his mother's old home. His mother remained on in New York and remarried a non-Catholic Englishman, who was a coachman to a wealthy family in Rochester, New York. They lived over the stables and there they had two children who grew up as Catholics: Annie (1889–1997) and Thomas (1890–1946), who became a Redemptorist priest.

De Valera began his education at the local national school in Bruree. He went on to attend the Christian Brothers school in Charleville, North Cork, and then won a scholarship to Blackrock College in Dublin. This was the beginning of Éamon de Valera's rise on the social scale. He loved Blackrock College, and indeed continued to live close to it for most of his life. At Blackrock, de Valera proved to be a diligent student and he won middle-grade and senior-grade exhibitions in 1899 and 1900. He went on to attend Williamstown Castle, a centre for students to study for the examinations of the old Royal University. There he took the courses that offered a four-year degree in Arts. He graduated with a degree in Mathematics in 1901 from the Royal University. His first job was as a replacement teacher of Mathematics and Physics at Rockwell College near Cashel in Co. Tipperary.

While at Blackrock and at Rockwell, de Valera played rugby, and he played for Munster around 1905. He had a lifelong interest in the sport and attended all the international rugby matches until he died. De Valera also taught at Belvedere College (1905–1906) and at the Dominican College, Eccles Street (1906–1908). Other brief appointments included Castleknock College, Holy Cross College, and Carysfort Training College.

With the foundation of the National University of Ireland in 1908, the Irish language became a compulsory subject for matriculation and Carysfort also began to teach it. This put some pressure on de Valera to learn Irish and he moved into digs with a native Irish speaker from Mayo. In 1908, he joined Conradh na Gaeilge and changed his name from Edward to Éamon. While there he fell in love with his teacher, Sinéad Flanagan, who was four years older than him. She was a primary school teacher and an actor by profession. After a two-year courtship, they married on 8 January 1910 in St Paul's Church, Arran Quay, Dublin, and commenced their married life at No. 33 Morehampton Terrace, Donnybrook. They went on to have five sons and two daughters.

De Valera was interested in an academic career and applied for permanent posts at University College Galway in 1912 and at University College Cork in 1913. He withdraw his application for the Galway Chair in favour of a more highly qualified candidate, but was defeated by a candidate for the UCC post with higher academic qualifications, Edgar Harper (1880–1916), from Dungannon, Co. Tyrone.

De Valera joined the Irish Volunteers in 1913 and the Irish Republican Army in 1915. He was involved with the 1916 Rising, too, when he commanded the garrison at Boland's Mills. Sentenced to death for his part in the Rising, this was commuted and he was released from prison in 1917. As the most senior member of the Rising to survive, he became MP for East Clare in a by-election that year. Thus began his leadership career as he became President of Sinn Fein in 1917 and held this post until 1926. In 1917 also de Valera became President of the Irish Volunteers (the IRA).

A conscription law was passed in England in 1918 but it was never put into effect, so no one in Ireland was drafted into the British military. As a result of his opposition to conscription, de Valera's status increased considerably in Ireland. While it was not introduced to Ireland, the British Government did arrest seventy-three Sinn Fein leaders 'on trumped up allegations of plotting with German agents'. De Valera therefore spent a short time in Gloucester Prison and was then transferred to Lincoln Gaol. He made a dramatic escape from Lincoln on 3 February 1919, which was engineered by Michael Collins and Harry Boland. This produced worldwide headlines.

On 1 April 1919, de Valera attended his first meeting of Dail Éireann and was elected President. The War of Independence against the British forces in Ireland began in 1919. As the conflict spread, de Valera decided to go to the United States and take Ireland's case for self-determination to President Woodrow Wilson and the large numbers of Irish Americans. His aim was to achieve American support for Ireland in their battle for freedom from British rule. Meanwhile, he left his 29-year-old Minister for Finance, Michael Collins, in charge of day-to-day government in Ireland. De Valera returned to Dublin in January 1921 and at his first appearance in the Dail he introduced a motion calling on the IRA to stop its war tactics and to use conventional military methods to defeat the British forces in Ireland.

De Valera visited Lloyd George in London in 1921 in the hope of a truce but no agreement was reached. It was quite extraordinary that de Valera refused to head the Irish delegation that signed the Treaty in December 1921 to confirm the effective independence of twenty-six of Ireland's thirty-two counties as the Irish Free State, with Northern Ireland's six counties remaining under British rule. The delegation was led by Arthur Griffith and Michael Collins. De Valera had not authorised the signing of a treaty and he argued that the Dail should reject it. This led to the Civil War in Ireland (June 1922–May 1923). De Valera enlisted in his old battalion of Volunteers, now the IRA, and he formed a rival government. He remained in hiding for a number of months after the ceasefire was declared, but in August he emerged to stand for election in Co. Clare. In Ennis, de Valera was arrested on a platform by the Free Staters, and was interned at Arbour Hill Prison until 1924.

The year 1926 was a significant one in Irish politics because de Valera was persuaded by Séan Lemass to form a new Republican party. In March 1926, along with Lemass, Constance Markievicz and others, de Valera formed Fianna Fáil, and from the beginning it made clear that they did not consider the oath of allegiance to the British King binding. By 1932, Fianna Fáil was the largest party in the Irish Government. De Valera led the party and held office until 1948. The oath of allegiance to the British Crown was abolished in 1933 and in 1936 de Valera exploited the abdication crisis to pass an External Relations Act that largely abolished the role of the crown in Ireland. In 1937, de Valera introduced a new constitution, which reflected Catholic social policy as well as Republicanism.

Ireland remained neutral during the Second World War under de Valera's leadership. He also managed to protest successfully in 1941 against a proposal to extend conscription to Northern Ireland. In the 1948 election, de Valera lost the majority he had enjoyed since 1933. This led to the formation of the first Inter-Party Government with John A. Costello of Fine Gael as a compromise candidate for Taoiseach. The following year (1949), John A. Costello declared Ireland as a republic. However, de Valera returned to power with the general election of 1951, but without an overall majority. Faced with defeat in the Dail, de Valera called an election in May 1954, which he lost. The Second Inter-Party Government (1954–1957) was formed with Costello as Taoiseach again. This coalition only lasted for three years and at the general election of 1957, de Valera won a majority of nine seats. This led to another sixteen years of Fianna Fáil in office. By 1959, de Valera, at 75, was seen as too old and out of touch to remain as Taoiseach, so he decided to retire and instead seek the Presidency of Ireland. He won the 1959 Presidential election and was re-elected President again in 1966, at the age of 84.

He retired in 1973 at the age of 90 and he and his wife, Sinéad, retired to Linden Convalescent Home in Blackrock. In retirement de Valera continued his interest in Mathematics. He died from pneumonia and heart failure on 29 August 1975 at Linden Convalescent Home, aged 92. Sinéad had died in the previous January, on the eve of their sixty-fifth wedding anniversary.

Further Reading

Coogan, T.P., *De Valera: Long Fellow, Long Shadow*, Cornerstone, London, 2015.

Ferriter, D., *Judging Dev: A Reassessment of the Life and Legacy of Éamon de Valera*, Royal Irish Academy, Dublin, 2007.

McCullagh, David, *De Valera: Volume 1 Rise (1882–1932), Vol. 2 Rule 1932–1975*, Gill, Dublin, 2018.

De Valera, Sinéad (1878–1975)
Teacher, Author and Playwright
33 Morehampton Terrace, Donnybrook, Dublin 4

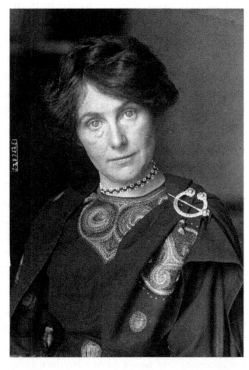

Born in Balbriggan, Co. Dublin, to Laurence and Margaret Flanagan, Jane (or Jennie) was one of a family of four children – three girls and one boy. Her parents had spent some time in Scotland and in the United States of America but returned to Balbriggan in 1873. Jane was born on 3 June 1878. The family moved to Phisborough in Dublin in 1885, when her father (a carpenter) obtained a post of clerk of works at the time of the building of a new church there, St Peter's Church. Jane always retained a great affection for Balbriggan as she spent holidays each year with her Aunt Kate, who ran a shop. Jane was educated locally and then trained as a teacher. Her first post was in Edenderry, Co. Offaly. She returned to Dublin in 1899 and took up at post at the Francis Xavier School that she had attended as a child. The census for 1901 has her living with her family at No. 6 Richmond Cottages in Dublin. Outside of school, she joined the Gaelic League. There she became involved in a number of plays, for example a tableaux staged by Alice Milligan, *The Tinker and The Fairy* by Douglas Hyde, and a play in Irish called *An Posadh (The Proposal)*. All her life she retained her interest in the theatre.

When Jane or Jennie Flanagan became interested in the Irish language she changed her name to Sinéad Ní Fhlannagain and attended classes at the Gaelic League in Dublin. She also spent time in the Mayo Gaeltacht learning Irish and went on to teach the language at Gaelic League classes in the city. She remained an enthusiastic promoter of the Irish language all her life. Sinéad joined Inghínidhe Na hÉireann (Daughters of Ireland), which was a radical women's organisation founded by Maud Gonne from 1900 to 1914. It then merged with a new organisation called Cumann na mBan. Sinéad acted in Irish language plays and taught the language to beginners, among them Seán T. O'Kelly, Ernest Blythe and Éamon de Valera. Sinéad and Éamon spent a holiday at the Irish College in Tourmakeady, Co. Mayo, in the summer of 1909. They were married in January 1910 at St Paul's Church in Arran Quay, and the ceremony was conducted in both English and Irish. They spent their honeymoon in Hotel Woodenbridge, Co. Wicklow. Éamon was 28 and Sinéad was 32 years old when they married. Sinéad devoted most of the rest of her life to her family, and remained in the background, playing little or no public role during her husband's fifty years in public office. Their family consisted of five sons and two daughters, one of whom, Brian, was killed in a riding accident in Phoenix Park in February 1936 when he was aged 20.

Sinéad was the backbone of the de Valera family when Éamon was involved in the 1916 Rising, after which he was jailed and sentenced to death. This was later commuted to penal servitude for life. With no financial income at that time, Sinéad had to leave her home in Donnybrook and return to her family home in Phisborough with some of her children. There she took care of her mother and invalid sister. Three of her children went to live with their Auntie Kate, Sinéad's sister, who lived in Balbriggan, and they remained with her for several months.

Éamon was released in the general amnesty of June 1917. When the family's financial situation improved somewhat, Sinéad moved with her children to Greystones, Co. Wicklow. There the de Valera family lived at Edenmore, Kinlen Road, Greystones. During her time in Wicklow, Sinéad was visited on a weekly basis by Michael Collins, who came with money for her (she had no income) and news of her husband. Between 1916 and 1923 Sinéad and her children saw very little of Éamon. This was due in the main to him being in prison or on the run, together with his various political activities and his fund-raising tour of the United States. They did manage to meet up in America in 1920 thanks to a false passport provided for her by Collins. She spent six weeks in the USA, but because of her husband's busy work schedule she did not see all that much of him. For many years Éamon and Sinéad were friends of the former Archbishop of Dublin, John Charles McQuaid, who had also been President of Blackrock College where Éamon was educated. He was a regular visitor to the de Valera home.

With her family reared, Sinéad turned to writing and she produced thirty-one books for children in both English and Irish. It is said that she could recite poetry at will. She translated fairy stories for children from Irish into English and wrote plays as well as poems for children. Her works include *Fairy Tales for Ireland* and *More Irish Fairy Tales*. Her fairy tales always seemed to end with glorious weddings and great feasts!

Sinéad was quite a distinguished intellectual, as was her husband. She was a quiet, shy and retiring woman, who was always a great support to Éamon during his political career. Over the years, she continued her interest in the Irish language and attended functions organised by the Gaelic League as well as children's drama competitions. There is a well-known all-Ireland trophy for Ceol Drama called the Sinéad de Valera All-Ireland Trophy for Ceol Drama, which is competed for every year. When her plays were produced in Dublin schools, she would frequently attend a performance.

Many tributes were paid to Sinéad de Valera on her death, and she was described as cultured, gracious and self-effacing. During her husband's Presidency of Ireland, she remained entirely in the background and made very few public appearances with him. A collection of love letters between Éamon and Sinéad surfaced in 2000. They were written between 1911 and 1920 and show a very different side of Éamon. Despite the hitherto description of de Valera as a stern, austere and remote father figure, the letters show that he was a warm individual with a great love for his wife. When he retired from the Presidency they both moved to Linden Convalescent Home in Blackrock. Sinéad died on 7 January 1975, aged 96. Her husband died almost eight months later, on 29 August 1975, aged 92. They are both buried in Glasnevin Cemetery.

Further Reading
Obituary, Sinéad de Valera, *Irish Press*, 8 January 1975.

O Tallamhain, Caitlin: *Sinéad: Sceal Shinead Bean de Valera*, Baile Atha Cliath, FNT, 1979.

McCoole, Sinéad, Ward, Margaret. *No Ordinary Women: Irish Female Activists in the Revolutionary Years 1900–1923*, O'Brien Press, Dublin, 2003.

Ward, Margaret, *Unmanageable Revolutionaries: Women and Irish Nationalism*, Pluto Press, London, 1983.

Dunlop, John Boyd (1840–1921)
Veterinary Surgeon and Inventor
Leighton, 46 Ailesbury Road, Donnybrook, Dublin 4

John Boyd Dunlop was born on a farm at Dreghorn in Ayrshire, Scotland, to John Dunlop, a farmer, and his wife, Agnes (*née* Boyd), on 5 February 1840. As a child he was considered delicate and not suitable for farm work. He attended the local parish school first and then studied at Irvine's Academy in Edinburgh. He went on to study Veterinary Medicine at the Royal School of Veterinary Science in Edinburgh (known as the Royal Dick after its founder William Dick). Dunlop graduated at the age of 19 and practised as a vet in Edinburgh before moving to Belfast in 1867, where he established a substantial practice. While living in Northern Ireland, he married Margaret Stevenson, the daughter of a farmer, James Stevenson. They had two children; a boy John, and a daughter Jean.

Dunlop's practice as a veterinary surgeon involved a great deal of travelling over roads in Belfast and the nearby counties of Antrim and Down, where he established the Down Veterinary Clinic together with his brother, James. Territories over which he travelled were often very rough, and since wheels in those days had rims of iron or wood, travelling was very uncomfortable. His 9-year-old son, Johnny, complained to his father that the hard cobbled streets of Belfast made riding his tricycle very uncomfortable. He started experimenting with the aim of making cycling more comfortable for his son. He began by fastening an air-filled rubber tube to a disk of wood with a strip of linen. In February 1888, he tested the tricycle using this tyre, which could be inflated with air and which was capable of absorbing the shocks transmitted from the roads and pathways. Johnny was very pleased with this invention and his friends were all envious of his new tricycle. Dunlop had never ridden a bicycle and at that time there were no bicycle or rubber factories in Ireland. The cycle agents in Belfast were called Messer's Edlin & Sinclair. Dunlop demonstrated his new invention to them, and it met with their approval. In July 1888, Dunlop applied for a provisional patent and this was granted in December of the same year.

A Mr W. Hume, who was the captain of a local cycling club, ordered a racing bicycle with pneumatic tyres and rode it in 1889 at a local sports meeting, beating a number of riders who rode solid-tyre bicycles. The President of the Irish Cyclists' Association was William Harvey Du Cros, who was most impressed by the pneumatic tyres and contacted the inventor Dunlop.

With the invention of the pneumatic tyre, the name Dunlop entered the English language. However, this was not the first of its type. A Robert William Thomson (1822–1873), also a Scot, had patented the first pneumatic tyre in England in June 1846 and in the USA in 1847. This was a hollow leather tyre enclosing a rubberised fabric tube filled with air, and the invention was confined to horse-drawn vehicles.

Harvey Du Cros and Dunlop became business partners and set up a company in Dublin called the Pneumatic Tyre and Booth's Cycle Agency. This partnership became one of the most important in the history of transport. On 18 November 1889, the Dunlop Rubber Company was born and the production of pneumatic tyres began at a factory in Dublin. In 1896, Dunlop had transferred control of his patent and the company to Du Cros and in return he received 1,500 shares in the new company. The firm Dunlop Tyres expanded greatly due to the demand that increased with the development of the internal combustion engine and so it became a multinational company.

Within a short time, the original factory building in Dublin became too small, so the manufacturing business was transferred to Coventry. This also became too small and a new factory was built in Birmingham. Further expansion led to the company acquiring an additional 400 acres. Thus, Fort Dunlop was born. The focus of the company was in England, however, Irish Dunlop was involved in the distribution side of the business. The invention of the pneumatic tyre by Dunlop meant bicycles and cars could provide greater comfort for people travelling on terrains of all types and quality. His tyre therefore revolutionised road traffic, and in the long term, the future development of the motorcar.

When Dunlop first moved to Dublin, he lived off Mount Merrion Avenue in Blackrock and then moved to a house called Leighton on Ailesbury Road, where he lived for the rest of his life. His son Johnny, who was brought up a Presbyterian, and Harvey Du Cros's son, George, attended Blackrock College at the same time, and Johnny demonstrated the new tyred tricycle in the grounds of Blackrock College. Johnny married Constance Mary Moore and they lived on Eglinton Road but later they decided to purchase the house next to his parents on Ailesbury Road. Today, the two houses are home to the Belgian Embassy. When he retired, John B. Dunlop invested in Irish industries and became a Director and Chairman of Todd, Burns & Co. He was also a chairman of Messrs. A. Percy & Co, cycle and motor factors, and of Messrs. D.H. McDowell and Co., motor dealers in Armagh. Dunlop was also very interested in sport and attended regular meetings of the Royal Irish Automobile Club.

In August 1916, an Old Timers Fellowship of Cyclists was formed in Dublin and John B. Dunlop was one of the founding members. This was modelled on the English Fellowship and an Old Timer was described as someone over military age who had ridden before 1890. Its first outing to The Scalp took place on 19 April 1916, when riders started from the Bridge at Donnybrook Church at 3.30 p.m. The outing saw almost 100 cyclists set out on that day with John B. Dunlop one of the leaders. However, he dropped out fairly early on due to his age.

John B. Dunlop lived until 1921, almost a year longer than his son, Johnny, who died in 1920. He is buried in Dean's Grange Cemetery. His wife survived him, as did his daughter, Jean McClintock, who in 1923 became the co-author of the *History of the Pneumatic Tyre*, her father's autobiography. Dunlop did not make a great deal of money from his invention. When he died his estate was valued at £9,867 gross, which was small in comparison to the value of the Dunlop Company.

Further Reading

Cook, J., *John Boyd Dunlop*, Royal Automobile Club, Dublin, 2000.

Dunlop, John Boyd, and McClintock, Jean, *History of the Pneumatic Tyre*, A. Thom, Dublin, 1925.

Lunney, L., 'Dunlop, John Boyd', in *Dictionary of Irish Biography*, edited by James McGuire and James Quinn, Cambridge University Press, Cambridge.

Best, B.W., *Dunlop, John Boyd (1840–1921)*, rev. Trevor I. Williams, *Oxford Dictionary of National Biography*, University Press, Oxford, 2004.

FitzGerald, Garret (1926–2011)
Politician, Taoiseach and Economist
75 Eglinton Road, Donnybrook, Dublin 4

Garret FitzGerald was born in 1926 into a political family. His father was Desmond FitzGerald, Minister for External Affairs in the Irish Government at the time of his son's birth. His mother, Mabel McConnell FitzGerald, was a Northern Ireland Presbyterian, who had been born in Belfast, and who was also involved in politics. She was a nationalist and a Republican during her days at Queen's University. Both his parents were involved in the Easter Rising and the Independence Movement. All his life, Garret FitzGerald had a strong interest in cross-border politics, and always kept in touch with his mother's family. As a child, he spent a year at Coláiste na Rinne in Waterford, where he acquired fluency in the Irish language. Returning to Dublin, he continued his education at Belvedere College. FitzGerald became a student at University College Dublin, and he graduated with a first-class honours BA in History and French, in 1946. He also attended King's Inns and qualified as a barrister but he never practised. FitzGerald's father would have liked him to pursue a career in law after he was called to the Bar in 1947. Later in life, he obtained a doctorate (1968) from UCD and honorary doctorates in Law from two American universities. Among his fellow undergraduate students at UCD was Charles J. Haughey, who later became a political rival. At UCD he also met Joan O'Farrell, who was born in Liverpool and who became his wife. They were married in Booterstown Church in October 1947. Garret and Joan had a very happy marriage and she was a great asset to him in his political career as his confidante and hostess. They were the parents of three children: John, Mary and Mark.

FitzGerald always had a great interest in transport and had a tremendous knowledge of the railway system. He could speak in detail about the various routes and train timetables throughout Ireland and Europe. In 1947, FitzGerald began working at Aer Lingus and became an authority on economic planning.

His work included working on rates and fares, aircraft scheduling, the sale of charter flights and he was also involved in the purchase of aircraft. He began writing newspaper articles and articles for economic journals during the 1948 general election and became the Irish correspondent for *The Economist*. Later on, he began writing on world affairs for the *Irish Independent*. He was then encouraged to write on university and Government finances, writing initially under a pseudonym for the *Irish Times*. On leaving Aer Lingus in 1958 he received a Research Assistantship at Trinity College Dublin, where he examined the inputs of materials into Irish industry between 1953 and 1957. After this Assistantship at Trinity, he became a Lecturer in Economics at University College Dublin, where he remained for a number of years.

With a family background in politics FitzGerald, too, was keen to enter politics. Members of Fianna Fáil including Charles Haughey and Michael Yeats were keen that he should join their party. However, out of loyalty to his father, it was Fine Gael that he joined – he had been impressed with a Fine Gael journal, *The National Observer*, published by Declan Costello and Alexis FitzGerald in the 1950s and '60s. He became impressed, too, with the 'Just Society' programme of Declan Costello. There was pressure on him to stand for Fine Gael in Dublin South-East in 1965 but he declined. However, he did run for the Senate on the industrial panel and was elected as a Fine Gael Senator.

FitzGerald's relationship with Liam Cosgrave, the leader of Fine Gael (1965–1977), was difficult for a number of years. Disagreements mainly centred on whether the party should endeavour to get into power on their own, or whether they should focus on doing so with a partner. When John A. Costello retired in 1969, FitzGerald was selected as a Fine Gael candidate in the Dublin South-East constituency, where he was duly elected, topping the poll. The 1973 general election saw Fine Gael coming to power with Labour in a coalition Government, with Liam Cosgrave as Taoiseach. FitzGerald had great hopes of taking over the Finance portfolio but was offered instead the post of Minister for Foreign Affairs, previously held by his father. He proved to be outstanding in the role, and this probably helped him to achieve the leadership of the party. He firmly believed in Europe, and his continued interest in Northern Ireland meant that he was a frequent visitor there. He was quite successful in establishing some rapport with a few of the Northern Unionists. In 1977, when the Fine Gael–Labour coalition suffered a disastrous defeat in the general election, Cosgrave resigned as leader of the party and FitzGerald was the unanimous choice to succeed him. On becoming leader, FitzGerald began by modernising and revitalizing the party. He sought new younger members, many of whom were essentially liberals.

The 1980s were periods with the greatest number of general elections ever held in Ireland in any single decade. There were five contests in all. In the 1981

Election, Fine Gael came back into power with the aid of Labour. A Fine Gael–Labour Party minority coalition government was formed, and FitzGerald became Taoiseach. It was a time of great economic crisis and Fine Gael had to introduce a draconian budget almost at once. Their second budget led on 27 January 1982 to a defeat for the Government on the proposal to impose VAT on children's clothes and shoes. Fianna Fáil came back into power. In the third general election within eighteen months in November 1982, FitzGerald became Taoiseach for a second time with the support of the Labour Party. He remained in office from December 1982 to March 1987, when there was a change of Government again, with Fianna Fáil returning with Charles J. Haughey as Taoiseach. After that defeat, FitzGerald left front-line politics, and in 1992 he resigned from the Dail.

While in office, FitzGerald endeavoured to liberalise Irish laws on divorce, abortion and contraception. He also attempted to build bridges to the Northern Ireland Protestants. His most successful achievement, the Anglo–Irish Agreement of 1985, was to provide a foundation for the 1998 Good Friday Agreement, which led to the power-sharing administration in Northern Ireland. He returned to his earlier career as a journalist, writing for British, Irish and American newspapers. He also re-joined the business world as Director of the International Institute for Economic Development and he became a Director of Guinness Peat Aviation. He was always a great supporter of Ireland's membership of the European Union, and campaigned in 2002 for the Nice Treaty, and in 2009 for the Lisbon Treaty.

Throughout his political life, FitzGerald's fluency in French, and one or two other European languages, made him a popular figure with the various European and world organisations with which he had to deal, both as Taoiseach and as Minister for Foreign Affairs. He developed strong relationships with the European Community and he held all the high offices open in Europe to people from Ireland.

The FitzGerald family lived for a number of years in Eglinton Road in Donnybrook. It was while living there that Garrett launched his political career, and he held meetings with national and international political figures in this house including Jim Callaghan, British Prime Minister from 1976 to 1979, leaders of the SDLP, and many other distinguished politicians. Joan FitzGerald died in 1999 and Garret himself in 2011. They are both buried in Shanganagh Cemetery, Shankhill, Co. Dublin.

Further Reading

FitzGerald, Garret, *All in a Life: An Autobiography*, Papermac, London, 1992.

Garret FitzGerald obituary, *Irish Times*, 9 May 2011.

Fanning, Ronan, *Garret FitzGerald and the Quest for a New Ireland*, NUI, Dublin, 2002.

French, William Percy (1854–1920)
Engineer, Writer and Artist
35 Mespil Road, Dublin 4

William Percy French was born in 1854 in Cloonyquin House, Co. Roscommon. His father, Christopher, was a landowner of considerable wealth, and his mother was Susan Emma (*née* Percy). He was their third child and second son, and he had three brothers and five sisters. His education began at home, where he had access to his father's large library. The family spent a number of years in England, where Percy attended schools in Derbyshire and Cumbria. When the family returned to Ireland, French attended Foyle College in Derry before going on to study civil engineering at Trinity College, Dublin. While in Trinity he developed his music skills and the seeds of his later talent developed. He is perhaps best known as the writer of humorous songs, but he was also an active concert promoter, painter, writer of sketches, poet, banjo player and public entertainer. During the years 1889 and 1890, French wrote and edited a comic magazine in Dublin called *The Jarvey*, soliciting contributions from some of his friends. While a student at Trinity, he organised concerts and entertained fellow students at parties in the college. At home in Roscommon, he often entertained spectators at cricket and tennis matches.

One of his famous songs, 'Abdulla Bulbul Ameer', was written while he was a student at Trinity. This describes a dual between a Turk and a Russian during the Russo-Turkish war. The song became very popular over several continents, but French did not receive any of the millions of pounds it made as he had not taken out copyright on it. His first job as a civil engineer was with the Board of Works, where he held the post of Inspector of Drains for Co. Cavan. It was during his time in Cavan that he wrote some of his best songs. French was a brilliant cartoonist, and an excellent watercolour painter. Over his lifetime he painted tens of thousands of paintings, most of them landscapes in watercolour. He exhibited regularly at the Royal Hibernian Academy in Dublin and after his move to London he became a regular exhibitor at London galleries. It is said that he believed art was his true vocation. Some of his best watercolours date from his time working in Cavan. Today, his paintings sell for several thousands of euros, and they are still very much sought after. French was impractical and disorderly in terms of finance and other organisational matters, and, indeed, relied on others to organise his schedules.

As an entertainer and performer, French travelled the length and breadth of Ireland on a regular basis with his banjo, as well as performing regularly in the United Kingdom. Percy French wrote the lyrics for his operas and Dr Houston Collisson (1865–1920) who wrote the music. They toured together internationally, giving recitals of their work, the best-known French song being 'The Mountains of Mourne', arranged by Dr Collisson.

The popularity of French, and in particular his songs, meant he had a wide variety of audiences, including an invitation to perform at the Viceregal Lodge in Dublin to entertain the Lord Lieutenant's guests. He also received an invitation to perform before the Prince of Wales (later Edward VII), leading to his continuing popularity with other members of the Royal Family, who frequently commissioned and purchased his paintings. Most French songs were written for his stage shows and many of them were actually inspired by a particular event, including the well-known song 'Are You Right There Michael, Are you Right'. French was due to perform in Kilkee, Co. Clare, on 10 August 1896, but arrived too late and the audience had left. He was travelling by the West Clare Railway, which he later lampooned in the song. Legend has it that he was sued by the railway company as a result and when he arrived for the court case in Clare, he again travelled by the West Clare Railway and again was late. When he used the train as the excuse for being late, the judge is reputed to have thrown out the case. 'Come Back Paddy Reilly to Ballyjamesduff' was said to have been written as a result of a visit to Cavan, where he heard that one of the local jarveys had left for America. En route to Canada by boat with Collisson on a tour of Canada, the eastern USA and the West Indies, French heard a young man remark to his companion that they would be cutting the corn in Cresslough that day, leading him to compose the song 'The Emigrants Letter'.

Later in his career, French toured in Switzerland raising money for a Church of England charity (Waifs and Strays) in which his collaborator Collisson was active. While there he spent time skiing and painting. In Britain, French travelled the length and breadth of the country performing. He was also extremely generous to charities, donating a generous proportion of the proceeds of his concerts to the Red Cross. He also gave performances to the troops in both England and France.

French was married twice. His first wife, Ethel Armytage Moore (1871–1891), died several weeks after the birth of their daughter, who only survived for one month. His second wife was Helen Sheldon from Warwickshire. There were three daughters of this marriage: Ettie, Mellie and Joan. Later in life French suffered from ill health and he broke a rib after falling down the stairs of his home in London. Later in the same year, he lost his footing jumping on a moving train at the railway station in Blackrock, Co. Dublin. His family advised him to retire, but he continued to tour theatres and music halls. In 1920, while touring in Scotland, he became ill in Glasgow and went from there to the home of a cousin in Formby, Lancashire, where he died from pneumonia on 24 January 1920 at the age of 65. He is buried in the graveyard at St Luke's Church, Formby.

French's sister, Emily Lucy De Burgh Daly (1859–1935), published the first extensive collections of his songs, poems and parodies in 1922. Included are letters and autobiographical fragments, with a foreword by Katharine Tynan, the well-known Irish writer, who was a family friend. Two Percy French festivals were hosted at his former home Cloonyquin House in 1957 and 1958, before the house was demolished in the early 1960s. Today, the annual Percy French Festival and Summer School takes place at Castlecoote House in French's native Roscommon. Brendan O'Dowda, a popular Irish tenor, specialised in interpreting French's songs. O'Dowda went on to develop a one-man show based on French's songs. A Percy French Society in North County Down was established in 1983 and is still active today. Other such societies are to be found in Cavan, at Moyasta, Co. Clare, and at Formby on Merseyside.

Further Reading

De Burgh Daly, M., *Chronicles and Poems of Percy French*, Talbot Press, Dublin, 1922.

O'Dowda, B., *The World of Percy French*, Blackstaff Press, Belfast, 1981.

McCabe, D. and White, L.W., 'French (William) Percy', in *Dictionary of Irish Biography*, edited by James McGuire and James Quinn, Cambridge University Press, Cambridge, 2019.

O'Neill, B. *Tones that are Tender: Percy French 1854–1920*. Dublin: Lilliput Press, 2016.

Fuller, James Franklin (1835–1924) Architect

83 Eglinton Road, Donnybrook, Dublin 4

James Franklin Fuller was born in Co. Kerry in 1835, near Derryquin, in a house called Nedanone (Bird's Nest) to Thomas Fuller of Glashnacree (a landowner), by his first wife, Frances Diana, daughter of Francis Bland of Derryquin Castle. His family could be considered as minor gentry. James inherited Glashnacree when his father died. He was educated in Blackrock, Cork City, and he moved to Dublin when the school moved to Baggot Street. One of his school friends was Thomas Newham Dean (1792–1871), the well-known Irish architect.

In 1850, Fuller moved to England and spent some time working as an actor. He also spent a year apprenticed to a firm of mechanical engineers in Southampton. He then moved to London and was apprenticed to the architect Frederick William Porter. He worked for a number of other architectural firms in London, including Horace Jones, T.R. Smith and William Burges. He spent time in Manchester, too, working for Alfred Waterhouse, before moving on to Sheffield and then to the firm of Henry Dawson in London.

While in London he contributed some literary work to journals such as *Truth, Dark Blue* and *Once a Week*. It appears from his autobiography *Omniana,* which he wrote when he was in his 80s, that he was very proud of his achievements as a writer, an antiquarian and as a genealogist, rather than as an architect. While working in both London and Sheffield, he became a member of Volunteer regiments.

Fuller returned to Ireland in 1861 from England, with his wife, Helen Prospere (1838–1925), daughter of J.P. Gouvion and granddaughter of the Marquis St Cyr Gouvion, who had been one of Napoleon's generals and who was also a Marshal of France. It seems from his autobiography that he was most interested in pedigrees and social connections. He claims never to have owned a razor, hence all photographs of him show him with a bushy beard. In 1862, Fuller was appointed Architect to the Irish Ecclesiastical Commissioners and moved to Killeshandra, Co. Cavan, the centre of his area of responsibility.

He worked in this area for eight years, looking after a number of different Anglican churches in the region.

When the Church of Ireland was disestablished by British Prime Minister William Gladstone in 1869, Fuller received compensation for the loss of his position, so he set up his architectural practice in Dublin at No. 179 Great Brunswick Street (now Pearse Street). This remained his business address for his entire life. It is interesting to recall that, according to his autobiography, he never kept ledgers or books of any kind, or financial records in relation to his practice. There are therefore very few archival records relating to his practice or his life. One of his earliest commissions was the restoration in 1870 of Annamoe House, Co. Sligo. He also worked on Mount Falcon, a Victorian Gothic manor house near Ballina, Co. Mayo, which is now a luxury hotel.

Having worked previously with the Church of Ireland, he was fortunate to be appointed as architect to the Church of Ireland Representative Church Body, and he continued to work with them for more than forty years. He also became architect to St Patrick's Cathedral in Dublin. Working for the Church of Ireland, Fuller was architect for the dioceses of Dublin & Glendalough, Kildare, Ossory, Ferns, Leighlin and later for Meath. His principal works were the Churches of Clane, Co. Kildare; Durrow, Co. Meath; Arthurstown, Co. Wexford; Rattoo, Co. Kerry; Kylemore, Connemara; Syddan, Co. Meath; and Rathdaire, Co. Laois. These works all took place between 1878 and 1880.

Many of Fuller's clients were wealthy landowners who were seeking to either enlarge their mansions or wanted him to design a new house for them. These included Lord Ardilaun, for whom Fuller designed his mansion St Anne's, at Clontarf in Dublin. The gardens at St Anne's included a number of follies, including a Herculaneum temple and a Pompeian water temple of Isis by the duck pond. When the house was finished it looked like a 'gargantuan Italianate palazzo'. His other work included the new town hall in Dalkey, the Coombe Maternity Hospital, and several schools in Dublin. He restored Kylemore Castle, Ashford Castle and Tinakilly House, Co. Wicklow. The Great Southern Hotel at Parknasilla, Co. Kerry, is by Fuller, and he was also responsible for major changes to Farmleigh House, in Dublin's Phoenix Park. Fuller was also architect to the Benchers of the King's Inns, and to the National Board of Education. Another one of his commissions was in St Stephen's Green, where he designed the Steward's house. A list of twenty-seven Fuller commissions were detailed in the *Irish Builder* (1870–1904).

Fuller was present at the inaugural meeting of the Architectural Association of Ireland in 1872, and that same year he became an elected Fellow of the Royal Institute of British Architects. Fuller wrote books and articles on a number of different topics, including several novels and articles on genealogy, heraldry and antiquarian subjects. He contributed to such journals as *Miscellanea*

Genealogica et Heraldica, *The Genealogist* and *Walford's Antiquarian Magazine*. With his interest in archaeology and antiquarian subjects he became a Member (1876) and a Fellow (1915) of the Royal Society of Antiquaries of Ireland. He was also a Fellow of the Society of Antiquaries (London).

In 1916 Fuller published his autobiography, *Omniana: The Autobiography of an Irish Octogenarian*. He included five appendices in this book, with each one dedicated to press reviews from his previous novels – he wrote melodramatic novels such as *Culmshire Folk* (Cassel, 1873) and *John Orlebar, Clerk* (Cassell, 1878). He was always very proud of his pedigree and claimed to be able to trace his ancestry back to Charlemagne. Although Fuller covers a great many subjects in his autobiography, there is very little mention of the buildings he designed. The Irish Architectural Archive held an exhibition of his work in 2015, and recently at Farmleigh House.

Over the years Fuller lived at a number of different addresses including Mornington Crescent, London, and Killeshandra, Co. Cavan. On his return to Dublin, he moved to No. 5 Sydenham Road, Dundrum, and then in 1898, he moved to Donnybrook, to a house called Lissatier, Eglinton Road. James Franklin died at his home on Eglinton Road, Donnybrook after a short illness on 8 December 1924 and is buried with his wife and daughter in Mount Jerome Cemetery. Evelyn Millicent Fuller, his daughter, continued to live in her father's house on Eglinton Road until her death in 1958.

Further Reading

James Franklin Fuller (1835–1924), Irish Architectural Archive database, Dublin, in progress.

Fuller, James Franklin, *Omniana: The Autobiography of an Irish Octogenarian*, Jarolds, London, 1920.

O'Brien, Andrew and Lunney. Linde, 'Fuller, James Franklin (1835–1924)', in *Dictionary of Irish Biography*, edited by James McGuire and James Quinn, Cambridge University Press, Cambridge, in progress.

Goodfellow, Kathleen (1891–1980)
Writer, Poet and Translator
4 Morehampton Road, Donnybrook, Dublin 4

Kathleen Goodfellow was born into a Quaker family on 20 August 1891. Her parents were George Goodfellow (1852–1925) and his wife, Susan Goodfellow (*née* Nicholson) (1861–1931). Her father was a builder and, together with his brother Jack, he had built Nos 2, 4, 6, 8, 10 and 12 Morehampton Road, Donnybrook. The Goodfellow family home was No. 4 Morehampton Road, a house Kathleen lived in for the rest of her life. She was educated at Alexandra College, at that time located in Earlsfort Terrace, and she went on to graduate with an Arts degree from Trinity College Dublin. She eventually inherited Nos 2 and 4 Morehampton Road from her parents, along with other property in Dublin. When her mother died in 1932, she inherited from her mother the estate of her grandfather and other property in England and Ireland. She was therefore a very wealthy woman and was always in the very fortunate position of never having to earn her own living!

Goodfellow was a writer, poet and translator. She mostly wrote under the pseudonym Michael Scot, and was known to her friends as either Goodfellow or Michael. Her book *Three Tales of the Times* describes life in Ireland under the Black and Tans. She contributed many articles, poems and reviews to the *Dublin Magazine* owned by Seumas O'Sullivan (James Starkey), the husband of her great friend Estella Solomons. Goodfellow and Solomons were inseparable friends for more than fifty years, so it is hardly surprising that Estella painted Kathleen several times. It seems Goodfellow was very shy and hated being photographed. It was therefore unusual for her to allow anyone to paint her. Two of these paintings, bequeathed by Goodfellow, are in the Model and Niland Collection in Sligo, and another one is in the National Gallery of Ireland. In a way it was an unlikely friendship, with one a Quaker (Goodfellow) and the other, of the Jewish faith (Solomons).

Goodfellow and Solomons were both members of Cumann na mBan. They joined the Rathmines branch in 1915, where they were taught first aid, drilling and signalling by Phyllis Ryan, who became the wife of the President of Ireland, Seán T. O'Kelly. Both Goodfellow and Solomons became devoted to the cause of Irish nationalism and were involved with the Republican cause. Solomon's studio became a refuge for many who were active in political and national activities.

Goodfellow knew Seumas O'Sullivan, an Abbey actor and member of the Methodist Church. He was also a writer and publisher, and was the owner of the *Dublin Magazine,* a well-known literary journal that he had founded in 1923. This was a most influential magazine from its foundation, which played a considerable role in encouraging Irish art and literature. The *Dublin Magazine* survived until O'Sullivan's death in 1958. The magazine was reissued between 1970 and 1975 by John Ryan (1925–1992), a well-known man of letters. Over the years, Kathleen contributed many poems, book reviews and articles to the journal. Goodfellow and Solomons worked tirelessly in sourcing advertising, and in addition Goodfellow provided considerable financial support to it for many years. It could possibly not have survived so long without this backing, which was always in the background.

Estella and Seumas, who had known one another for years, did not marry until 1926. They had not done so out of respect for her parents, who would not have liked their daughter to marry a Gentile. The O'Sullivans spent the early part of their married life in Rathfarnham, where their home in Grange was frequented by the Dublin literati during their Sunday afternoon salons. As a close friend of the couple, Goodfellow was always part of these salons. Salons have always played an important role in shaping literary culture in Ireland and elsewhere. Women always had powerful influence over them, inviting political men and intellectuals, with whom ladies present could exchange ideas, receive and give criticism, and discuss their own work and ideas with other intellectuals.

The O'Sullivans ran into a problem with their house as it was damp and Seumas was worried that his large library of books would become damaged. Goodfellow offered them the house next door to her, No. 2 Morehampton Road in Donnybrook, which she owned, for a nominal sum. There was space in the garden of this house for a studio, where Estella continued her painting and engraving. She frequently used the adjacent grove of trees as her subject in several of her paintings. Goodfellow was always generous with her money and contributed to numerous good causes, in particular children's charities. She was also a member of the Board of Governors for The Royal Hospital in Donnybrook in Bloomfield Avenue that is, literally, across the road from her home.

During the early twentieth century, many Anglo–Irish people became interested in the Irish language. Goodfellow was no exception and was encouraged to take up the study of it by Dr Douglas Hyde (1860–1949), an Irish academic, scholar of the Irish language, politician and President of Ireland. However, when it became very popular to do so, Goodfellow appears to have dropped it! One thing she never dropped was her interest in literature. She continued to write poetry and was also a translator of French poetry, in particular that of Francois Villon. In general, Goodfellow was a patron of the arts, and of the *Dublin Magazine* in particular.

Goodfellow also owned a woodland area covering a fifth of a hectare located at the corner of Morehampton Road and Wellington Place. It is quite close to the underground Swan river, which runs for about 10 miles and 'forms the drainage backbone ... of the Terenure, Rathmines and Pembroke districts'. The Grove is an oasis of tranquillity, and during her lifetime Goodfellow and Solomons spent a lot of time in it, with Estella painting there for pleasure. At one stage Dublin Corporation wanted to place a compulsory purchase order on it to build a fire station. Goodfellow got in touch with the Upper Leeson Street Residents Association and with them came up with the idea of giving it into the ownership of An Taisce, 'a charity that works to preserve and protect Ireland's natural and built heritage'. Goodfellow bequeathed the Grove to An Taisce on condition that it be maintained forever as a place of refuge for birds and plants. In the years after Goodfellow's death in 1980, the Grove became derelict and overgrown. However, in recent years a substantial management programme has been introduced. Bird nesting boxes, for example, have been built, and new trees and wild flowers now grow there. The Upper Leeson Street Residents Association has paid for some of its maintenance, and there is some support from Dublin City Council. Also involved are Conservation Volunteers Ireland and Birdwatch Ireland. This is an excellent example of urban conservation.

In 1939, Goodfellow had a fall when getting off a tram at the top of Waterloo Road. She injured her leg badly, and there was some delay before it was firmly established that she had a bad break. She had cause to remember this for the rest of her life because it left her with a limp. She was described as a shy person, and not very good at talking to people face to face. As a result, she became an avid telephone user and kept in touch with her many friends that way. Goodfellow died on 20 May 1980 and is buried with her parents George and Susan Goodfellow in Mount Jerome Cemetery.

Further Reading

Clarke, Dardis, 'The Dark Lady of the Dublin Magazine', the *Irish Times*, 13 February 1981.

Morehampton Road Wildlife Sanctuary, www.newsfour.ie/2016/10/the-grove-sanctuary-a-little-wilderness-in-development, accessed 7 November 2019.

Pyle, Hilary, *Portraits of Patriots*, Dublin, Allen Figgis & Co. Dublin, 1966.

Russell, Jane, *James Starkey/Seumas O'Sullivan*, Associated University Presses, 1981.

Heaney, Seamus (1939–2013)
Poet and Translator
Strand Road, Sandymount, Dublin 4

Seamus Heaney was one of Ireland's most distinguished poets, and the winner of the 1995 Nobel Prize in Literature. Born in Northern Ireland on a farm called Mossbawn near Castledawson, Co. Derry, Heaney's family later moved to Bellaghy, some miles from his birthplace. His parents were Patrick Heaney (1901–1986), a farmer and cattle dealer, and Margaret McCann (1911–1984). There were nine children in the family and Seamus was the eldest. Seamus grieved greatly for his brother, Christopher, who died aged 4 in a road accident in 1953. 'Mid-Term Break', one of Seamus's early poems, was written as a result of his death. Heaney returned to this theme later in life with 'The Blackbird of Glanmore'. Heaney attended the local national school and when he was 12 years old he won a scholarship to St Columb's College, a Catholic boarding school in Derry city.

Heaney won an Exhibition awarded by the State to Queen's University Belfast, where he studied English Language and Literature. He was a brilliant student and graduated with a first-class honours degree in 1961. After graduating from Queen's, despite being encouraged to apply to Oxford, Heaney decided to take a teaching qualification at St Joseph's Teacher Training College in Belfast. One of his placements was to a secondary school in West Belfast, called St Thomas's Secondary Intermediate School (Ballymurphy), where the headmaster was a well-known writer from Co. Monaghan, Michael McLaverty. It was he who introduced Heaney to the poetry of Patrick Kavanagh and greatly encouraged him to write his own.

Heaney became a member of the staff of St Joseph's Training College in 1963 as a lecturer in English. There he met Marie Devlin, a teacher from

Ardboe, Co. Tyrone, in 1962, and they married in 1965. He remained in St Joseph's Training College for three years and then moved to a similar position at Queen's University in 1966, where he remained until 1972. While at Queen's, Heaney was a regular attender at a writing workshop set up by the poet and academic Philip Hobsbaum. Among his contemporaries there were the playwright Steward Parker and poets Joan Newman and Michael Longley, as well as the literary critic Edna Longley. During the 1960s, Heaney and members of this group began publishing their poems in English language literary journals and newspapers.

Faber & Faber published Heaney's first volume of poetry, *Death of a Naturalist*, in 1966, to wide acclaim. It was in this year, too, that his son, Michael, was born. He was followed by Christopher (1968) and Catherine (1973). His poetry is often concerned with our daily experiences, but they also contain motifs from history. He appears to have had an interest in Celtic history and the pre-Christian period. His poetry appeals to everyone, and he has a very big following. During his lifetime he was recognised as one of the major poets writing in English in both the twentieth and twenty-first centuries. His subject matter has been greatly influenced by his native heath and details of his upbringing in Co. Derry. His poetry is about Northern Ireland, the farms with which he was so familiar and towns and cities, and includes accounts of civic strife. His work in general reflects the Northern Ireland Troubles, and in particular, the violent political struggles that plagued his native area. He wrote elegies too for some of his friends and acquaintances, many of whom died during the Troubles.

Heaney's second volume of poetry was published in 1969, and its title was *Door into the Dark*. The poems describe in great detail the author's rural background, for example, descriptions of the local forge and fishermen on the banks of Lough Neagh. This book of poetry concludes with Heaney's poem 'Bogland', which provides a detailed description of his native place. The Heaney family moved to California, where Heaney spent a sabbatical year at the University of California, Berkeley (1970–1971). On his return to Belfast, Heaney resigned his Lectureship at Queen's University, and the family moved to Co. Wicklow. He intended to devote himself to writing full time, but in 1976 he was offered the post of Head of the English Department at Carysfort Teacher Training College in Dublin, which would provide him with a secure income. During their time living in Wicklow full time, Heaney found time to write some of his most notable poems, including those in *North* (1975). His fourth book was *Field Work* (1979), which contains some of his most famous poems on politics in Northern Ireland.

Heaney returned to America in 1976, when he again spent time at Berkeley. He was on leave of absence from his post in Carysfort for a year. In 1981 Heaney decided to resign his post at Carysfort, and he secured an arrangement with Harvard University where he would agree to teach there for the spring semester for the following three years. His post at Harvard became a tenured one in 1984, when he was appointed Boylston Professor of Rhetoric and Oratory. He resigned this post in 1996 and was appointed Emerson Poet in Residence at Harvard, which only required him to spend six weeks there in alternative years. However, in 1987 and 1988, Heaney spent the entire academic year at Harvard. Heaney was elected to the Chair of Poetry at Oxford University in 1989. He held this post for a five-year term until 1994. He was able to keep his commitments to Harvard, along with his new role in Oxford.

Of great significance in Heaney's life was the award of the Nobel Prize for Literature that he received in 1995 for 'works of lyrical beauty and ethical depth, which exalt everyday miracles and the living past'. From as early as 1983, Heaney became a prolific translator from several different sources that included two plays by Sophocles, *The Cure at Troy* from *Philoctetes* (1990) and *The Burial at Thebes* (2004). The Seamus Heaney Centre for Poetry at Queen's University dates to 2003. It contains the media archive, together with a full catalogue of his radio and television presentations. In 2003, Emory University in Atlanta, Georgia, acquired for their Irish literary archive letters Heaney had received from other writers between 1964 and 2003. Heaney suffered a stroke in August 2006 and, although he recovered, he cancelled all his public engagements for several months.

In 2011, because he wanted his literary archive to remain in Ireland, Heaney deposited the manuscripts of his published work in the National Library of Ireland. The collection includes poetry, prose, drama and translations. In 2018 the National Library of Ireland, the Irish Government Department of Culture and the Bank of Ireland opened an exhibition of the Seamus Heaney archive held by the Library entitled Listen Now Again. The exhibition has been curated by Professor Geraldine Higgins, Director of Irish Studies at Emory University, Atlanta. The exhibition will ultimately transfer to a permanent home at the National Library of Ireland. The BBC broadcast a documentary in 2013 called *Seamus Heaney and the Music of What Happens,* which featured interviews with Heaney's wife, Marie, and his three children, who read some of the poems he wrote for them.

Heaney died in the Blackrock Clinic in Dublin, on 30 August 2013. He was 74 years old. He was in hospital for a medical procedure, but he died suddenly before this had taken place. He sent a text message to his wife just before he died saying 'Noli timere – Do not be afraid'. Heaney is buried in his native Bellaghy, Co. Derry, close by his parents and other family members.

The Seamus Heaney Home Place in Bellaghy was opened in 2016. It is full of personal stories and artefacts, relating to the poet together with a collection of family photographs, video recordings from his friends and neighbours, as well as the voice of the poet reading his poetry.

Further Reading

O'Donoghue, Brendan, 'Heaney, Seamus Justin', in *Dictionary of Irish Biography*, edited by James McGuire and James Quinn, Cambridge University Press, Cambridge.

O'Driscoll, Denis, *Stepping Stones: Interviews with Seamus Heaney*, Faber & Faber, London, 2009.

Parker, Michael, *Seamus Heaney: The Making of the Poet*, Palgrave Macmillan, Basingstoke, 1994.

Vendler, Helen, *Seamus Heaney*, Harper Press, New York, 2012.

Hearn, Lafcadio (1850–1904)
Writer and Translator
73 Upper Leeson Street, Dublin 4

Patrick Lafcadio Hearn was born in Greece on the island of Levkas, one of the Ionian Islands, on 27 June 1850. He used his Greek name exclusively from his early 20s. His father was Charles Bush Hearn, from Offaly, an Anglo-Irish man who was an officer surgeon in the British Army. He married a Greek woman, Rosa Antonia Cassimate from Cerigo in Greece, but the marriage did not last. Lafcadio was abandoned by his parents and went to live with a great Aunt, Mrs Sarah Brenane, who became his official guardian. She lived at No. 73 Upper Leeson Street in Dublin. She was a Catholic, so Hearn was educated by the Jesuits in Paris and Yvetot in France and became a fluent French speaker. He also attended St Cuthbert's College at Ushaw near Durham, where his name appears in the school records as Patrick Hearn. There he lost one of his eyes due to a schoolboy fight as a result of bullying.

Hearn emigrated to the United States at the age of 19, and eventually he became a newspaper reporter, first in Cincinnati, Ohio, and later in New Orleans. In Cincinnati he was a reporter for *The Cincinnati Enquirer* and *The Cincinnati Commercial*. He contributed prose, poems and scholarly essays. In Cincinnati, too, he translated stories from French into English by the writer Theophile Gautier, and also stories by Gustav Flaubert. He was also well known for his lurid accounts of local murders and developed a reputation as a sensational journalist and a writer of horror stories. In 1874, at the age 23, he married a 20-year-old African-American woman called Althea (Mattie) Foley, a cook and former slave, which was in violation of Ohio anti-miscegenation laws at that time. The marriage did not last and they divorced in 1877. They had no children.

From Cincinnati, Hearn moved to New Orleans in 1877, from where he wrote articles on the 'gateway to the Tropics' for the *Cincinnati Commercial* newspaper. Hearn spent almost ten years in New Orleans, contributing articles to the *Daily City Item* and later on for the *New Orleans Times Democrat*, where, by 1881 he had become a successful literary editor. During this time, he translated items of interest from French and Spanish newspapers as well as editorials. As a literary editor, he created and published almost 200 woodcuts of daily life and the people of New Orleans. These cartoons helped increase the circulation figures of the paper. His first book was published in 1882 and was called *One of Cleopatra's Nights,* which was a translation of six of Gautier's stories. While in New Orleans, he contributed to well-known American magazines such as *Harper's Weekly* and the *Century.* These writings contributed in no small way to the reputation of New Orleans as a city with a culture that was more European and Caribbean than that of the rest of North America.

Hearn was sent to the West Indies as a correspondent for *Harper's* in 1887. He lived in Martinique for two years, and besides writing for the magazine he also wrote two books there – *Two Years in the French West Indies* and *Youma, The Story of a West-Indian Slave,* which were both published in 1890. This was the same year that he went to Japan as a newspaper correspondent. His contract did not last so he took up a teaching post in 1890 at the Shimane Prefectural Common Middle School and Normal School in Matsue, a town in the west of Japan. Today there is a Lafcadio Hearn Memorial Museum at his old residence, and it is one of Matsue's popular tourist attractions. During his time there he married Koiziumi Setsu, the daughter of a local samurai family. They had four children: three sons and a daughter, named Kazuo, Iwao, Kiyoshi and Suzuk. In 1896 Hearn became a Japanese citizen, taking the name Koizumi Yakumo; Koizumi being his wife's family name. That year, too, he wrote some of his best prose, collected in *Glimpses of Unfamiliar Japan* (1894), *Kokoro* (1896), *Gleanings in Buddha Fields* (1897), *Exotics and Retrospectives* (1898), *In Ghostly Japan* (1899), *Shadowings* (1900) and *Kwaidan* and *Japan* (1904). In 1896 Hearn obtained a teaching post as a lecturer at Tokyo University, where he remained until 1903. During this time, he wrote prose that included detailed examinations of Japan, its people and its folk ways. The following year (1904) he took up a post as a professor at Waseda University, a private, independent research university in central Tokyo.

In total, Hearn published thirteen books on Japan, and these have proved to be of incredible value to students of Japanese history and literature. In his writings he condemned the westernisation of his adopted country. He also described in detail Japan in the throes of Meiji transformation, which is of great significance to students of the country. Some of his stories are still in use in Japan to teach children English and one of his other books, *Kwaidan*, was made into a film by the Japanese director Masaki Kobayashi and was a winner at the Cannes Film Festival in 1965.

A plaque commemorating Hearn was unveiled by the Mayor of Matsue, who was on a visit to Dublin, in 1988 at No. 73 Upper Leeson Street, the home of his guardian, Mrs Sarah Brenane and where he spent his childhood. Mrs Brenane had property in Waterford, too, and Hearn spent summer holidays with her in Tramore. There is a beautiful garden called The Lafcadio Hearn Japanese Gardens in Tramore that is open to the public all year and commemorates Hearn's life and work. It is a very attractive venue for tourists.

Hearn is well known for his writings on Japan and is a cult figure in France and in the United States. He died from heart failure at the age of 54 in September 1904 and is buried in the Buddhist Zohigaya Cemetery in Tokyo.

Further Reading

Murray, Paul, *A Fantastic Journey: The Life and Literature of Lafcadio Hearn*, Japan Library, Sandgate, Kent, 1993.

Murray, Paul, 'Hearn, Patrick Lafcadio', in *Dictionary of Irish Biography*, edited by James McGuire and James Quinn, Cambridge University Press, Cambridge.

Ronan, Sean, ed., *Irish writing on Lafcadio Hearn and Japan*, Global, Kent, 1997.

Heath, Mary Lady (1896–1939)
Aviator and International Athlete
Pembroke Road, Dublin 4

Born into an Anglo–Irish family in Newcastle West, Co. Limerick, on 17 November 1896, and named Sophie Catherine Mary, her parents were Jackie Peirce-Evans and his wife, Kate Doolin. Their home was Knockaderry House and was built on 350 acres, which her father had inherited from his maternal grandfather. Tragically, Sophie's father murdered her mother when Sophie was not much more than a baby. She was therefore brought up by her maiden aunts, and sent away to boarding school, first at Rochelle School in Cork, then at Princess Gardens School in Belfast, and finally at St Margaret's Hall, on Mespil Road in Dublin. At school she was considered a brilliant student, and she also excelled at sport. She went on to study agriculture at the Royal College of Science in Ireland, a third-level institution in Dublin that existed from 1867 to 1926, when it was absorbed into University College Dublin.

Peirce-Evans became a dispatch rider in the First World War and while in London she had her portrait painted by the distinguished Irish painter Sir John Lavery. She became a university graduate, lecturer, author, champion and Olympic competitor in the high jump, and a female aviation pioneer. While a student at the Royal College of Science, her aunts were involved in arranging her marriage to a British Army captain, who was some twenty years her senior, called William Davies Eliott-Lynn. He owned a coffee farm in Kenya and she moved to East Africa with him. The marriage only lasted about eighteen months and she returned to England. As Sophie Mary Eliott-Lynn, she became a founder of the Women's Amateur Athletic Association. She excelled in several sports, including the high jump and the javelin. She became Britain's first women javelin champion and set a record for the high jump that was later disputed. She was extremely tall, almost 6ft, weighed 11 stone and was always very active and healthy. She also competed for Britain in two world games, and at the Monte Carlo games in 1923 she took part in eight events.

Sophie helped to set up the Women's Amateur Athletic Association in 1922, and became its Chair. Her interest in athletics continued for many years, and she published a coaching manual in 1925 called *Athletics for Women and Girls*. She was invited by the International Athletics Federation to argue the case for women's inclusion in track and field events in the International Olympic Games. As a result, within three years, women were able to take part in three athletic events in the Amsterdam games, where she was invited to be a judge.

With her first experience of flying in 1925, when she flew to Prague to address a conference of the Olympic Committee, Sophie became enamoured with aviation. She became a member of the London Light Aeroplane Club and obtained a private pilot's licence quite quickly. She became the first woman in the world to make a parachute jump and landed in the middle of a football pitch while a match was in progress. At that time, women pilots were not permitted to carry passengers, or earn their living as a pilot. The two-tier system was unjust, and indeed many men actually supported her claim. She was finally awarded a commercial pilot's licence in 1926 – the first woman in Britain and Ireland to hold one. She broke the world altitude record for British light aircraft in 1927. By now, she was recognised as a celebrity and gave lectures on aviation all over Great Britain, and her talks were published by *The Times*.

Sophie now needed her own aircraft and she found herself a wealthy husband who could finance her flying activities. She married Sir James Heath, who was forty years her senior, in October 1927, and thus became Lady Heath. He bought her an Avro Avian and it was assembled in South Africa where they were honeymooning. She was determined to fly her new plane from Cape Town back to London, and she left there in January 1928. The plane was an open-cockpit aircraft and the journey that she expected would take her three weeks in fact took her three months, from January to May 1928. She ran into many difficulties during her arduous flight. Suffering from heat stroke, she had to land in Southern Rhodesia (now Zimbabwe), and spent a few weeks in a nursing home recovering. Back in the air once more, Lady Mary had to make a number of other landings due to the inclement weather. During her many stop overs, she was entertained royally, played tennis and went on safari.

On 17 May 1928 she finally arrived at Croydon, then the main airport for London. Her journey had taken her 10,000 miles from Cape Town. She carried out all her own maintenance to the aircraft, and later took a mechanic's qualification in the USA, the first woman to do so. On arrival from South Africa, Lady Mary stepped out of the plane like a model, in a fur coat and pearls. On her return, she toured Britain, giving lectures and talks on her achievements. She became a pilot with KLM (Royal Dutch Airlines) and she flew the London–Amsterdam route regularly. She went on to tour the USA, where thousands attended her lectures. She set up home in New York and very soon began competing in air races throughout the USA. While competing in the National Air Races in Cleveland Ohio in 1929, she crashed and the plane was totally destroyed. Lady Mary was pulled unconscious from the aircraft and was in a coma for several weeks. She had surgery that involved putting a metal plate into her skull. Very soon after that she and her husband, Sir James Heath, separated and were divorced. After her accident, it took her a long time to recover her health, however, she still continued to give lectures and talks in various parts of the United States. She began to fly again in 1931, and that year too she met Jack Williams, a fellow aviator, who became her third husband.

Lady Mary never lost touch with Ireland, making regular trips back to her homeland. She promoted the Irish Flying Club and in 1931 returned to Dublin. In 1934 she became the first female flying instructor at Kildonan Aerodrome in Finglas. Kildonan had been established in 1931 as Ireland's first civilian airport. She bought Iona National Airways, and set up her own company called Dublin Air Ferries Ltd. Unfortunately, within four years her airline went into bankruptcy and Lady Mary lost all her money. The setting up of Aer Lingus in 1936 led to the demise of Dublin Air Ferries in 1938 and Kildonan closed.

Lady Mary moved back to London, and by now was estranged from her third husband. In May 1939, while travelling by public transport, she had a very bad fall. She suffered major head injuries and died without gaining consciousness at St Leonard's Hospital in Shoreditch, London, at the age of 43. She was cremated and her ashes were scattered over Newcastle West, Co. Limerick. Ireland finally recognised her when the Irish Post Office created a stamp in her honour in 1998.

Further Reading

Hourican, Bridget, 'Evans, Sophie Catherine Peirce', in *Dictionary of Irish Biography*, edited by James McGuire and James Quinn, Cambridge University Press, Cambridge.

Naughton, Lindie, *Lady Icarus: The Life of Irish Aviator, Lady Mary Heath*, Ashfield Press, Dublin, 2004.

Traynor, Michael, *Petticoat Pilots. Vols. 1 & 2*, M. Traynor, Dublin, 2019.

Hooper, Patrick Joseph (1873–1931)
Barrister and Journalist
102 Morehampton Road, Donnybrook, Dublin 4

Patrick Joseph Hooper was born in Cork on 1 June 1873. His parents were John Hooper (1846–1897), an Irish nationalist journalist, editor and owner of the *Cork Herald* until 1889, and MP for South East Cork (1885–1887). John Hooper was also an editor of the Dublin *Evening Telegraph*. Patrick's mother was Mary Jane Buckley and he was the eldest of nine children. There were four boys and five girls in his family. Patrick was educated in Cork by the Christian Brothers and graduated with a BA from the Royal University. In 1892, he joined the staff of *The Freeman's Journal*, at that time one of Dublin's most influential newspapers

The Freeman's Journal dates from 1763, and it was Ireland's first national newspaper. It lasted for 166 years and it is a vital resource for reports of Irish social, political and historical events. Over the years of its existence, this newspaper's political tone changed with its various owners from policies emanating from London to a much more Irish focus from the 1830s. In 1841, it was sold to Sir John Gray (1815–1875) and for fifty years the paper was associated with this family. The final member of the Gray family involved was Edmund Dwyer Gray (1870–1945), who went on to become Prime Minister of Tasmania. When *The Freeman's Journal* merged with the *National Press*, there emerged bitter struggles for the control of the paper between the anti-Parnell factions led by Tim Healy and John Dillon, who were both directors of the newly merged companies, and the proprietors of *The Freeman's Journal*.

Patrick Hooper had transferred to the office of *The Freeman's Journal* in London in 1897 and remained there until 1912 as Assistant Correspondent, and then as Chief Correspondent until 1916. While he worked full time in London, he studied law part time, and was called to the English Bar by Gray's Inn in 1915. He is said to have had a junior brief in the trial of Roger Casement. Hooper was very popular among the Irish in London and was active in both the Irish literary and language movements. While working as a journalist there he gained wide experience in Parliamentary procedures and affairs, which proved useful to him later when he was a member of the Irish Seanad. He was also Chief European representative of *The New York World,* a newspaper published in New York City (1860–1931). This publication played a major role in the history of American newspapers and was a leading national voice of the Democratic Party.

The following year, 1916, Hooper was appointed editor of *The Freeman's Journal* and returned to Ireland, where he had the major task of rejuvenating the title. He also became a Director of the Freeman Company (1918–1919). The offices of *The Freeman's Journal* on North Prince's Street were destroyed during the Rising of 1916 and new premises were found in Townsend Street. Hooper carried out a huge amount of work outside the ordinary editorial duties, in that he had to secure new premises, purchase the plant and reorganise the staff. The new office was well equipped and fresh capital was found from associates of the Irish Party who lived overseas. The daily circulation of the revitalised paper increased under Hooper's editorship, and at its height 40,000 copies a day were produced. Hooper's task of revitalising the paper appears to have been very successful. However, *The Freeman's Journal* was tied to the Nationalist Party and when that organisation was displaced by Sinn Fein, it began to lose readers and influence. Hooper fought against heavy odds, but finally had to acknowledge defeat. *The Freeman's Journal* had strong competition from William Martin Murphy's *Irish Independent,* which was half the price of *The Freeman's Journal*. It was a more popular format and it very soon began to erode the circulation figures of its rival.

The last owners of *The Freeman's Journal* were Martin FitzGerald, a Dublin wine merchant and a prominent Dublin businessman, and Hamilton Edwards, a British journalist. They purchased the paper in October 1919 and continued to publish it for another five years. Hooper was retained as editor and under his guidance it was a voice of 'moderate nationalism'. The proprietors, however, constantly sought to influence the editorial balance and Hooper had difficulty in containing the more aggressive approach to the activities of the day sought by the proprietors. *The Freeman's Journal* was suppressed by the British military authorities between December 1919 and January 1920 for questioning the deaths of those in custody and the general brutality of the British forces in Dublin. In December 1920, Hooper was sentenced by court martial (along with two other directors of the paper) to one year in prison. However, they were released after four weeks in Mountjoy Prison due to an outcry in the British press. The paper supported the Anglo–Irish Treaty of 1921 and during the Civil War, probably as a result, its printing presses were smashed by Republican raiders (anti-Treaty forces) in March 1922. When the Treaty was signed it was hoped that *The Freeman's Journal* would again prosper but, just before Christmas 1924, it ceased publication. Due to a lack of investment, the last edition appeared on 19 December 1924. It then merged with the *Irish Independent* and William Martin Murphy bought its assets including the title, together with its archive.

It is interesting to note that *The Freeman's Journal* featured in James Joyce's *Ulysses*. A chapter called 'Aeolus' is set in the *Freeman's* office in North Prince's Street and Hooper and the previous editor, William Henry Brayden, are mentioned in it.

When *The Freeman's Journal* closed down, Hooper secured a job as correspondent for the *Philadelphia Public Ledger* and also became a freelance journalist. He was elected to the Free State Senate in March 1927 to fill the vacancy created by the death of Martin FitzGerald, the former proprietor of *The Freeman's Journal*. Hooper had taken part in the senate election of 1925 but had been unsuccessful. During his time in the Seanad he sat as an Independent member, and while there he opposed aspects of the Censorship of Publications Bill 1928, and the Juries (Protection) Bill 1929. He served as Leas Chathaoirleach (Deputy Chairman) of the Seanad from 6 May 1931 until his death.

In 1904, Hooper married Margaret Ryan (1872–1951) from Ballincollig in Cork, a daughter of James Ryan and his wife, Catherine (*née* Buckley). Margaret had been a nurse in London before her marriage. They had two sons and a daughter. Their eldest son, Seán (1906–1961), was a well-known barrister in Dublin, and their son Laurence was a distinguished economist with the National Bank. Like his father, Laurence and his family lived in Donnybrook. Hooper died suddenly from a heart condition at his home, No. 102 Morehampton Road, on 6 September 1931. Although some of his death notices in the daily papers stated that his funeral was private, it was reported elsewhere that it was attended by many of the leading political figures of the day including the President of the Free State, W.T. Cosgrave, and four of his Ministers, the Lord Mayor, the Chief Justice and the Attorney General. Hooper and his wife are buried in Glasnevin Cemetery.

Further Reading

Larkin, Felix M, 'Hooper, Patrick Joseph', in *Dictionary of Irish Biography* edited by James McGuire and James Quinn, Cambridge University Press, Cambridge.

Larkin, Felix M., 'A Great Daily Organ: The Freeman's Journal, 1763–1924', *History Ireland*, 14:3 (May/June 2006).

Hooper, Richard, *Hooper's in Ireland* (unpublished).

Humphreys (Ui Dhonnchadha), Sighle (1899–1994) Republican Activist

18 Eglinton Park, Donnybrook, Dublin 4

Sighle Humphreys was born in Limerick on 26 February 1899, the only daughter of David Humphreys and Nell (*née* Rahilly). Her father was an eye surgeon and her mother was a sister of Michael Joseph, The O'Rahilly, who was killed during the 1916 Rising in Dublin. Her brother was Richard Humphreys (1896–1968), who was also a revolutionary. He too, fought in the 1916 Rising. David Humphreys (Sighle's father) died in 1903 from tuberculosis. His wife, together with their three children, moved to live with her mother at Quinsborough House, Parteen, Co. Limerick. Sighle's aunt, Aine Rahilly, who was an out-and-out nationalist and Republican, lived with the Humphreys family for most of her life. The children were heavily influenced by their aunt's strong nationalist views. Sighle's brothers both attended Pearse's school at St Enda's and later on they joined the Irish Volunteers. Sighle also took part in some of the pre-1916 Volunteer activities.

In 1909, Nell Humphreys moved her family to Dublin to No. 54 Northumberland Road, Ballsbridge. Sighle began her education with the Sacred Heart nuns in Lower Leeson Street, and later she went to Mount Anville as a boarder, where she was head of the school. On finishing school, she spent a year in Paris (1919–1920), studying French civilisation. Later on, she used to give voluntary classes in Irish in Scoil Bhride, a well-known primary school founded by Louise Gavan Duffy on St Stephen's Green in 1917. The family had a holiday home in Muirioch in the Kerry Gaeltacht, and Sighle spent many holidays there and on the Blasket Islands. She was a fluent Irish speaker all her life. She joined Cumann na mBan in 1919 and was over the years Secretary, Director of Publicity and National Vice President. She worked, too, for the Committee of the Irish Volunteer Dependents' Fund after the Rising.

Sighle's mother engaged Batt O'Connor (1870–1935), builder, revolutionary and politician (who lived in Donnybrook), to build her a new house at

36 Ailesbury Road opposite the French Embassy. The house included a secret room on the first floor that was used to hide fugitives during the War of Independence. During this war, despite many intensive raids by British Army Auxiliary Forces and units of the Black and Tans, the secret room was never discovered. The house also contained a number of secret drawers under the floorboards that were never discovered by those raiding the house. During the War of Independence this house was essentially the headquarters of the IRA (Irish Republican Army) and weekly meetings of the Cabinet were often held there. Ernie O'Malley (1897–1957), a revolutionary and writer, was dramatically captured (and badly wounded) in the Humphreys' family home (November 1922) by Free State forces. Aine O'Rahilly, Sighle's aunt, was wounded, and Sighle was fired on by the soldiers. The entire family was arrested and Sighle and Nell, her mother, were sent to prison. Sighle spent the next year in jail, and during her time there was moved from one prison to another. She spent three months in solitary confinement after taking part in a protest in Mountjoy Prison. The Humphreys family took the Republican side in the Civil War, so Sighle was anti the Free State and had organised safe houses for those on the run, and painted slogans on walls at night. Sighle went on hunger strike, with the main one lasting thirty-one days during the Civil War in 1923. She told the young girls in Cumann na mBan afterwards that her skin was never better!

Sighle Humphreys was very active in Cumann na mBan and in 1926 she became its Director of Publicity. She tried to keep Cumann na mBan going after the Civil War by organising lectures, first aid and demonstrations. She became their representative on the Republican Council in 1929. Because of her many Republican activities, Sighle was imprisoned several more times – in 1926, 1927, 1928 and 1931. She was also known to have endeavoured to influence jurors in Republican cases in the courts. She was the author of a pamphlet called *Ghosts*, which she distributed to jurors in Republican cases, telling them why an accused should not be found guilty.

Saor Éire was a far-left political group dating from 1931 and was founded by communist-leaning members of the IRA. Humphreys joined it and served as co-treasurer from 1931. It aimed 'to overthrow British imperialism and Irish capitalism'. She believed 'this micro-group had the potential to link Republicanism to the concerns of ordinary people'. Saor Éire, the IRA and Cumann na mBan were made illegal under the Government of W.T. Cosgrave in October 1931. Sighle was arrested once again on 2 November 1931 and charged with having Saor Éire and Cumann na mBan documents.

Between 1932 and 1933 Humphreys became a leading member of the Boycott British League set up to boycott British goods. They also attacked premises that sold Bass beer, a well-known English brand. By the 1940s,

Cumann na mBan had died a natural death. Humphreys continued to be active in other walks of life, for example she was a member of the Ladies Association of Charity of St Vincent de Paul. She also became involved with the Prisoners Dependents campaign in 1951–1989. She was active, too, in the Irish Sovereignty Movement in the 1970s and '80s. Other causes she espoused were those of Sinn Fein – she was anti the EEC and she had a strong spiritual faith. She was also interested in promoting the Mass in Irish on Irish Television. Always a Republican sympathiser, Humphreys corresponded with Republican prisoners in the 1970s and '80s and endorsed Sinn Fein and the H-block campaign.

In 1935, Humphreys married a prominent IRA activist, Donal O'Donoghue (1897–1957), when she was 36 years old. He was a veteran of the IRA Dublin Brigade. He was interned during the Civil War and he also participated in the 1923 hunger strike of anti-Treaty prisoners. He was appointed editor of *An Phoblacht* in 1934 and went to prison for making seditious speeches. Later he became active in Clann na Poblachta as Chairman of its National Executive and Standing Committee. Their first child, a boy, Dara, died shortly after his birth. Their daughter, Croine, still lives in Donnybrook, having grown up in the family home in Eglinton Park. After her marriage, Humphreys became known as Sighle Bean Domhnaill O Donnchadha or Sighle Bean Ui Donnchadha.

Humphreys remained a loyal Republican until the day she died on 14 March 1994 in Our Lady's Hospice, Harold's Cross in Dublin. She is buried along with her husband and son in Glasnevin Cemetery. She lived most of her life in Donnybrook; in Ailesbury Road before her marriage, and after that in Eglinton Park. Her papers were presented by her daughter, Croine Magan, to the Archives Department at University College Dublin. In 2003, her grandsons, Ruan and Manchan Magan, made a documentary called *The Struggle*, which was received with much acclaim. It covered significant events in the Civil War, and the role played in it by their grandmother.

Further Reading
HumphreysFamilytree.com, Genealogy research by Mark Humphreys, 1983–2019.

Kyte, E., *Sighle Humphreys: A Case Study in Irish Socialist Feminism 1920s–1930s*, *Saothar* 36 2011, pp.27–36.

Manley, T., *Sighle Humphreys, Her Republican Beliefs*, MA thesis, NUI, Maynooth.

Maume, P., 'Humphreys, Sighle', in *Dictionary of Irish Biography*, edited by James McGuire and James Quinn, Cambridge University Press, Cambridge, 2002.

Jones, Sir Thomas Alfred (1823–1893)
Portrait Painter
41 Morehampton Road, Donnybrook, Dublin 4

Thomas Alfred Jones's parents are unknown – he was a foundling. He appears to have been adopted by a well-known Dublin philanthropic family called the Archdales, who lived in Kildare Street in Dublin. Mr Archdale and his sisters were known in Dublin for their charitable and philanthropic activities. Thomas's date of birth is not certain, but his talent for art was recognised early on and in 1833, at the age of 10, he became a student at the Dublin Society schools, where he stayed until 1840. He was taught landscape and ornamental drawing, together with figure drawing. The Dublin Society Art Schools had been founded in 1746 and for more than 100 years were the centre for the teaching of art, drawing and sculpture in Dublin. Tuition was free, and the school was very popular with people from a wide variety of trades and backgrounds. In 1867, the Government took over the RDS schools, and they went on to become the Dublin Metropolitan School of Art, and later the National College of Art and Design.

Thomas Jones contributed a picture called 'Vision of Kings' – a subject from *Macbeth* – to the 1841 exhibition of the Royal Hibernian Academy. He became a student at Trinity College Dublin the following year (1842) but there is no evidence that he ever graduated. In 1846, he spent three years travelling on the Continent, possibly through the generosity of his adoptive family. While in Italy he drew a number of peasant subjects and he exhibited some of these, which included studies of children and other Italian topics, at the Royal Hibernian Academy in 1849. Some of his early work included drawing in watercolours and pastels, often of small figure subjects. During his lifetime he travelled throughout the west of Ireland and there he painted watercolours of country girls in both Limerick and Galway. However, it is as an oil painter, and in particular as a portrait painter, that he is best known.

In the latter part of the nineteenth century, Jones had almost a monopoly on portrait painting in Ireland. He showed portraits at the RHA from 1851 onwards, and he also took part in a number of individual exhibitions in Dublin. These included the Great Industrial Exhibition of 1853, an Exhibition at the Royal Dublin Society in 1858, as well as the Exhibition of Fine and Oriental Art (1861) and at two more – an Exhibition of Irish Manufacturers Machinery and Fine Art (1864) and the Dublin Industrial Exhibition of 1865. He had become an Associate of the Royal Hibernian Academy in 1860, and nine years later (1869) was elected President of the Academy. During his time as President he worked hard to advance the Academy's interests. Due to his distinguished career as a portrait painter, and as President of the Royal Hibernian Academy, Jones had the honour of being knighted by the Lord Lieutenant at the time, the Duke of Marlborough, George Spencer Churchill (1844–1892). He was the first President of the RHA to be so knighted, although his successor was as well (Thomas Farrell, 1827–1900).

Portrait painting became popular in Ireland during the late seventeenth and early eighteenth century, approximately fifty years before landscape painting became popular. Jones became the most distinguished portrait painter working in late nineteenth-century Ireland. Most portrait painters receive commissions for public and private persons, and they are very often commissioned by the State or by a family, and so their work forms important historical records as well as remembrances. From the beginnings of portrait painting in the seventeenth century, the paintings have memorialised the rich and powerful in society. Jones's sitters were such people. He painted most of the eminent members of the aristocracy, judges, Lord Chancellors, Lord Lieutenants, military men, and well-known medical men, business men and writers. He also painted the wives of distinguished members of society including Mrs Eccles (1856), Mrs Exham and children (1861), Augusta Countess of Kingston (1873), Frances Countess of Granard (1877) and Lady Randolph Churchill (1878) among others. He painted the Lord Lieutenant John Winston Spencer Churchill, 7th Duke of Marlborough (1822–1883), who was the grandfather of Sir Winston Churchill. He also painted Sir Arthur E. Guinness (Lord Ardilaun) and Lady Olive Guinness (Lady Ardilaun).

During the late nineteenth century, Jones acquired patrons in Belfast. His subjects included Belfast businessmen, the Belfast Town Council and other well-known industrialists of the day. There was some suggestion in 1883 that he would be offered a commission to paint Queen Victoria, but this never materialised. Jones was popular during his lifetime, and he is included in

Walter Strickland's *Dictionary of Irish Artists* (1913). However, Strickland was quite critical of Jones's work, writing, 'his art was commonplace, and though his pictures satisfied his sitters as faithful likenesses, they were poorly painted, mechanical in execution and without any artistic merit'. This may account for why he is not as prominent today as he was during his very successful career.

Besides his portrait painting, Jones also continued to paint watercolours of literary subjects including Dante, Shakespeare and Goethe. Some of his paintings were sentimental paintings, which were again in watercolour. Examples of this genre include 'A Prayer for the Absent' and the 'Babes in the Wood', as well as 'Molly Macree' and 'The Galway Girl'. He painted a number of sympathetic portraits of Irish emigrants, for example his 'Limerick Lassies' and 'A Galway Girl', which appear to convey a sympathy for the less well off in Irish society. The latter painting appeared in an art gallery catalogue recently with a price of €26,500.

Jones was married twice. His first wife was Susan Lucinda Casey, who died in 1876. She was the daughter of William Casey of Seafield, Co. Clare. They had one son. After her death, Jones married Florence Mary Quinan, daughter of Henry Quinan. Besides his work as a portrait painter, Jones was interested in music and was a Governor of the Royal Irish Academy of Music. In his later years, Jones suffered from ill health and he died at his home, No. 41 Morehampton Road, on 10 May 1893 aged 70. He is buried in Mount Jerome Cemetery.

Further Reading

Hussey, Mary Olive, 'A century of Dublin portrait painters 1750–1850', *Dublin Historical Record*, xviii, Sept. 1956, p.31.

Minch, Rebecca, 'Jones, Sir Thomas Alfred', in *Dictionary of Irish Biography*, edited by James McGuire and James Lynch, Cambridge University Press, Cambridge, in progress.

Sir Thomas Alfred Jones Portrait Painter, www.libraryireland.com

Kane, Sir Robert (1809–1890)
First President of Queen's College Cork
2 Wellington Road, Ballsbridge, Dublin 4

Robert Kane was born in Dublin to John and Eleanor Kean. His mother was a sister of the well-known Archbishop of Dublin, John Thomas Troy (1739–1823). His father was a chemist who studied in Paris as a result of fleeing Ireland due to his membership of the United Irishmen. On his return to Dublin, John Kean changed his name to Kane and set up a manufacturing company called the Kane Company based at the North Wall, which specialised in the manufacture of sulphuric acid. Robert was the second son, born on 28 April 1809. He seems to have inherited his father's love of chemistry from an early age. As a schoolboy, he attended the chemical and other afternoon science lectures held at the Royal Dublin Society.

From a very young age, Kane expanded his interest in chemistry and commenced research in this subject. His first paper appeared in the *London Quarterly Journal of Science, Literature and Art* in 1828, so his research would have taken place when he was only 18. The following year (1829) Kane was in print again in the same journal with a paper on what is a natural arsenide of manganese and is now known as Kaneite in his honour.

Kane studied Medicine at the Apothecaries Hall and qualified in 1829. In 1831, at the early age of 22, he was elected a member of the prestigious Royal Irish Academy. The same year he founded *The Dublin Journal of Medical & Chemical Science*. This was the first successful journal published in Ireland during the nineteenth century and it is interesting to note that it still continues under the title of the *Irish Journal of Medical Science*. Between 1832 and 1837 Kane published as many as twenty scientific papers, half of which appeared in the journal he had founded.

Kane became a student at TCD in 1829 and graduated with a BA in 1834. At the same time, he was studying and working in the Meath Hospital, where he was a clinical clerk with the distinguished physicians William Stokes and

Robert Graves. His first book was published in 1834 and was called *Elements of Practical Pharmacy*. As a result of its publication he was appointed to the Chair of Chemistry at the Apothecaries Hall while still only 21. After this, Kane devoted himself entirely to the study of Chemistry, though he did become a became a Licentiate of the Royal College of Physicians of Ireland in 1835 and in 1843 Fellow of the College. His famous textbook entitled *Elements of Chemistry* was published in 1841 and 1842, with a second edition in 1849. After this he became more interested in the role and development of industry in Ireland.

Kane joined the staff of the Royal Dublin Society as a lecturer in Natural Philosophy in 1834 and some five years later he became Professor of Natural Science there for thirteen years. His lectures were very popular, and he also delivered them in a number of provincial towns in Ireland. His famous book *Industrial Resources of Ireland*, published in 1844 with a second edition in 1845, was based on his RDS lectures. His time with the RDS, and the research he carried out there, established his reputation as one of the leading chemists of the day. In 1840, he became editor of the *The Philosophical Magazine*, a post he held for the remainder of his life. As a result of his standing in research, and as a leading chemist of his day, Kane was awarded the Royal Medal by the Royal Society, and in 1849 he became a Fellow of this Society.

While still Professor of Natural Philosophy at the RDS, Kane continued to teach at the Apothecaries Hall and when a medical school was established at Cecilia Street (later it was sold to the Catholic University) he became involved in the organisation of its courses. By 1845 he became involved with the Museum of Economic Geology in Dublin, which later became the Museum of Irish Industry and a forerunner of the Royal College of Science, which was founded in 1867. In 1845, too, Kane was appointed by the Government, in conjunction with Professors Lindley and Playfair, to examine the causes and means of preventing the potato blight – the cause of the Great Famine of 1845–1849. He was also appointed as one of the Relief Commissioners.

Kane's interest in industrial chemistry and the industrial resources of Ireland was of great significance for the country. He was aware of the potential of water power from Ireland's major rivers. He was interested in peat and the cultivation of sugar beet, which was later recognised. He believed that by-products of potatoes, for example, potato starch and alcohol, could have great industrial value.

In 1838, Kane married Catherine Baily from Newbury in Berkshire, who was the author of *The Irish Flora*. Nine children were born to them, including Robert Romney Kane, an Irish country court judge, Admiral Sir Henry Coey Kane, and Dr Francis Baily Kane, who practised medicine in San Francisco.

The Queen's Colleges (Ireland) Act of 1845 set up the Queen's Colleges in the hope that they would provide for the Catholic demand for third-level education.

With the appointment in 1845 of Kane as the first President of Queen's College Cork, it appeared that the ideal man had been chosen for this prestigious post. The appointment was significant in that he was a Catholic. The three colleges in Belfast, Cork and Galway were set up as non-sectarian, third-level institutions. Referred to as the godless colleges, they were considered to be dangerous to faith and morals, in particular, by the Synod of Thurles (1850).

Queen's College Cork (QCC) opened in October 1849. Due to his many professional commitments in Dublin, Kane made it a condition of his appointment that he would not be required to live in the city. He continued to be Dean of the Royal College of Science in Dublin along with his duties as President of the Cork College. The new President was extremely enthusiastic about his new role in third-level education, and this caused him to interfere with the professors in regard to the details of their work. Kane's absences from the college campus caused a number of difficulties in respect to its government. In 1856 an unfortunate article appeared in the *Cork Daily Reporter* criticising the President for the few public lectures delivered under the auspices of the college. He was also attacked publically for devoting too much of his time to his more favoured institutions in Dublin. The criticism in print came from none other than Professor George Boole, the famous mathematician who held the chair of Mathematics at QCC. As a result, a Royal Commission was set up to inquire into the progress and conditions at the college. One of its recommendations was that residence in the college should be obligatory for the President. As a result, Kane did move to Cork for a number of years (1849–1852). However, in 1852 he claimed that family circumstances had forced him to move back to Dublin – a change that was not popular. In May 1862, the east wing of the college was destroyed by fire and the evidence suggested it had been caused maliciously. Unfortunately, this brought further trouble for the President, particularly with the Professor of Surgery, Denis Bullen, who claimed that the blaze had been started by a college official. This led to a bitter dispute between the two gentlemen and it only ended with Bullen's resignation and admission that his accusation was unfounded.

Kane finally resigned his Presidency of Queen's College Cork in 1873 after twenty-eight years as President. He then became Commissioner of National Education, Vice Chancellor of Queen's University, and later first Dean of the Royal University. In 1875, Trinity College Dublin gave him an honorary LLD and elected him to its Academic Council, one of the first Catholics ever elected to this esteemed body. After his retirement from Queen's College Cork, Kane devoted much of his time to the Royal Irish Academy, which he served diligently for five years, retiring in 1882. In 1889, he moved his home from Killiney to No. 2 Wellington Road, Ballsbridge, where he died on 16 February 1890 after a brief illness. He is buried in the family grave in Glasnevin Cemetery.

Further Reading

Geoghegan, Patrick M., (2009). 'Kane, Sir Robert John', in *Dictionary of Irish Biography*, edited by James McGuire and James Quinn, Cambridge University Press, Cambridge, 2009.

Kane, R., *Industrial Resources of Ireland*, The Development of Industrial Society series, Irish University Press Shannon, Ireland, [1844] 1971.

Kerr, J.J., 'Sir Robert Kane: an apostle of Irish industries', *Dublin Historical Record*, 5, 1942, pp.137–146.

Wheeler, T.S., 'Sir Robert Kane: life and work', *Studies: An Irish Quarterly Review*, 33, 1944, pp.158–168, 316–330.

Wheeler, T.S., 'Sir Robert Kane: First president of Q.C.C.' *Cork University Record*, 3, 1945, pp.29–38.

Kavanagh, Patrick (1904–1967)
Poet and Journalist
62 Pembroke Road, Ballsbridge, Dublin 4

Patrick Kavanagh was a native of Inniskeen, Co. Monaghan. He was born on 21 October 1904 to James and Bridget Kavanagh and was the fourth of their ten children. His father was a cobbler and after attending primary school in Inniskeen, Patrick was apprenticed to his father's trade. He also helped out on the farm his parents bought in 1910. His family were Catholic, and he was brought up as a practising Catholic.

The family bought a second farm and Patrick began gradually to take over his father's work, and indeed he did some cobbling, too. While working as a farmer, Patrick started writing. He also began reading and had access to literary works such as the poetry of Shelley and Goldsmith. He read widely, and in particular *Palgrave's Golden Treasury* was important to him. At the age of 21, he came across the weekly journal of arts edited by George Russell called *The Irish Statesman*. He contacted Russell and had three of his poems published in this august publication. Unfortunately, this journal closed in 1930 and Kavanagh then wrote regularly for the *Dublin Magazine*. He first visited Dublin in 1931, and there he contacted Russell, who very generously gave him a number of books to read. He continued to work on the family farm and studied and read widely in the evenings. Four of his poems were accepted by the *Irish Times* in 1935, and his first collection of poems called *Ploughman and Other Poems* was published by Macmillan in 1936.

Kavanagh decided to abandon farming and in 1937 he moved to London. There he received a commission to write his autobiography, which was published under the title *The Green Fool* in 1938. This was well received in both London and Dublin. In 1939, Kavanagh moved to Dublin from London. His uncouth manner and heavy boots did not endear him to the Dublin literary set. However, he became a regular drinker in the Palace Bar in Fleet Street, a well-known haunt of journalists from the *Irish Times* in particular. Today a bronze sculpture of Kavanagh stands outside this bar. In Dublin he became friendly with Seán Ó Faoláin and Frank O'Connor, and in 1940 he began contributing to *The Bell*, an Irish monthly magazine that had Ó Faoláin as the editor and O'Connor as poetry editor.

Kavanagh could not have survived in Dublin without the financial support of his brother, Peter, who was a school teacher. Kavanagh began writing columns as a freelance journalist for the Dublin-based daily papers, the *Irish Times, Irish Independent* and *Irish Press*. The publication in 1942 of 'The Great Hunger' by the Cuala Press in Dublin very quickly established him as a major Irish poet. This poem was quickly followed by another long poem called 'Lough Derg' that was published posthumously in 1971 and in 1978.

During the 1940s, Kavanagh continued to work as a part-time journalist. He wrote a gossip column in the *Irish Press* under the pseudonym Piers Plowman between 1942 and 1944, and was a film critic for the *Irish Press* between 1945 and 1949. John Charles McQuaid, Archbishop of Dublin, found a job for Kavanagh on the staff of the Catholic magazine *The Standard*. The Archbishop became a friend of Kavanagh and continued to support him during his life.

John Ryan, founder of a literary publication called *Envoy*, engaged Kavanagh to write a monthly diary for this publication. Ryan became a lifelong friend and benefactor of Kavanagh. The offices of *Envoy* were located on Grafton Street but much of the business was carried out in McDaid's, a nearby pub, which ultimately became Kavanagh's local. There he met up with the Dublin literary circles of poets and writers.

Despite his poems being published regularly and writing for other journals, Kavanagh did not have economic security, which appears to have been something that he craved, and he spent most of his life living in poverty, spending his money on cigarettes, gambling and alcohol. His brother, Peter, was always a great support to him and together they published *Kavanagh's Weekly: A Journal of Literature and Politics* that attacked almost every Irish institution and did not endear the brothers to the many cultural institutions and influential Irish people. *Kavanagh's Weekly* lasted from April 1952 to July the same year.

The year 1954 was dramatic for Kavanagh – he sued *The Leader* because it published a portrait of him as an alcoholic sponger. Unfortunately for Kavanagh, one of Ireland's leading barristers John A. Costello, Attorney General (1926–1932) and later Taoiseach (1948–1951 and 1954–1957), acted on behalf of *The Leader* and Kavanagh lost his case. However, he and Costello eventually became good friends. A short time after this court case, Kavanagh was diagnosed with lung cancer and had to have a lung removed. He became a regular visitor to Parson Bookshop on Baggot Street Bridge and he also began relaxing on the banks of the Canal, where a statute to his memory now sits.

Every St Patrick's Day a group of his friends meet there to pay tribute to this great poet.

Kavanagh obtained an extramural lectureship in poetry at University College Dublin from 1955, which helped his financial position. He also wrote a weekly column for *The Irish Farmers Journal* between 1958 and 1963 and for the RTÉ *Guide* between 1964 and 1967.The production of Kavanagh's *Tarry Flynn* at the Abbey Theatre in 1966 was a box office success. His poem 'On Raglan Road' was popularised by the singer Luke Kelly of The Dubliners and became a very well-known ballad.

Kavanagh married his long-term companion and friend Katherine Moloney, who was a niece of Kevin Barry, in 1967, and they lived in Waterloo Road. In November the same year, Kavanagh died of pneumonia in a Dublin Nursing Home, and he was buried at Inniskeen. An annual poetry competition in honour of the poet called The Patrick Kavanagh Poetry Award is competed for each year. There is also an annual Patrick Kavanagh weekend held in September each year at The Patrick Kavanagh Centre in Inniskeen, Co. Monaghan. The centre was set up to commemorate the local poet. University College Dublin now holds The Patrick Kavanagh Archive. Its purchase was enabled by a public appeal for money organised by the late great Professor Gus Martin of UCD. Substantial collections of his manuscripts are also in the National Library of Ireland.

Further Reading
Kavanagh, Peter, *Sacred Keeper*, Goldsmith, Newbridge, 2003.

Nemo, John, *Patrick Kavanagh*, Prior, London, 1979.

Smith, Stan, *Patrick Kavanagh*, Academic Press, Dublin, 2009.

Quinn, Antoinette, *Patrick Kavanagh*, Gill & Macmillan, Dublin, 1993.

Kelleher, Kevin D. (1921–2016) Headmaster
St Conleth's College, Ballsbridge, Dublin 4

Kevin Kelleher was born in Drumcondra, Dublin, on 18 October 1921. His father, David, was a civil servant from Charleville, Co. Cork, and he played for the Dublin team that won the All-Ireland football championship in 1906 and in the following two years. These medals were subsequently melted down into a chalice for his brother, who became a priest. The chalice is now in the possession of St Conleth's College, where Kevin was headmaster for fifty-six years. His mother, Susan (*née* Kavanagh), was from Co. Wicklow. Kevin was educated by the Christian Brothers at O'Connell schools, where he and his brother Dermot played hurling and rugby. He grew up in Drumcondra on the north side of Dublin at No. 17 Claude Road, the family home, where there was great emphasis placed within his family on education and sporting activities. He won hurling medals with the Fenians in Croke Park while still a schoolboy.

Kelleher attended University College Dublin, where he graduated in Latin, Irish and English. He also obtained his Higher Diploma in Education at UCD. On leaving UCD, Kevin's first job was with a private school in Clontarf called

Kostka College. He joined the staff of St Conleth's College on Clyde Road in 1944. St Conleth's continues to be a thriving Catholic primary and secondary school, founded by the late Bernard Shepard in 1939. Since its foundation the school has thrived and has continued to imbue in its students the robust Christian values of its founder and the school's patron St Conleth, a sixth-century Irish saint. Kelleher was a keen rugby player and was a long-standing member of Lansdowne Rugby Club. At St Conleth's, he coached the boys at rugby and other sports along with his teaching duties. In the mid-1950s, Bernard Shepherd, the school's founder, suffered increasing ill health and he died in 1957. His wife, Patricia, was an American from Seattle, whom he met while she was working in Dublin at the American Embassy. After their marriage and until her death, she was very active in the running of the school and was determined to continue the good work started by her late husband. In 1960, Kelleher became headmaster at St Conleth's and remained in this role for fifty-six years. In the same year, he and Patricia Shepherd, Bernard's widow, married. He became a kind stepfather to Ann, Bernard and Patricia's daughter. For many years, Ann taught French and Spanish in the school and was principal teacher between 1988 and 2001. She is now the senior administrator of St Conleth's with the title of Chief Executive Officer (CEO).

Beyond the school walls, Kelleher forged a wonderful career in Irish and international rugby. He became President of his club, Lansdowne Road RFC, and President of the Leinster Branch of the Irish Rugby Football Union. He was deeply involved in many rugby competitions and acted as secretary of the Leinster Rugby School's Committee for fifty-two years. He was at the forefront of Ireland's entry into schools' internationals in 1975, and for three years he served on the selection committee. He was one of the most distinguished and respected rugby international referees of his era. He began refereeing when he was thirty years old and rose very quickly to the top within five years. He always said that he favoured the 'silent whistle' approach, which would allow the game to proceed with as few stoppages as possible. He refereed twenty-three international rugby matches between 1960 and 1972. In 1967, for example, he refereed no fewer than four internationals. Kevin always wore the distinctive striped socks of Lansdowne when refereeing. He was referee on the day of a match between the All Blacks and Scotland at Murrayfield in 1967, where there was a legendary encounter between himself as referee and Colin Meads, an All Blacks star, whom he sent off for kicking an opponent. Kelleher's decision outraged many of the All Blacks fans, and this persisted for many years. Being sent off a rugby field in those days was 'more like a national scandal than a sporting disciplinary measure'. Twenty years later, New Zealand television were doing a *This is your Life* programme on Colin Meads, and they flew Kelleher out to New Zealand to appear in it. He and Meads became firm friends and they visited each other's homes in New Zealand and Ireland in later years. Kelleher gave Meads the whistle he used when sending him off the playing field and it is now in a museum in Palmerston North, New Zealand. As a referee, Kelleher always took a firm line on dangerous play. In an interview in the *Irish Independent* in 2001 with Sean Diffley, he said he was not a tough referee, and that in twenty-seven years of refereeing he only sent off two players, the aforementioned Meads, and a Leinster player in a cup match who ran across the rugby pitch to punch someone! He earned the reputation as being one of the most popular post-war referees. He was known to be firm and fair with all players on the field. Kelleher remained active in rugby after he retired as an international and Irish rugby referee. He became Honorary Secretary of the Leinster Schools Committee, where he served for fifty-two years. His contribution to Leinster schools' rugby was quite exceptional.

Kelleher's dedication to St Conleth's College was quite remarkable. Known affectionately as KD, he was involved with everything to do with the school. He was also the patron of the Past Pupils Union. He had a great love for St Conleth's and its current and past pupils. He lived on the premises, closing the school at night and opening it early every morning. He took responsibility for the school's finances and, even though he was an administrator in later years, he still managed to run the school's tuck shop, thus keeping in touch with the pupils of St Conleth's until the very end of his life. He was a devoted family man, loved by his wife, his stepdaughter Ann, his siblings Norah and Con, as well as his son-in-law Seán, and Ann and Seán's son, Cian. He devoted his entire life to the education of hundreds and thousands of students at St Conleth's over the years. The school has been attended by several generations of Dublin families. Bernard Shepherd, founder of St Conleth's, had made a point of wooing the various ambassadors who spent time in Dublin, and many of their children attended St Conleth's. The school continues to thrive. One of its past pupils, Michael O'Dea, designed a new kitchen area in 1959 and further classrooms were built in 1963. In 1974, a new laboratory and resource centre was built. All these developments took place without any Government grants. In 1975, girls were admitted into the sixth-year leaving certificate class. Prior to this, students from Pembroke School (Miss Meredith's) attended classes in Chemistry, Physics and Applied Maths at St Conleth's. By 1999, 200 girls had graduated from St Conleth's, demonstrating what an innovative school it had become.

Further developments in the fabric of the school took place in 1999, when a major extension was completed. In 2017, the building of the Kevin D. Kelleher wing (costing €1.7 million) was completed without any Government grants. It included a fully equipped multi-purpose sports hall with viewing gallery, showers, changing facilities, a fitness suite, a performance area for drama, a conference room, lecture hall and a revamped junior school learning and exploration area. This building was essentially funded with generous contributions from the students' parents.

Kelleher died at his home St Conleth's College on 27 October 2016 at the age of 95. He was beloved by students and teachers alike and was always available to students and staff as a guide, philosopher and friend. His funeral from Clyde Road to St Mary's Church Haddington Road was one of the largest seen in that area. He was buried after Requiem Mass in Haddington Road, in Shanganagh Cemetery. 'His intense awareness of humanity and his gentle good humour have left a wonderful legacy in one of the most remarkable Catholic schools in the Country.'

Further Reading

St Conleth's College, *Reflections 1990–1996*, St Conleth's College, Dublin.

St Conleth's College, *80th Year Anniversary*, St Conleth's College, Dublin, 2019.

Walsh, Brendan, *Essays in the History of Irish Education*, Palgrave Macmillan, London, 2016.

Kellett, Iris Patricia (1926–2011)
International Showjumper
Mespil Road, Dublin 4

Iris Kellett was born on 8 January 1926 to Thomas Kellett (1890–1964) and his wife, Dolly (1895–1944), who died when Iris was a teenager. Iris's father was a veterinary surgeon who worked in the Veterinary Corps of the British Army for a number of years. His family owned Kellett's a large drapery business at Nos 19–21 South Great George's Street in Dublin. He took over as Managing Director when he was decommissioned from the army. He was always interested in horses and took part in many point-to-point races. In 1924, he opened a riding school in Mespil Road in Dublin, which was formerly the British Army cavalry stables. Thomas Kellett seems to have passed on his skills and his great love and care of horses to his daughter. Iris grew up in Mespil Road was educated at nearby St Margaret's Hall (a Church of Ireland school for girls), where she played hockey and tennis. This school was also located on Mespil Road, which was described in nineteenth-century advertisements as being 'a high-class boarding and day school for girls'.

On her return from school, Iris would help out at the stables and riding school belonging to her father. Both her parents fell ill during her teen years, and Iris took over the running of the riding school with great success. Her riding skills were very soon recognised, and she began teaching aspiring riders while she was still at school. On leaving school, she obtained a place at Trinity College Dublin to study science, but she decided to pursue a career as a showjumper instead.

One of Kellett's early successes in the riding arena took place in 1936, when she won a silver hunting crop for the best girl pony rider on her pony Sparkle, which she walked from her home on Mespil Road to the RDS's spring show in Ballsbridge that year, at the age of 9. She was a keen rider from an early age and hunted, as well as being a point-to-point rider. She also competed in one-day events, including winning at Castletown. This was all before she decided to devote her time to showjumping. Kellett was a member of the Kildare Branch of the Pony Club and she became a regular competitor in junior competitions. She first competed in an adult competition at Dundalk in 1941.

By 1945, Kellett was Ireland's leading female international showjumper. Early in her career her favourite horse was Starlet, which she rode and competed on to a level people thought was impossible. Rusty, her most famous horse, was a half-bred chestnut gelding. He was originally a hunter and plough horse, but under Kellett's tutelage and training, he became an international star. She rode Rusty as a member of the Irish civilian jumping team in 1947 and also won the British Showjumping Association's national championship at Blackpool in England. She and Rusty continued to compete at the annual RDS Spring and Horse Shows, and together they had great success in winning the show's main international competition in 1948. In the previous year she had won in Holland, defeating the very distinguished British rider Colonel Harry Llewellyn.

As a 22-year-old, Kellett won the prestigious Princess Elizabeth Cup at the White City in London in 1949, and she won it again in 1951. The International Horse Show at the White City required all countries to have a female rider on their team. Kellett therefore became the first Irish civilian to accompany an Irish Army team abroad, though she was restricted to individual events. Kellett also accompanied the Irish Army to the UK Horse of the Year Show in 1949 and 1950. Riding Rusty, she won the Diana Stakes competition for women riders in England in 1949. She also rode to victory in four events abroad on another of her horses called Starlet.

Between 1947 and 1951, Kellett was the leading showjumping rider in both the United Kingdom and Ireland. Unfortunately, she was unable to compete in the Nations Cup held annually at the RDS because this competition was for male army riders only. Finally, in 1963, civilian riders were able to compete in this very prestigious competition. The Olympics, too, were closed to women riders until 1956.

Kellett suffered a major accident in 1952 when she fell from a horse. This resulted in a shattered ankle as well as a bout of tetanus. The following year she had another fall from her horse, breaking her leg, shoulder, wrist and ribs. This halted her riding career for a number of years. Kellett was always an astute breeder and purchaser of horses, and she owned most of the horses she rode herself in national and international competitions. It took almost ten years before she was back in the saddle, in tiptop form, competing for the Irish team in the Nations Cup at the RDS during the 1960s and winning the European Ladies Championship on Morning Light at the 1969 RDS Horse Show. Kellett retired from showjumping after this to devote her time to her riding school.

In the 1950s and '60s, the Mespil Road Riding School was a great centre for Irish showjumping, and Kellett's influence set standards for showjumping and riding both in Ireland and abroad. She was an inspiration for generations of Irish riders. Many distinguished businessmen learned to ride at Kellett's stables. Charles J. Haughey for example, a former Irish Taoiseach (Prime Minister), learned to ride there. Kellett was always generous with her skills and her time; for example, she taught members of the Trinity College Equestrian Club free of charge. She also took a great interest in Riding for the Disabled.

Eddie Macken was Iris's star pupil, benefiting greatly from her strict tutelage and her top-class horses. So taken was she by him, that that she even paid for his board and lodgings in Dublin. When Kellett retired from international showjumping after winning the Ladies European championship in 1969, Eddie became the rider of Morning Light, her champion horse, and he competed very successfully on this horse for a number of years. Another of Kellett's star pupil was Paul Darragh. He was on the winning team in the Aga Khan Trophy at the RDS annual Horse Show three years in a row from 1977 to 1980.

Besides being an international showjumper, Kellett also had a deep understanding, love and knowledge of horses. She was a great teacher and had a shrewd business brain. Besides running the riding school, she also ran the Eblana bookshop in Grafton Street, with her husband, Ben Brennan, whom she had married in 1952. During her lifetime she was one of the most influential and highly respected persons in Irish showjumping and her reputation also spread worldwide. In 1972, she sold her premises in Mespil Road and bought instead a 91-acre farm at Kill, Co. Kildare, where she set up her riding school again. Her students came from all over the world to study with her and that included Middle Eastern royalty. At Kill she could house eighty horses and had accommodation for staff and some forty students. In general, her facilities were excellent, and from there she sold on many horses to rich Arabs. She also trained the Kuwaiti showjumping team that went on to win gold, silver and bronze at the Asian games in 1982.

Kellett became a world authority on the breeding and training of horses and was appointed a director of the State's Bord na gCapall in 1976. She was also active in the Showjumping Association of Ireland. In 1998, Iris sold her Kill riding school and developed a smaller facility at her farm near Naas. Married twice, Iris separated from her second husband in 1990 – she had no children from either marriage. In 1997, she was inaugurated into the Texaco Sports Hall of Fame. The University of Limerick honoured her with an honorary doctor of Science in 1999, for her assistance in setting up a degree course in Equestrian Science.

Kellett's contribution to the equestrian world is unparalleled, and her reputation as an outstanding trainer and breeder of horses will be difficult to surpass. She was always very proud of her many successful students who went on to have international careers in the equestrian world. In the latter part of her life she developed Alzheimer's disease and she died in a Naas nursing home on 11 March 2011. She is buried with her parents in Mount Jerome Cemetery in Dublin.

Further Reading

Clavin, T., 'Kellett, Iris', in *Dictionary of Irish Biography,* edited by James McGuire and James Quinn, Cambridge University Press, Cambridge.

Mullins, N., *Horse Tales and Hunt Talk*, NDM Publications, Dublin, 2006.

Slavin, M., *Showjumping legends (1868–1998),* Irish American Book Company, Dublin, 1999.

Kettle, Thomas Michael (1880–1916)
Parliamentarian, Writer and Soldier
119 Upper Leeson Street, Dublin 4

Thomas Kettle was born in Artane, Dublin, to Andrew Kettle (1833–1916), and his wife, Margaret (*née* McCourt). His father was a progressive farmer, a leading nationalist politician, and a founding member of the Irish Land League. Tom Kettle was educated at O'Connell School in Dublin, and at Clongowes Wood College in Co. Kildare. At Clongowes, he proved to be an excellent student, and a good debater. He was also a keen sportsman with a great interest in cricket, athletics and cycling. In 1897, he became a student at University College Dublin, where his friends included Padraig Pearse, Con Curran, Padraig Colum, Francis Sheehy-Skeffington, Oliver St John Gogarty and James Joyce. He very quickly became a well-known student politician and was elected Auditor of the Literary and Historical Society for the session 1898–1899.

During his time in UCD, Kettle suffered from ill health, and he spent time out of university on his father's farm, in Innsbruck, and in Switzerland, where he improved his knowledge of French and German. This illness appears to have been a form of nervous breakdown. He is known to have suffered in this respect throughout his life. On returning to UCD, he obtained a BA in Philosophy in 1902. The following January he enrolled at the King's Inns to become a barrister. He qualified in 1905 but only practised from time to time. His great interest lay in political journalism. That year too he became the editor of the UCD magazine, *St Stephen's,* and in 1905, became editor of the short-lived weekly review of Irish thought and affairs called *The Nationalist.*

Kettle was a supporter of Home Rule and the Irish Parliamentary Party. He co-founded and became President of the Young Ireland branch of the United

Irish League in 1904. The United Irish League, with the motto 'The Land for the People', was founded in 1898 by William O'Brien (1852–1928). In 1906, Kettle was persuaded to become the candidate for a vacant parliamentary seat in the East Tyrone district. He won the seat by a very narrow majority and represented the Irish Party in the British House of Commons. He was seen as a potential leader of the Irish party, and went to America on its behalf, where he took part in a number of propaganda and fund-raising meetings. In Westminster, after his maiden speech, he was seen as a born speaker, and leading orators such as Asquith, Balfour and John Redmond increasingly accepted him as their equal. In 1908, in Parliament, Kettle supported the Irish Universities Bill, and he criticised heavily, the maladministration of the Old Age Pension Act in Ireland. Kettle was very much a European, and he said at one stage, 'My only counsel to Ireland, is, that to become deeply Irish, she must become European.' In 1909, Kettle married Mary Sheehy, a graduate of University College Dublin and a sister-in-law of his friend, Francis Sheehy Skeffington. In 1913, their daughter, Elizabeth (Betty), was born.

While still in Parliament, Kettle was appointed in 1908 to the Chair of National Economics at University College Dublin, then a new constituent college of the new National University of Ireland. Very soon he found it difficult to combine his academic work as a professor with his work as a Member of Parliament. He retained his seat in East Tyrone in the general election of January 1910 but did not contest it in the second election of December of the same year. Though no longer a member of Parliament, he continued to support the Irish Parliamentary Party, and he was delighted with the 1912 Home Rule Bill. However, he totally underestimated the rising belligerence of Ulster. During the 1913 Workers Strike and the lockout, Kettle supported the workers and wrote a number of articles demonstrating the appalling living conditions of the poor. In 1913, too, Kettle became involved with the Irish Volunteers, which was formed in response to the creation of the Ulster Volunteers. With his knowledge of continental languages, it was hardly surprising to find that in 1914 he was in Belgium on behalf of the Irish Volunteers, purchasing arms and ammunition for the organisation. He sought a nomination as a nationalist candidate in the Galway East by-election of December 1891 but was unsuccessful. By this time, Kettle's alcoholism had become a major health problem. He was not in favour of the 1916 Rising in Dublin, which he saw as madness, and in fact, destructive to parliamentary nationalism. However, with the execution of the Leaders of the Rising he was moved to indignation and pity. 'These men will go down to history as heroes and martyrs and I will go down – if I go down at all – as a bloody British Officer.'

It was while Kettle was in Belgium that the First World War broke out, and he stayed on there as a war correspondent for the *Daily News*. Many of his reports warned of the dire threat to Europe from the Germans. He was outraged by the invasion of Belgium, which he believed was a crime against civilisation. He felt it his duty to join the war effort, and in November 1914 he joined the Dublin Fusiliers. Due to his poor health and his gift of oratory, he remained in Ireland as a recruiting officer for the British Army. When his health improved somewhat, he applied for and received a commission into the 9th Battalion of the Royal Dublin Fusiliers, and in early 1916 he was sent to France. It was in the Battle of the Somme that Kettle was destined to die. This battle was fought between the British and the French against the Germans, and it lasted from 1 July to 18 November 1916. It has been described as the largest battle on the Western Front and was fought on both sides of the River Somme. Three million men fought in it and almost one million were either wounded or killed. Thus, it was one of the bloodiest battles in the history of war. During the war in France, before Guillemont, Somme, on 4 September 1916, Kettle wrote the celebrated sonnet to his young daughter, Betty, entitled 'To my daughter Betty, The Gift of God'.

Kettle was killed in action with B Company of the 9th Battalion of the Royal Dublin Fusiliers on 9 September 1916. He was 36 years old, and he was buried in a battlefield grave that is no longer identifiable. Kettle is commemorated on the Thiepval Memorial, in northern France, which is dedicated to the missing. It contains the names of more than 72,000 officers and men of the British Army who died in the Somme sector and have no known grave. Kettle is commemorated in Dublin by a bronze bust by Albert Power (1881–1945), which was placed in St Stephen's Green in 1937. The UCD Literary and Historical Society holds an annual wreath-laying ceremony there. Kettle is remembered, too, by the Economics Society in UCD, which has named their life membership award in memory of their former auditor. There is another memorial in the Irish Peace Park at Messines, Belgium, where a stone tablet commemorates Kettle. He is listed too on a bronze plaque in the Four Courts in Dublin, which commemorate twenty-six Irish barristers who died in the Great War. His name also appears on the Parliamentary War Memorial in Westminster Hall in London, which commemorates twenty-two former members of Parliament who lost their lives during the First World War. The Tom Kettle Papers were deposited in UCD Archives by Dr Conor Cruise O'Brien in 1987.

Further Reading

Burke, Tom, 'In Memory of Lieutenant Tom Kettle, B Company 9th Royal Dublin Fusiliers', *Dublin Historical Record* 57 (2), pp.164–173.

Lyons, J.B., *The Enigma of Tom Kettle: Irish Patriot, Essayist, Poet, British Soldier, 1880–1916*, Glendale Press, Dublin, 1983.

Paseta, Senia, *Thomas Kettle,* Dublin University Press, Dublin, 2009.

Kiely, Benedict (1919–2007)
Writer and Journalist
119 Morehampton Road, Donnybrook, Dublin 4

Born Thomas Joseph Benedict Kiely near Dromore, Co. Tyrone, on 15 August 1919, Benedict (or Ben) was the youngest in a family of six children born to Thomas Kiely (a British Army veteran) and his wife, Sarah Anne (*née* Gormley). The year following Ben's birth, the family moved to Omagh, and there Ben received his primary and secondary education. He attended the Christian Brothers Schools (Mount St Columba's) in Omagh, and he always retained very fond memories of some of  his teachers there. Ben was an Ulsterman all his life, and even though he spent the greater part of his life in Dublin, Omagh and Co. Tyrone had a lasting influence on his entire life and writings.

Between 1936 and 1937 Kiely worked as a sorter in the local post office before entering the Jesuit novitiate at Emo Park in Co. Laois. Due to a back injury (a tubercular lesion of the spine) he spent eighteen months in Cappagh Orthopaedic Hospital in Dublin. At the end of that period, he decided that he did not have a vocation for the priesthood, and so left the Jesuits. He acquired a lifelong habit of rising early each morning from his time in the novitiate, and he carried out several hours of work every morning before breakfast.

Kiely began writing essays for the *Father Matthew Record* when still young. His elder brother was a self-made businessman and Kiely borrowed money from him to allow him attend University College Dublin. He became a mature student in the Faculty of Arts, studying History, English and Latin. During his time in college he became a part-time assistant on *The Standard,* a well-known Catholic newspaper.

When he graduated from UCD in 1943, Kiely commenced an MA in History, but soon abandoned it when he was recruited by Peadar O'Curry (the editor of *The Standard*) to a full-time post. While working there he also worked for Radio Éireann on musical and literary programmes. Then, two years later (1945), Kiely joined the editorial staff of the *Irish Independent* as a leader writer, and in 1951 he became literary editor of the *Irish Press*. When he was offered a post at a university in the United States, he requested leave of absence from his work at the *Irish Press,* but this was refused, so he went to the States anyhow. He had been at the *Irish Press* for thirteen years when he applied for the leave of absence. During these years he reviewed books for Irish periodicals as well as on Radio Éireann. He was a regular contributor to a popular radio programme on a Sunday morning on RTÉ Radio called *Sunday Miscellany.* His Northern Ireland accent still rings in many an Irish ear.

During the 1940s, Kiely began to write seriously and his first publications were all non-fiction. *Counties of Contention* was published in 1945, and it is essentially a study in the origins and implications of the partition of Ireland. In 1947 he wrote *Poor Scholar: A Study of the Works and Days of William Carleton (1794–1869),* a biography of the Irish writer and novelist from Co. Tyrone, who is best known for his *Traits and Stories of the Irish Peasantry.* In his later years Kiely was a patron and a regular attender at the Carleton Summer School, held in Clogher, Co. Tyrone.

Kiely's early novels are set in what appears to be Omagh, during the period 1938–1940. These include *Land Without Stars* (1946) and *In a Harbour Green* (1948). His third novel, entitled *Call for a Miracle*, published in 1950 is set in Dublin in 1942. Many of his books cover such subjects as marital separation, prostitution and suicide, and a number of them were banned in Ireland. He continued to write novels into the 1950s and more were banned by the Irish censor – a verdict Kiely seems to have accepted with good humour.

From the early 1950s, Kiely began publishing in the *New Yorker* magazine and during this period he made many contacts with American academics. He spent a year as writer in residence at Hollins College in West Virginia between 1964 and 1965. He became Professor of Creative Writing at the University of Oregon in Portland Maine from 1965 to 1966. He was also writer in residence at Emory University in Georgia. While in the United States, Kiely contributed a fortnightly column to the *Irish Times* commenting on American society in general, as well as the civil rights movement. He spent some time again in the United States in 1976 as a distinguished visiting professor, at the University of Delaware. From 1968, Kiely became a full-time writer. He began to focus on short stories, and indeed, he became a master of the form. These collections became his most popular works of fiction.

During the 1970s, Kiely wrote more novels and they became angrier and more embittered; for example, *Proxopera* published in 1977, and *Nothing Happens in Carmincross*, published in 1985. The latter has been described as 'a masterpiece by one of Northern Ireland's greatest writers'. The former contains the history of a town and a country. Throughout his life, Kiely drew on his own experiences for the themes of his stories, especially on his childhood in Co. Tyrone. His writings give us a unique history of Northern Ireland, the problems of sectarianism, political failure and political violence. His writings also reflect the time he spent in the 1960s and '70s at various universities in the United States. It has been suggested by a number of critics that Kiely's writings on the Troubles is his most outstanding work.

From the time he moved to Dublin, Kiely very soon became part of the Dublin literary scene, counting among his friends writers such as Francis MacManus, Seamus O'Sullivan, Austin Clarke, Padraic Fallon and Patrick Kavanagh, whom he would meet regularly in the Palace Bar. This is a famous pub on Fleet Street in Dublin (still in existence), which for many years was close to the *Irish Times* offices, and was for generations the favoured haunt of journalists and with leading Irish writers.

The National University of Ireland (of which he was a graduate) awarded Kiely an Honorary Doctorate in 1982. He was also a Council member and President of the Irish Academy of Letters, which had been founded in 1932 by W.B. Yeats and George Bernard Shaw. In 1996, he was made a Saoi of Aosdána, one of the highest awards bestowed on an Irish artist. No more than seven living members can be honoured at one time. Over the course of his life, Kiely wrote ten novels in total, with the last one, *Nothing Happens in Carmincross*, published in 1985. Kiely's *Collected Short Stories* first appeared in 2001, but there were earlier collections including A *Journey to the Seven Streams* (1963), *A Ball of Malt and Madame Butterfly* (1973), *A Cow in the House* (1978), *The State of Ireland: A Novella and Seven Short Stories* (1980) and *A Letter to Peachtree* (1987).

Kiely published his autobiography or memoir, *Drink to the Bird*, in 1991. This book covers his boyhood in Co. Tyrone as well as his early life as a journalist. His final work was *The Waves Behind,* a memoir that is set for the most part in Dublin just after the Second World War. It describes Kiely's adventures and encounters as a young journalist and writer.

Kiely was married twice. In 1944, he wed Maureen O'Connell and they had three daughters and one son. He married his second wife, Frances, in 2005, after Maureen's death. Kiely died in Dublin at St Vincent's Hospital on 9 February 2007 and is buried with his parents and family in Omagh. The annual Benedict Kiely Literary Weekend takes place each year in Omagh, Co. Tyrone. Kiely's main collection of papers is in the National Library of Ireland. Emory University in the United States also holds a small collection.

Further Reading

Casey, Daniel J., *Benedict Kiely*, Bucknell University Press, Pennsylvania, 1974.

Kiely, Benedict, *Drink to the Bird: A Memoir*, Methuen, London, 1999.

Kiely, Benedict, *The Waves Behind Us*, Methuen, London, 1999.

Maume, Patrick, 'Kiely, Benedict', in *Dictionary of Irish Biography*, edited by James McGuire and James Quinn.: Cambridge University Press, Cambridge.

Larkin, Delia (1878–1949)
Trade Unionist and Journalist
41 Wellington Road, Ballsbridge, Dublin 4

Delia Larkin was born in Liverpool in 1878 to Irish emigrants James Larkin and Mary Ann McNulty, who were both originally from Armagh. She was the fifth child and was a sister of James (Big Jim) Larkin (1876–1947), a Labour leader. Her father died in 1887 when Delia was 9 years old. Delia attended the local elementary school in Chipping Street. She was always interested in education, although she did not have the chance of further education after leaving primary school. Due to the family's poor financial circumstances after her father died, Delia left primary school early and took a job in a hospital. From the time she was young she had a great interest in politics and in literature, which may have been due to the influence of her brother James.

In 1907 Delia moved to Northern Ireland, to Rostrevor, Co. Down, not far from the original Larkin family home. While living there she managed a hotel for a while, and then she moved to Dublin and stayed with James and his family. In 1909, Jim Larkin founded the Irish Transport and General Workers Union (ITGWU). Delia was a great support to her brother politically from the time he had set up a trade union in the Liverpool dockyards. She continued to support him for most of his life and it was through this that she moved to Dublin. Although originally sceptical of the idea, she agreed to become involved in the setting up of a women's trade union as part of her brother's ITGWU. Delia contributed numerous articles to the *Irish Worker*, the newspaper of the ITGWU. It was here that the first advertisement for the Irish Women Works Union (IWWU) appeared. The union was based at Liberty Hall, the headquarters of the ITGWU, and Delia became its first secretary. Delia's biographer, Theresa Moriarty, has pointed out that at this time women trade unionists were very isolated. Their numbers were small in comparison to the men's unions and they appeared to lack the organisational experience of their male counterparts. Delia was totally committed to the IWWU and worked unceasingly for it.

The Irish Women Workers Union had branches in a number of Irish cities and towns including Belfast, Dundalk, Wexford and Cork, but the main focus of the union was in Dublin. Professor Diarmaid Ferriter has pointed out that an office was provided for the IWWU in Liberty Hall in Dublin, where Delia worked unceasingly to acquire better working conditions for domestic and factory workers, waitresses, printers and dressmakers. There was only one large factory in Dublin where there were several hundred members of this union and that was Jacob's biscuit factory in Dublin. Female employees there were subsequently locked out by their employers for supporting their male colleagues, who were on strike. With the help of the IWWU, the men secured better working conditions and pay from their employers.

In 1913, the IWWU then became involved in the great lockout of workers that followed the tramway strike. The Dublin tramways strike was a dispute between 20,000 workers and 300 employers, which took place in Dublin and lasted from August 1913 until January 1914. Central to this dispute was the right of workers to belong to a trade union. When her brother, James, went to England to seek British support for the strikers it was Delia who helped to organise support for them at Liberty Hall. She ran the soup kitchens and with the help of Countess Markievicz and volunteer members of the IWWU, she ensured that between 2,000 to 3,000 starving Dublin children received breakfasts and lunches every day. Delia was responsible, too, for a plan to bring strikers' children to England to be cared for during the lockout but ran up against the wrath of the then Archbishop of Dublin William Walsh. He stated:

> I can only put it to them that they can be no longer held worthy of the name of Catholic mothers if they so far forget their duty as to send away their little children to be cared for in a strange land, without security of any kind that those to whom the poor children are to be handed over are Catholics, or indeed are persons of any faith at all.

During the lockout, Delia ran an undertaking to feed the union members on strike and their dependents for its duration. When her brother was sent to prison in October 1913, Delia became more or less the public face of Liberty Hall and was a frequent speaker at rallies. When the lockout ended, almost 400 members of the IWWU were sacked. With a view to raising funds, Delia went on tour of England with a drama group that consisted of some of the sacked workers as well as the Irish Workers Choir that she had founded. Unfortunately, the tour was not a success and very little money was raised. When her brother left for the United States in 1914, Delia did not get on with his successor as the new secretary of the ITGWU. There were tensions between the IWWU and the ITGWU, and the results of the tour brought these tensions to the fore. In September 1914, the IWWU were ordered to leave Liberty Hall and In 1915 Delia left Dublin for London to work as a nurse. She returned to Dublin in 1918 and worked for a time in the insurance section of Liberty Hall. She applied to re-join the IWWU, but her application was refused, and she was also refused admittance to the Irish Clerical Workers Union.

After a number of conflicts with the Irish Transport and General Workers Union, she helped her brother, James, and another brother, Peter, to found the Workers Union of Ireland (WUI) in 1924. This union was formed as a consequence of clashes between James and the incumbent leadership of the ITGWU.

A rift occurred between Delia and James that appears to have begun in 1924. The cause may have been the fact that her husband, Pat Colgan, had broken the picket line of the strike at Kingsbridge Station with his Rapid Transit Company (which was a haulage company) while the workers were on strike. She had married Pat, a former trade unionist and member of the Irish Citizen Army, in 1921. It is reputed that James never spoke to his sister again following Pat's actions, although they lived in the same house for a number of years. Delia's activity in running a game of House at Langrishe Hall in Dublin may have also helped to damage relations between them. James was of the opinion that this was an activity that could be used to embarrass him at a critical stage in the fortunes of the Labour movement in Ireland.

Larkin made a major contribution to the history of the Labour movement in Ireland. She led the IWWU to several strike victories and spoke at several important trade union conferences between 1912 and 1914. As a journalist, she provided women with an outlet to vent their frustrations in her column Women Workers in the *Irish Worker*, a well-known trade union newspaper.

Larkin suffered from ill health in later life and died at her home on Wellington Road on 26 October 1949. She is buried in Glasnevin Cemetery.

Further Reading

Ferriter, Diarmaid, 'Delia Larkin', in *Dictionary of Irish Biography*, edited by James McGuire and James Quinn, Cambridge University Press, Cambridge, in progress.
Larkin, Emmet, *James Larkin*, Pluto Press, London, 1989.
MacCurtain, M. and Corrain, D.O., *Women in Irish Society*, Arlen Press, Dublin, 1984.

Laverty, Maura (1907–1966)
Writer and Broadcaster
25 Pembroke Road, Dublin 4

Maura Laverty was born Maura Kelly to Michael Kelly and his wife, Mary Ann Kelly (*née* Tracey) in Rathangan, Co. Kildare on 15 May 1907. Maura's father owned a drapery shop, but he ran into financial difficulties and her mother set up a dressmaking business to maintain the family of nine children. Maura seems to have spent a good deal of time with her maternal grandmother, who instilled a love of cooking into her granddaughter. She was educated in a boarding school run by the Brigidine nuns in Tullow, Co. Carlow, where she also trained as a teacher.

In 1924, Maura moved to Spain to work as a governess to the young Princess Bibesco. While there she taught herself shorthand and typewriting and she later became secretary to the Bibesco family. Maura became a journalist and a foreign correspondent in Madrid. There she wrote for a paper called *El Debate* as well as working as a freelance correspondent. While in Spain she also worked for a short time at the Banco de Bilbao and contributed poems, stories and translations from the Spanish to several Irish magazines. Through her work as a journalist she met up with a fellow journalist, James Laverty. They corresponded for a number of years and they were married in 1928 after a whirlwind romance. They had three children, one of whom became the very well-known artist Barry Castle (1935–2008). Maura continued working as both a journalist and broadcaster at RTÉ, while she was married and had the three children. Her husband worked as a sub editor for the *Irish Times*, and occasionally wrote articles for the paper. Maura continued writing in order to contribute to the running of the household and the education of her family. The two girls were sent as boarders to the Loreto Abbey in Rathfarnham, and the boy went to Terenure College.

While working in 2RN (as RTÉ was previously known), Laverty gave talks on a number of different topics including Irish legends and folklore, religion and literature, Spain and cooking. She also wrote regularly for Irish newspapers and women's magazines, as well as booklets for the Catholic Truth Society of Ireland. During the 1930s, Laverty was involved in *Woman's Life*, a magazine that began in July 1936. There she wrote not only under her own name, but as an agony aunt called Mrs Wyse, and she wrote too as Dr Garry Myers, who advised readers on matters of health. She also wrote under the pseudonym Delia Dixon, a beauty expert, for *Women's Life*. She was the first agony aunt in *Woman's Way*, a popular Irish women's magazine. Laverty not only wrote for Irish publications, but she contributed magazine articles to British magazines and to the English newspaper *Sunday Empire News*, which was banned in Ireland. Laverty also contributed to *The Bell* (1940–1954), a monthly magazine of literature and social comment that was very popular with generations of Irish people. It was the most important literary and intellectual journal published in Ireland during the twentieth century.

Laverty became well known in Ireland for her first book published in 1941 – a cook book called *Flour Economy* for Emergency conditions in Ireland, which was commissioned by the Irish Government. Between 1942 and 1946 she wrote four novels, all of which were published in London by Longmans Green. Her first novel, *Never No More*, was largely autobiographical and was very well received by critics. However, it was not so well received in her native Rathangan, where people felt they could be identified in the book, and it was publically burned. The preface to this novel was written by the well-known Irish writer Seán Ó Faoláin, who wrote, 'For me the book was a case of love at first sight.' This novel was followed by *Touched by the Thorn* in 1943, *No More than Human* in 1944, and *Lift Up your Gates* in 1946. *Touched by a Thorn* (also published as *Alone we Embark*) was banned by the Irish censor. However, it won the Irish Women's Writers Award the year it was published. *No More than Human* was another semi-autobiographical novel set in Spain, and this and *Lift Up your Gates* (set in the inner city of Dublin) were also banned. Laverty also wrote children's books, with perhaps the most successful one *The Cottage in the Bog* (1946). Others were *The Green Orchard* (1949) and *The Queen of Aran's Daughter (1997)*. The latter was illustrated by her daughter, Barry Castle, and was published posthumously.

Two of her plays, *Liffey Lane* (1951), which was adapted from her novel, *Lift Up your Gates* (1946), and *Tolka Row* (1951), were both produced at the Gate Theatre. *Tolka Row* went on to become one of the most successful television series on RTÉ. It was the station's first soap opera, which ran between 1964 and 1968, with the script for each episode written by Laverty.

Laverty was also a cookery writer. Besides her first book, *Flour Economy* (1941) her second book was *Kind Cooking* (1946), illustrated by Louis le

Brocquy. Her final cookbook, *Full and Plenty*, was published in 1960 and made her a household name and a legend in Irish kitchens. The book also contains bits of home economics. It is part fiction, a type of creative memoir, and it contains an assortment of historical and folk tales. Besides recipes this book contains food-related romantic stories. Her great love of cookery shines through in her novels, too. Her advice of a minimum daily ration included egg, cheese, butter, bread, vegetables, fruit and 'a serving of meat or fish or bacon'. Throughout her life, Laverty wrote in various genres and for national and provincial newspapers as well as for British newspapers and women's magazines. Of her four novels, three of them were banned in Ireland. Books could be banned under the Censorship of Publications Acts of 1929 if they were considered to be indecent or obscene,

Laverty worked for a while with Séan MacBride's political party, Clann na Poblachta, as a type of publicist. She became a member of their National Executive and wrote the script for *Our Country*, one of the first party political broadcasts on film in Ireland. Sarah Binchy, a niece of the late Maeve Binchy, made a documentary about Laverty in 2011. Brendan Behan and Maeve Binchy were also admirers of her work and Maeve wrote the foreword to two of Laverty's books that were republished by Virago in the 1980s. Bairbrie Ní Chaoimh and Yvonne Quinn wrote a play in recent years about Laverty, which was called *Maura Laverty – This was your Life*. Directed by Joan Sheehy and starring Bairbre Ní Chaoimh and Patrick Ryan, it was staged at the Viking Theatre in Clontarf, Dublin, in 2019 and was on a nationwide tour in 2020.

Laverty lived in Dublin from the time she was married. The family seem to have moved around Dublin. They lived at various times in Raheny, Fairview, Merrion Square, Leinster Road in Rathmines, Pembroke Road, and finally to Butterfield Crescent in Rathfarnham. Unfortunately, there are no plaques on any of these Dublin houses to commemorate Laverty, who was an outstanding female novelist and playwright. However, there is now a monument to her memory in Rathangan, Co. Kildare. Laverty's marriage was not always happy, and she and James were living separate lives when she died of a heart attack in 1966 in her home in Butterfield Avenue. She is buried in Glasnevin Cemetery. Her papers are in the National Library of Ireland.

Further Reading

Clarke, Frances, 'Laverty (Kelly) Maura', in *Dictionary of Irish Biography*, edited by James McGuire and James Quinn, Cambridge University Press, Cambridge, in progress.

Kelly, Seamus, *The Maura Laverty Story from Rathangan to Tolka Row*, Naas Printing, Naas, 2018.

'Maura Laverty, Profile', *RTÉ Guide*, 13 May 1966, p.15.

Lavin, Mary (1912–1996)
Short Story Writer and Novelist
5 Guilford Place, Sandymount, Dublin 4

Mary Lavin, daughter of Thomas Lavin and Nora Lavin (*née* Mahon), was born on 11 June 1912 in Massachusetts, USA, where her parents had emigrated. When she was 10 years old, both mother and daughter returned to live with her mother's family in Athenry, Co. Galway. Later they bought a house in Dublin and Mary's father returned from the USA to manage a demesne and large property, Bective House, in Co. Meath, for a wealthy American family, the Birds of East Walpole, Massachusetts.

Mary Lavin lived mostly with her mother on Adelaide Road in Dublin. She was sent to school with the Loreto nuns, on St Stephen's Green, where she was a keen hockey player. She went on to University College Dublin, then located on Earlsfort Terrace, and near her home at No. 38 Adelaide Road. Though not an educated man himself, Tom Lavin firmly believed in education, and wanted it above all for his daughter. He was always very proud of the fact that she went to UCD.

According to Mary's daughter, the late Caroline Walsh, she loved UCD and it was there she met her two husbands, William Walsh, who studied Law, from Co. Kildare. Her second husband was Michael McDonald Scott, a former Jesuit who came from Australia. Scott returned to Australia after his time at UCD and was ordained a Jesuit priest. During Mary's time at UCD, there were many students there who later became writers, including Donagh MacDonagh, Denis Devlin, Brian O'Nolan, Mervyn Wall, Lorna Reynolds and Roger MacHugh. The latter two became distinguished university professors of English.

Lavin's primary degree from UCD was in English and French and she received an MA in English in 1936 – her thesis was on Jane Austen. She intended doing a PhD on Virginia Woolf, but instead wrote her first short story on the back of a typed draft of her thesis and then abandoned the thesis altogether. Called *Miss Holland*, this story was published in 1939 in the *Dublin Magazine*. Tom Lavin was very proud of his daughter's writings and he asked the well-known Anglo–Irish writer and dramatist Lord Dunsany (1878–1957), who lived at Dunsany Castle in Co. Meath, to read some of her unpublished work. Dunsany was most impressed with the quality of Lavin's writing and became her mentor for many years. Her short story, *The Green Grave & the Black Grave*, was published in the *Atlantic Monthly* in 1940. This was her introduction to American audiences, who later became very familiar with her writing.

In 1942, Lavin married William Walsh, by then a qualified solicitor, and they had three daughters. They bought land near Bective House, in Co. Meath and built the Abbey Farm, which became their main home. William, Mary and their family divided their time between this farm and a house on Clyde Road in Dublin. The same year, Lavin had her first collection of short stories published, called *Tales from Bective Bridge*. It won the James Tail Black memorial prize, one of the oldest British Literary awards, and thus established her reputation. Her novel, *The House in Clewe Street*, appeared in serial form in the *Atlantic Magazine*, an American publication, before it was published as a book in 1945. Her next novel, *Mary O'Grady*, was published in 1950.

During her marriage to Walsh, who died in 1954, Lavin wrote two novels, a novella and further collections of short stories. Included were *The Becker Wives and Other Stories (1946) The Patriot Son and Other Stories* (1956), *The Great Wave and Other Stories* (1961*), In the Middle of the Fields and other stories* (1967), *Happiness and Other Stories* (1969) and *A Memory and Other Stories* (1972). Her stories were mostly about families, the emotional challenges of widowhood, and the domestic world in general.

After Walsh's death, Lavin moved her family to Dublin and she bought a mews at No. 11 Upper Lad Lane, just off Lower Baggot Street. Her house was always a centre for gatherings of writers and artists and her parties were famous among the literati of Dublin.

Trying to write and bring up three children at the same time was extremely time consuming for Lavin. She always wrote in longhand as she never learned to type, and she used the National Library of Ireland on Kildare Street on a regular basis. She more or less wrote wherever she could, in coffee shops such as Bewleys and in St Stephen's Green. More often than not was accompanied by her youngest daughter, the late Caroline Walsh, who would become a literary editor of the *Irish Times*. During her widowhood Lavin had a contract with the *New Yorker* magazine, which provided her with great editors and a fairly regular pay packet that was most welcome.

Lavin has been described as one of the most important writers of the twentieth century, although it was not until the 1970s that she received any significant recognition. By that time, she had been writing for about thirty years. Her short stories are all rooted in a certain time and are, in fact, social commentaries on life in Ireland during the late twentieth century. Many of her short stories appeared in the *New Yorker* magazine. Lavin received the Guggenheim Fellowships in 1959 and 1961, and in 1962 she won the Katherine Mansfield Prize. Her alma mater, University College Dublin, honoured her with an honorary doctorate in 1968, and she was awarded the Ella Lyman Cabot Award in 1972, and the Eire Society Medal and the Gregory Medal in 1975. She received the American Irish Literary Award in 1979. Her published output included nineteen books of short stories and two novels. Lavin was President of the Irish Academy of Letters (1971–1975) and she became a member of Aosdána. The latter was established in 1981 by the late Charles Haughey as an organisation of Irish-based artists, some of whom would receive a state-funded stipend. Lavin was elected as Saoi, the highest honour that Aosdána can bestow.

Eventually Lavin's social and financial life improved and she was contacted by one of her former university friends, Michael McDonald Scott, who had become a Jesuit but was laicised in 1968. The following year they were married in Bruges. They eventually sold the Mews in Lad Lane and moved to an apartment at No. 5 Guilford Place in Sandymount. Scott died in 1990 and Lavin died in a Dublin nursing home on 25 March 1996 aged 83. She is buried in St Mary's Cemetery, Navan, Co. Meath.

Further Reading

D'hoker, E., *Mary Lavin*, Irish Academic Press, Dublin, 2013.

McCormack, W.J., 'Obituary for Mary Lavin,' *The Independent*, 26 March 1996.

Peterson, R.F., *Mary Lavin*, Twayne Publishers, Boston, 1978.

Walsh, C., 'Mary Lavin (1912–1996)' in *The UCD Aesthetic, celebrating 150 years of UCD writers*, ed. Anthony Roche, UCD, Dublin.

May, Frederick (Freddie) (1911–1985)
Music Composer
38 Marlborough Road, Donnybrook, Dublin 4

Frederick May was born in 1911 to Frederick William May (1884–1969) and his wife, Jeannie McDonald Merrick (1879–1960). His parents were Protestants, and he grew up in an Anglo-Irish household on Marlborough Road, Donnybrook, where he lived for most of his life. His father worked in the Guinness Brewery in Dublin. Frederick Junior began his piano lessons with Madeleine and John Larchet at the Royal Irish Academy of Music on Westland Row. His other piano teachers at the Academy were Annie Lord and Michael Esposito. He continued to study harmony with Professor John Larchet. In 1930, May had his first piece of music published by McCullough Pigott and Co. with 'Irish Love Song'. He competed at the Dublin Feis Ceoil for several years and won the Esposito Cup. He was then offered a scholarship prize worth £100 that he could spend on furthering his piano studies. He completed his preliminary examination for a BMus at Trinity College Dublin in the same year and then took off for London to pursue his studies.

May enrolled at the Royal College of Music in London and among his teachers was Ralph Vaughan Williams, who was to have a great influence on his future compositions. One of his contemporaries at the RCM was Benjamin Brittain (1913–1976). The Feis Ceoil in Dublin renewed his scholarship for a second year to enable him to continue with his studies in Dublin. He returned to Dublin the following year (1931) and took his final examination at Trinity College for his BMus, which was conferred on him on 10 December 1931. The following year, the Royal College of Music awarded him the Foli Scholarship and later that year he obtained the Octavia Travelling Scholarship. The first performance of his *Scherzo for Orchestra* was performed on 1 December 1933 at the Patron's Concert in the Royal College of Music. The following year he went to Vienna for further study that initially was to be with Alban Berg (1885–1935), an Austrian composer of the Second Viennese School. Berg died in 1935 just before May arrived in Vienna, so instead he studied with a student of Berg called Egon Wellesz (1885–1974).

The fact that May spent up to ten months studying in Vienna has led him being called 'the least insular Irish composer of his generation'. The following year (1934) his *Four Romantic Songs* received their premiere in London. During this period, May appears to have had a great interest in the music of Alban Berg, the Austrian composer, although the evidence suggests that Williams (1872–1978) had a greater influence on his work.

May's *String Quarter in C Minor* was composed in 1935, and it was at this time too that he acquired the early symptoms of otosclerosis that can cause hearing loss, dizziness, balance problems or tinnitus. It is caused by abnormal growth of bone of the middle ear and causes hearing loss. Being diagnosed with such a condition was horrendous for a composer, and it was to torment May during his entire life. However, his most prolific period appears to have been between 1936 and 1942, when he produced his *String Quartet in C Minor* (1936), the *Symphonic Ballad* (1937), *Suite of Irish Airs* (1937), *Spring Nocturne* (1938), *Songs from Prison* (1941) and *Lyric Movement for Strings* (1942). He ceased composing for a number of years except for doing arrangements and revising some of his earlier compositions.

May returned to Ireland in 1936. About this time he started to deputise for Professor John Larchet, who was Director of Music at the Abbey Theatre in Dublin. He began writing in *The Bell* magazine (1940–1954), a well-known Irish monthly magazine of literary and social comment. His articles were mostly on the role of the arts and the artist in Irish society. At the beginning of 1936 he became Director of Music at the Abbey Theatre in Dublin in succession to Professor John Larchet, who proposed him for this post that he held until 1948. His work involved leading a piano trio called The Abbey Orchestra that performed during the intervals. Evidence from the theatre archive suggests that the role of Director of Music was considered by the Board to be a minor one. Such a role gave him plenty of time for his own composing. Unfortunately, May had a nervous breakdown in 1938. The cause of this was not clear, although there is some evidence that a problem with alcohol had gone out of control.

Despite being brought up in an Anglo–Irish household, May became very supportive of Irish Republicans and he counted Brendan Behan among his friends. He seems to have remained a great Republican supporter all his life. May always claimed to have had a great interest in Irish traditional music. Aloys Fleishmann, Professor of Music at University College Cork, with the University Orchestra, premiered his *Suite of Irish Airs* in Cork in 1937. Radio Athlone also broadcast it in December the same year. His *Lyric Movement for Strings* was premiered by the Dublin String Orchestra, conducted by the late Terry O'Connor Glasgow, at the Royal Dublin Society in 1943.

It was difficult to find biographical material on May. He was involved in the foundation of the Music Association of Ireland in the 1950s. He was also writing programme notes for the RTÉ orchestras' concerts and broadcasts. During the 1950s, the BBC Symphony Orchestra performed some of May's major compositions in Britain. He was keen too to have his *String Quartet* recorded but that did not happen at this time. Some of his music was performed on the Continent, such as in Sweden, when his *Lyric Movement* (1939) was conducted by Sixten Eckerberg in the presence of the composer.

During the 1950s, May made a number of arrangements for the RTÉ Singers. In 1956 he completed his final composition, *Sunshine & Shadow*, which was premiered in January 1956. During the 1950s, May's mental and physical condition deteriorated considerably. His deafness increased, and he had a bad nervous breakdown. By the 1960s, May had behavioural problems that rendered him unpredictable. For a number of years, he managed to continue working for RTÉ and he contributed a number of articles to Irish newspapers. By the early 1960s, his mental health was cause for great concern. When his parents died, he sold the family home on Marlborough Road and he disappeared from public view for a time. He appears to have been homeless for a time and was sleeping rough at night. Garech Browne of Claddagh Records wanted to record May's quartet and he ran him to ground at Grangegorman mental hospital. Browne very kindly took May out of the hospital and tried unsuccessfully, along with other friends, to rehabilitate him.

In the early 1970s he was living on a temporary basis with the Little Sisters of the Poor in Raheny. In 1975, May was involved in a car crash and he ended up in the Orthopaedic Hospital in Clontarf, where he spent the remaining years of his life. Financially he was not well off – he received a nominal pension from the Arts Council and had become a member of Aosdána, the Irish Association of Artists, in 1981 and that provided him with an annuity. He continued to live in the Orthopaedic Hospital until his death on 8 September 1985. He is buried in Mount Jerome Cemetery in Dublin. In 2011, at the time of May's centenary, five CDs of his orchestral work were released by RTÉ.

Further Reading

Deale, Edgar M. ed., *A Catalogue of Contemporary Irish Composers*, 2nd ed., Music Association of Ireland, Dublin, 1973.

Fitzgerald, M., 'Retrieving the Real Frederick May', *Journal of the Society for Musicology in Ireland*, 14, 2019, pp.31–73.

Ryan, Joseph J., 'May, Frederick (Freddie)', in *Dictionary of Irish Biography*, edited by James McGuire and James Quinn, Cambridge University Press, Cambridge.

McBride, Maud Gonne (1866–1953)
Irish Revolutionary
Floraville, Eglinton Road, Donnybrook, Dublin 4

Maud Gonne was born near Farnham in Surrey, England, the eldest daughter of Captain Thomas Gonne (1835–1886) and his wife, Edith Firth Gonne (*née* Cooke) (1844–1871). Her father's family were wealthy and they were importers of Portuguese wines. Both families had considerable social standing. Maud claimed the Gonnes were originally from Co. Mayo. In 1868, Thomas was appointed brigadier major at the Curragh Camp in Co. Kildare and they lived at Athgarvan House, the Curragh. While living in Ireland, the family resided at a number of different houses, including one in Howth, and in Floraville, Eglinton Road, Donnybrook. Edith suffered from tuberculosis and died in June 1871.

After Maud's mother's death she and her sister, Kathleen, were sent to live with her mother's aunt in London, and then on to a grand-uncle in Richmond Park. On her father's appointment as Military Attaché to the Austrian Court, the family moved to the south of France, where Maud acquired her love for that country and its language. In Provence, Gonne was educated by a governess. Her father was appointed as Assistant Adjutant General at Dublin Castle in 1882. Maud acted as a hostess for her father in Dublin from 1882 until his untimely death in 1885 from typhoid fever.

Before he died, Thomas had agreed to support her in her struggle for Home Rule as a result of her involvement in the Land League movement, when she had witnessed a number of horrific evictions in Donegal. Maude and Kathleen were the beneficiaries of a legacy of £80,000 from her mother's estate. Maud thus became a wealthy woman with the freedom to live as she wished. For many years she divided her time between France and Ireland. Contemporary descriptions of Maud describe her as almost 6 ft tall with beautiful auburn hair and fiery golden eyes. Sarah Purser painted her portrait in Dublin. W.B. Yeats fell madly in love with her at first sight in 1889, and thus began a mutually obsessive relationship, which would last almost half a century. She inspired Yeats to write some of the most beautiful poetry in the English language. Despite Yeats asking her several times to marry him, she refused.

Like her mother, Gonne suffered from tuberculosis (TB) throughout her life, and while recovering from a bout of illness in the Auvergne in France in 1887 she met and fell in love with Lucien Millevoye, a married journalist and anti-Semitic politician. It was Millevoye that inspired Gonne to become active in revolutionary politics and he was the father of her son, Georges. She was devastated when two and a half years later Georges died, possibly from meningitis, on 31 August 1891. He was buried at Samois-sur-Seine, south-east of Paris, where Gonne built a cemetery chapel with Georges buried in the crypt. She always pretended in Ireland that Georges was a child she had adopted. She was encouraged by George Russell (AE) to believe that an infant soul can be reincarnated within a family. She therefore contacted Millevoye again, and conceived a second child with him, a girl, reputedly in the crypt where her son was laid to rest. She brought her daughter, Iseult, up in France but did not acknowledge her publically as her child. When she was 23 years old, Yeats proposed to Iseult but was refused. Later, Iseult married Francis Stuart (1902–2000), the Irish Australian novelist.

Gonne continued to be active in various political areas. She travelled in the late nineteenth century throughout England, Wales, Scotland and the USA campaigning for the Irish nationalist cause. In 1897, together with Yeats and Arthur Griffith, she organised protests against Queen Victoria's Diamond Jubilee celebrations. Through Yeats's influence and the Gaelic revival, Gonne played the lead in his play *Cathleen Ní Houlihan* in 1902, to great acclaim. That year also saw Gonne convert to Catholicism and yet again she refused to marry Yeats. In 1903, however, she did marry Major John McBride, who had led the Irish Transvaal Brigade against the British during the Second Boer War. The following year she gave birth to a son, Seán McBride (1904–1988). The marriage was not a success and her attempt at a divorce in a Paris court was unsuccessful. What was finally granted to her in 1906 was a legal separation. Major McBride returned to Ireland and never saw his son again. Seán was raised in Paris by his mother and his father took part in the 1916 Rising in Dublin, where he was executed along with the leaders. It is interesting to note that Gonne spent more and more time in Paris after the separation. It had damaged her position in nationalist circles in Ireland.

Due to the fact that women were excluded from nationalist organisations in Ireland in 1900, Gonne founded Inghinidhe na hÉireann (Daughters of Erin), whose aims included complete independence from Britain, the popularisation of goods of Irish manufacture and the revival of the Irish language and culture. In 1914, this organisation merged into the newly formed Cumann na mBan, which was the female wing of the Irish Volunteers. Gonne added her late husband's name to her own after his death and became known as Maud Gonne McBride. While still living abroad in December 1917 Gonne McBride returned secretly to Dublin and was arrested for her alleged involvement in a pro-German conspiracy, the following year. She spent six months in Holloway prison with Kathleen Clarke (wife of Thomas Clarke), Constance Markievicz and other Irish revolutionaries. She was released on the grounds of ill health – she had a relapse of her TB.

Gonne McBride continued to be active politically during the Irish War of Independence (1919–1921). She originally accepted the 1921 Treaty, between Ireland and Britain, but when her friend Arthur Griffith died, she attacked the Free State Government and for this she was imprisoned in 1923 in Kilmainham Gaol, where she went on hunger strike. She had a relapse of her TB and this secured her release in twenty days. In 1922, together with Hanna Sheehy Skeffington and Charlotte Despard, Gonne McBride founded the Women's Prisoners Defence League for the 'help, comfort and release of Republican prisoners'. The organisation carried out good work but was banned a year later by the Irish Government.

In 1923, Gonne McBride was arrested again for parading peacefully carrying anti-Free State banners. Once again she was sent to Kilmainham Gaol, and together with ninety other prisoners she began a hunger strike that lasted twenty days until she was released due to ill health. Her great friend, Charlotte Despard, staged a lonely protest night and day outside the prison until Gonne McBride was released. In her later years, Gonne McBride was pro-fascism and communism, and by the outbreak of the Second World War she was very pro-German. In Dublin, she was close to Dr Eduard Hempel, the German Minister stationed in Dublin, and his wife, Evelyn. Irish military intelligence had her under surveillance and suspected her of being involved in the Herman Goertz affair that implicated not only Gonne McBride, but also her daughter, Iseult, and her husband, Francis Stuart.

Together with Charlotte Despard, who was a sister of Lord French, the Lord Lieutenant, Gonne McBride bought Roebuck House, where she ended her days together with her son, daughter-in-law Catalina Bulfin (1901–1976) and her grandchildren, Anna and Tiernan. Gonne McBride published her autobiography, *A Servant of the Queen*, in 1938. This only covers the period of her life up to her marriage to Major John McBride. She had plans to publish a second volume but this was never achieved. Gonne McBride was proud of her children, Seán and Iseult. She was close to Iseult, although she never acknowledged her as her daughter. She died in Dublin on 27 April 1953 at the age of 86. A pair of her son George's bootees were placed in her coffin at her request. She is buried in Glasnevin Cemetery in the Republican plot.

Further Reading

Cardozo, Nancy, *Maud Gonne*, Gollanz, London, 1979.

McBride, Maud Gonne, *A Servant of the Queen*, new edition, Smyth, London, 1994.

O'Callaghan, M., Dhaibheid, Nic, 'C. McBride, (Edith) Maud Gonne', in *Dictionary of Irish Biography*, edited by James McGuire and James Quinn, Cambridge University Press, Cambridge.

McCourt, Kevin (1915–2000)
Businessman and Director General of RTÉ

Harmony Cottage, Eglinton Road,
Donnybrook, Dublin 4

Kevin McCourt was born in Tralee on 14 April 1915 to Seán McCourt and his wife, Mary (*née* Small). When Kevin was 9 years old, the family moved to Dublin and it was there where he spent the rest of his life. His father was a keen Irish language enthusiast and that was the language spoken in the family home. His early schooling was with the Christian Brothers in Tralee and he attended their school in Dun Laoghaire when the family moved to Dublin. In 1930, he became a boarder at Blackrock College. Among his teachers at that time was Fr John Charles McQuaid, who later became Archbishop of Dublin. Unfortunately, due to his family's poor financial circumstances he had to leave Blackrock in less than one year to help his father with running the Post Office in Sandymount, together with a lending library, the Argosy Library.

In 1933, McCourt took a post as a junior wages clerk with Dublin United Tramways. While working there he enrolled in a part-time course in Accountancy at the College of Commerce in Rathmines. Studying for the accountancy examinations took up all McCourt's spare time but it led to a qualification as a certified accountant and that of Chartered Secretary. He worked with Kennedy Crowley, the well-known chartered accountants in Dublin, as Client Company Secretary (1937–1940) and later moved to C.E. Macaulay's, a wool merchant, as accountant and Company Secretary (1940–1944).

In 1941, McCourt married Margaret (Peggy) McMahon from Pembroke Road in Dublin. She was the daughter of a barrister, John McMahon. They had met a few years earlier at Anglesea Lawn Tennis Club in Donnybrook. They began their married life in a flat on Merrion Square, later moving to Shankhill, and later still to Harmony Cottage on Eglinton Road, Donnybrook. They had one son and three daughters.

In 1944, McCourt applied for and was successful in obtaining the post of Secretary of the Federation of Irish Manufacturers (FIM), which subsequently became the Federation of Irish Industry and then the Confederation of Irish Industry. As Secretary, he was required to make many public speeches promoting the Federation's view of economic life. Throughout his professional life he was always known as an effective and accomplished speaker.

Due to his work with the Federation/Confederation, McCourt came into close contact with the then Minister of Industry and Commerce, Séan Lemass, who later became Taoiseach. In 1949, McCourt was appointed a Director (1949–1951) and founder member of the Industrial Development Authority. In 1951, he took up a post with the tobacco manufacturer P.J. Carroll as Executive Director. The company was based in Dundalk, where there was a tradition of second, third and fourth generations of families working in Carroll's. The company was well known for its Sweet Afton brand of cigarettes as well as its tipped Carroll's No. 1. Dating back to 1824, the company had been founded by a Patrick James Carroll, who was the son of a prosperous farmer. The company became publicly quoted in the mid-1930s. For many years it remained a traditional family concern. During his time with P.J. Carroll & Co., McCourt became very aware of the problems of production and he helped modernise their rather antiquated manufacturing processes. He was very well aware of the importance of brand but had great difficulty in persuading the Carroll family to spend more money on advertising. Over the next few years, McCourt became a leading advocate of the importance of branding and marketing in general. He believed that the export market would be critical to the success of companies such as P.J. Carroll, which had a small competitive home market.

As a result of his espousal of the importance of exports, in 1955 the Irish Government appointed McCourt to the Board of Córas Tráchtála, the state export body. The following year he was a Government appointee to the Capital Investment Advisory Committee, which was an advisory body to the Government on the needs of the national economy. At the same time, McCourt was travelling the world on behalf of P.J. Carroll & Co., visiting export markets in countries such as India, Hong Kong, Singapore, Malaya, Thailand, China and Iraq.

Despite his success at P.J. Carroll's, by 1959 McCourt realised it was time for a change. He became Co-Managing Director of Hunter Douglas, Holland, a European affiliate of a major United States aluminium and plastics company. He spent three and a half years with this company in Rotterdam, although he and his family were based in The Hague. In 1962, the Taoiseach, Séan Lemass invited McCourt to become the second Director General of RTÉ, and he took up the post on 1 January 1963.

During his tenure as Director General, McCourt had to deal with Archbishop John Charles McQuaid, who was trying to interfere with various aspects of Irish television, as well as Lemass, who was of the belief that it should be an instrument of Government policy. McCourt, on the other hand, firmly believed that RTÉ should remain independent of both church and state. He remained as Director General of RTÉ for five years, during which time there was industrial unrest at the station. However, he oversaw great change within the organisation and brought it a sense of professionalism and order. He was succeeded by Tom Hardiman, who said that McCourt 'gave RTÉ a character, style and presence which would not have been created without him'.

On his retirement from RTÉ, McCourt became Group Managing Director of United Distillers of Ireland Ltd (later Irish Distillers) in 1968. This company was less than two years old, and was formed as a result of a merger between Cork Distilleries Co. Ltd, John Jameson & Son Ltd and John Power & Son Ltd. McCourt spent ten years with Irish Distillers and was responsible for the integration of the company from the amalgamation of the three distilleries. He rationalised it by moving all whiskey production to Midleton, Co. Cork. He purchased Bushmills Distillery in Northern Ireland too, and created a partnership with the Canadian firm Seagrams, which purchased 20 per cent of Irish Distillers. He was an outstanding Managing Director and when he retired the profits of the company had risen from £500,000 p.a. to £3.5 million. He remained a board member until 1983.

McCourt's career spanned more than forty years and he managed a number of large enterprises that encompassed tobacco, broadcasting, distilling and steel. He was a remarkable businessman who had a huge influence on Irish business. In retirement he became a non-executive Chairman of Irish Steel (1974–1986), Chairman of the Irish Agricultural Machinery and Hibernian Life Assurance, and he held directorships on the board of Jefferson Smurfit, Peterson Tenant Group, Baltimore Technologies and Bula Resources. He also became a Director and then Chairman of Gorta, the famine relief agency.

Throughout his long career, McCourt was constantly in demand as a non-executive director. He served on some eighteen different boards during his lifetime and brought his great business experience to bear to the many different company boards on which he served. His biographer, Eugene McCague, states that he was 'an extremely cultured man, a voracious reader and a lover of theatre, classical music and opera'. In April 2000, in his 85th year, McCourt suffered a stroke from which he did not recover. He died on 13 May 2000 and is buried in Shanganagh Cemetery, Shankhill, Co. Dublin.

Further Reading

Boylan, S., 'McCourt, Kevin', in *Dictionary of Irish Biography*, edited by James McGuire and James Quinn, Cambridge University Press, Cambridge.

Business & Finance, 30 March 1978, pp.6–7.

McCague, E., *My Dear Mr McCourt*, Gill, Dublin, 2009.

MacNeill, Eoin (1867–1945)
Nationalist and Politician
63 Upper Leeson Street, Donnybrook, Dublin 4

Eoin MacNeill was born in Glenarm, Co. Antrim, in 1867 to Archibald MacNeill, a businessman, and his wife, Rosetta (*née* Macauley). He was their fourth son and they had nine children. The MacNeills were a Catholic family and they lived in an area in the Glens of Antrim that was a Catholic enclave. Eóin's parents were keen that their children should be well educated. They attended the local national school and for his secondary education Eoin attended St Malachy's, a well-known Belfast Catholic secondary school and the oldest Catholic diocesan college on the island of Ireland. He obtained first place in all of Ireland in the intermediate examination. The school also had a collegiate division and in 1885 Eoin studied for the examination of the Royal University, which was an examining and degree awarding university similar to that of the University of London.

MacNeill received a Modern Languages scholarship to enrol at the Royal University and he obtained a degree in Constitutional History, Jurisprudence and Political Economy in 1888.

The previous year he obtained a post as a junior clerk in the accountant general's office in Dublin's law courts. He obtained this post by competitive examination rather than by patronage. About this time, he began to learn Irish and in 1890 he started to study Old and Middle Irish in his spare time. He became a student of Edmund Hogan S.J., who lectured on the Irish Language and History at University College Dublin, and he introduced him to Celtic scholarship. Between 1891 and 1908, he made annual visits to the Aran Islands to perfect his knowledge of the spoken language. He contributed a number of articles on the Irish language to the well-known Irish periodical the *Irish Ecclesiastical Record*, a monthly journal founded in 1864 by Paul, Cardinal Cullen (1803–1878). He also published in the *Gaelic Journal*, one of the first important bilingual Irish journals published in this country. MacNeill became its editor from 1894 until 1899. His other editorial activities included being co-editor of *Fainne an Lae* from 1898 to 1899, and he became the first editor of *An Claidheamh Soluis* from 1899 to 1901. The latter was an Irish nationalist newspaper published by Conradh na Gaeilge. MacNeill had taken a leading role in the formation of the Gaelic League and between 1893 and 1897 he became its unofficial and unpaid secretary. It was during this time that he became a friend of Padraig Pearse, whom he recruited to the Gaelic League executive. He and Pearse were very close friends and each one of them influenced the other.

One of the articles in *An Claidheamh Soluis* called for the formation of an Irish Volunteer force similar to the Ulster Volunteer Force that was founded in 1913. MacNeill was very involved in the setting up of this organisation and almost immediately became its leader. This was unusual as he was not a military figure. Whether he was made leader by the Irish Republican Brotherhood (IRB), and in particular by Tom Clarke and Padraig Pearse, as a respectable front while they prepared in secret for the Rising of 1916 is still a debatable question. It is interesting to note that members of the IRB held most leadership posts within the Irish Volunteers. This was a secret oath-bound organisation dedicated to the establishment of an 'independent democratic republic'. It was they who were responsible for organising the Easter Rising of 1916. The Irish Volunteers' stated purpose was not to establish a republic but the IRB's aim was to do so. Joseph Plunkett, Thomas MacDonagh and Padraig Pearse were co-opted on to the Supreme Council of the Irish Volunteers in 1915 and they were also members of the Military Committee who planned the 1916 Rising. Though not a member of the IRB, it appears MacNeill had separatist sympathies.

Within the Irish Volunteers there were two parties. MacNeill belonged to the group that advocated a defensive strategy aimed at resisting any effort to impose conscription or abandon the fight for Home Rule. The other group, essentially members of the IRB, secretly prepared for a Rising. It was directed by the IRB Committee led by Thomas Clarke and Seán Mac Diarmada, with Pearse as the figurehead. April 1916 saw the emergence of an alleged official document from Dublin Castle that showed a Government crackdown on the Irish Volunteers was imminent. Historians to this day differ on whether this was or was not a genuine document. It suggested military raids were planned, at an imminent unknown date, in which arrests would be made of the officers of the Irish Volunteers, National Volunteers and Gaelic League. As head of the Irish Volunteers, MacNeill ordered defensive manoeuvres but he was unaware that these were a cover for the landing of arms and an insurrection to begin on Easter Sunday. Preparations had gone too far for the Rising, so MacNeill was unable to cancel the manoeuvres as so many other activities were in place. News reached MacNeill that the German ship carrying arms for the Rising had been sunk by the British, and he then published an order in the daily papers cancelling the manoeuvres. The IRB group headed by Pearse ostensibly accepted this cancellation, but instead he brought out the Dublin units of the Volunteers on Easter Monday. MacNeill's role in the planning of the 1916 Rising is still controversial. On the one hand it is said that he prevented its success, but on the other hand he averted great slaughter.

MacNeill did not take part in the Rising but despite this he was arrested and tried by court martial and sentenced to penal servitude for life. He remained in gaol until there was an amnesty in 1917. On his release he joined the reconstituted Sinn Fein party and became a member of its executive. He was elected to the First Dail and was the agreed nationalist candidate for Derry City. He also stood as a representative of the National University of Ireland. In May 1921, he was re-elected to both of these posts. He became Minister for Finance in the first Dail, but when Michael Collins assumed control of finances he was demoted to the Ministry of Industry and Commerce. With a post-Bloody Sunday crackdown, MacNeill was arrested in November 1920 and was held in Mountjoy Prison until June 1921.

MacNeill supported the Anglo–Irish Treaty and was the Chair of the Dail debates that led to its ratification. He had been elected Speaker in August 1921. In 1922, he became TD for Co. Clare as a pro-Treaty candidate. During the Civil War that followed, MacNeill was a strong supporter of the Government's reprisal policy. He suffered a great personal loss when his second son Brian, who had joined the anti-Treaty forces, was killed during fighting in Sligo.

MacNeill became the first Minister for Education in the Free State. He was responsible for imposing Irish as a compulsory school subject, despite protests from Protestants, parents and teachers. In 1924, he was appointed to the Boundary Commission that was to determine the division of the Irish Free State and Northern Ireland. He was a defender of the Free State's claim to the nationalist majority areas but had eventually to acquiesce to the decision that only small areas should be transferred. As a member of this Commission, MacNeill failed to inform his colleagues of the trend of the discussions and likely outcome of its work. He saw the Commission's proceedings as being quasi-judicial and therefore confidential. Unfortunately, he was seen as the principal scapegoat in this respect. His political career ended in 1927 when he was unsuccessful in contesting a seat in the National University of Ireland constituency in the general election of that year. He then returned to the academic life.

As an academic and Professor of Early and Medieval Irish History at University College Dublin from 1909 until his retirement in 1945, MacNeill revolutionised Celtic scholarship. His book *Celtic Ireland* (1921) revised the framework of early Irish history. He was among the first to study early Irish laws, and he uncovered the nature of succession in Irish kingship. While holding the Chair in UCD, MacNeill was elected to the first Senate of the new National University of Ireland, where, together with Douglas Hyde, he campaigned to make Irish a compulsory subject for entry to the university despite opposition from most Catholic bishops. His publication *Irish in the National University* appeared in 1909.

On his return to academic life, MacNeill continued to work on place names, early Irish law and patrician studies. His work on early Irish laws appeared in 1932 under the title *Early Irish Laws and Institutions*. Some of his writings on St Patrick were collected posthumously and published as St *Patrick* (1964). MacNeill continued to be active in other professional organisations during his academic career. For example, he chaired the Irish Manuscripts Commission, he was President of the Irish Historical Society from 1937 and he became President of the Royal Society of Antiquaries in Ireland in 1937, a post he held until 1939. Between 1940 and 1943, MacNeill was President of the Royal Irish Academy.

MacNeill was married to Agnes Moore (1872–1953), a daughter of James Moore, who was a solicitor from Ballymena. They had four sons and four daughters. In the early years of his marriage, MacNeill suffered a nervous breakdown that may have contributed to his lack of energy later in life and his being passive in relation to later political crises. MacNeill died from cancer at his home, No. 63 Upper Leeson Street, on 15 October 1945. He is buried in Kilbarrack Cemetery, Sutton, Co. Dublin. According to the 1911, Irish Census he also lived at No. 19 Herbert Park, Donnybrook.

Further Reading

Hughes, Brian, *Eoin MacNeill: Memoir of a Revolutionary Scholar*, Irish Manuscripts Commission, Dublin, 2016,

Martin, F.X. and Byrne, F.J., *The Scholar Revolutionary: Eoin MacNeill 1867–1945*, Irish University Press, Shannon, 1973.

Maume, Patrick and Charles-Edwards, Thomas, 'MacNeill, Eoin (John)', in *Dictionary of Irish Biography*, edited by James McGuire and James Quinn, Cambridge University Press, Cambridge.

Mitchell, Susan Langstaff (1866–1926)
Writer and Poet
21 Wellington Road, Ballsbridge, Dublin 4

Susan Langstaff Mitchell was born in Carrick-on-Shannon on 5 December 1866 to Michael Thomas Mitchell and his wife, Kate (*née* Cullen). She was the fifth of seven children. Her father was the bank manager for the Provincial Bank of Ireland in Carrick-on-Shannon. Unfortunately, he died when Susan was 6 years old, and she was sent to live with her aunts in Dublin, while her mother and brothers moved to Sligo in order to have the boys educated there. Her aunts were strong Unionists. Nearby neighbours of her aunts on Wellington Road were the family of Sarah Purser, the well-known artist. Susan was educated at Ms Harriet Abbott's school at No. 78 Morehampton Road, which had been founded in 1875 by Ms Abbott and was a select boarding school for the daughters of gentlemen. It survived as a school until 1923. Later, she attended Trinity College Dublin, where she took the Trinity College Dublin's women's examination and obtained Honours.

While living in Wellington Road, Mitchell met the artist John Butler Years and she became close friends with him as well as with his daughter, Lily. A portrait of Mitchell by Yeats hangs in the National Gallery of Ireland. In 1884, she moved to Birr to live with her aunts. As a Protestant, she soon rebelled against their Unionist views and she became a Home Rule supporter despite her Protestant background. She spent some time with the Yeats family as Lily's companion at their home in Bedford Park, London. Mitchell suffered from tuberculosis for most of her life and she was quite ill with it during her stay in London. She later underwent several operations to treat it. While in London, she met many distinguished figures associated with the Irish literary renaissance such as Lady Gregory, Constance Markievicz, Katharine Tynan and Edward Martyn. Mitchell remained in London for eighteen months and returned to Ireland in 1899.

When she returned home she based herself in Dublin. In 1901, she became a sub-editor for the *Irish Homestead,* the organ of the Irish Agricultural Society (IAOS). The editor was George Russell (AE) and his influence can be seen in her mystic verse. They became lifelong friends and she contributed many essays, reviews, drama notes and poems, many of which were published under a pseudonym. Her poems were first published in the *Irish Homestead,* as well as in *New Songs (1904)* edited by Russell, which also contained pieces by Padraic Colum and Alice Milligan. Encouraged by AE, she published some of her poems in an anthology called *A Celtic Christmas* in 1902.

In 1905, Mitchell wrote a poem dealing with a controversy involving Hugh Lane, the art collector. It was called 'The Ballad of Shawe-Taylor' and was described as a comic ballad, which she herself performed at many a social evening in Dublin. Her social circle included such distinguished writers as William Butler Yeats, Padraic Colum, George Moore and others. Between 1909 and her death in 1926, she contributed a number of verses for cards produced by the Cuala Press. Some of these are still available at the National Library of Ireland.

Mitchell published two books, *A Celtic Christmas* and in 1908 two more works *The Living Chalice*, a collection of spiritual poetry, and her very popular *Aids to the Immortality of Certain Persons in Ireland Charitably Administered,* which demonstrated her great wit. In 1908, she wrote a poem called 'The Anti-Recruiting Song'. She published another volume of her verse, *Frankincense and Myrrh*, in 1912. In 1916, she wrote a critical biography of the writer, George Moore (1852–1933), with whom she was friendly.

Throughout her life, Mitchell held strong views on the role of women in Irish society. In 1910 she composed a song called *To the Daughters of Erin* to honour the members of the United Irishwomen (later the Irish Countrywomen's Association), of which she was a founding member. Mitchell was a pacifist, but her sympathies were with the condemned leaders of the 1916 Rising.

Mitchell continued to write ballads and she also became a literary critic. She also spoke at a meeting of the National Literary Society in December 1919 on John Butler Yeats. She continued to review regularly for *The Freeman's Journal* and contributed to *The Irish Statesman,* a weekly journal that merged with the *Irish Homestead* under the editorship of George Russell (AE). In 1921, Russell appointed Mitchell as assistant editor of the *Irish Statesman,* to which she contributed articles, book and theatre reviews.

In 1919, Mitchell moved with her sister, Jinny, and her mother to No. 77 Rathmines Road, where she lived for the rest of her life. Her mother dictated her memoirs to Mitchell and theses were later published. Ill health plagued her, and at times she was confined to bed for several weeks. She also became profoundly deaf but continued to publish her opinions on the current situation in Ireland during the 1920s. However, she still managed to maintain an active social life attending the select evenings hosted by the Yeats sisters. Gatherings of like-minded people called 'at homes' were popular during the Irish Literary Revival and Mitchell hosted her own on Saturday evenings between 8 p.m. and midnight. Attendees included members of the Irish Literary Revival such as James Stephens, Padraic Colum and AE. Tea, coffee and sandwiches were provided, but no alcohol. The entertainment consisted of conversations with the participants, singing ballads or playing charades. Mitchell was also a regular attender at opening nights in the Abbey Theatre.

In 1923, Mitchell composed a poem called 'The Wail of a Pseudo Gael', a satire that mocked the dreams of a cultural Ireland that she thought was never to be. In January 1926 she had an operation from which she never really recovered, and she died of cancer aged 60 in a Dublin nursing home on 4 March 1926. Among the attendants at her funeral in Mount Jerome Cemetery were members of the Yeats family, the Purser family, George Russell (AE) and Douglas Hyde, later President of Ireland from 1938–1945. Mitchell never married. In 2016, to mark the 150th anniversary of her birth and the ninetieth anniversary of her death, a monument was erected to her memory in Carrick-on-Shannon, her birthplace.

Further Reading

Geoghegan, Patrick M., 'Mitchell, Susan Langstaff', in *Dictionary of Irish Biography*, edited by James McGuire and James Quinn, Cambridge University Press, Cambridge, in progress.

Kain, R.M., *Susan L. Mitchell*, Bucknell University Press, Lewisburg, 1972.

Pyle, Hilary, *Red Headed Rebel: Poet and Mystic of the Irish Cultural Renaissance*, Woodfield Press, Dublin, 1998.

Nangle, Edward (1800–1883)
Church of Ireland Clergyman
23 Morehampton Road, Donnybrook, Dublin 4

Rev. Edward Nangle was a Church of Ireland Evangelical Protestant Minister know for the famous Achill Mission of the early nineteenth century. Born in Dublin in 1800 to Walter Nangle, a Catholic, and his second wife, Catherine Anne Sall, a Protestant (with whom he had eight children), Edward was brought up a Protestant. His father was descended from the powerful Nangle family, who had held the title of Barons of Navan for more than 600 years, and he was a commissioned officer in the British Army. When his mother died in 1808, he was sent to Cavan Royal School, a boarding school

Nangle attended Trinity College Dublin, graduating with a BA in 1823 and MA in 1862. He was mindful of becoming a doctor but was persuaded by friends to enter the Church of Ireland instead. Nangle became a deacon in 1824 and was ordained shortly afterwards. His first curacy was in Athboy, where he was for a short time, and he spent an even briefer time as a curate in Monkstown, Co. Dublin. At the age of 24, he moved to Arva in the Diocese of Kilmore as a curate. However, ill health forced him to resign after only two years. While convalescing from what may have been a nervous breakdown, he is said to have read Christopher Anderson's *Historical Sketches of the Native Irish,* which influenced him profoundly. Anderson. a Scottish clergyman had begun to convert people through their native language, and this inspired Nangle. It was during this period (1828) that he married Elizabeth Warner, from Marvelstown House, Co. Meath. They had eight children between 1835 and 1847, of whom five died in infancy.

Nangle became part of an extreme evangelisation movement in nineteenth-century Ireland. This developed in the 1820s to convert Catholics to Protestantism. It was known as the Second Reformation; an evangelical campaign organised by theological conservatives in both the Church of Ireland and in the Church of England. One of the main proponents of the evangelisation of the west of Ireland was the Protestant Archbishop of Tuam, the Rev. Power le Poer Trench.

With the failure of the potato crop in 1831, Nangle and his wife Eliza decided to travel to Achill on a steamer, the *Nottingham*, which was bringing provisions to the starving people in the west of Ireland and which came ashore in Westport. There he met the Rector of Newport, Rev. William Baker Stoney, who persuaded him to visit Achill Island to see for himself the poverty and the starving people. He then became resolved to begin his mission on Achill. He began by leasing 100 acres of land from the local landlord, Sir Richard O'Donnell of Newport, and many years later the mission bought out the estate. In Dublin, the Rt Rev. Robert Daly, later Bishop of Cashel, set up a committee to oversee the Achill mission's foundation. The Rev. Power Le Poer Trench also supported the proposed mission in Achill. Three years later, in 1834, Nangle, wife Eliza and their family moved permanently to Achill. His missionary aim was twofold: to lift the people out of poverty and to bring the Bible to the local inhabitants by speaking to them in their native language. He also wanted to convert them from Catholicism to Protestantism.

From the very beginning of his mission on Achill, Nangle was anti-Catholic despite his family background. During the 1830s and '40s, Nangle's settlement saw donations to his mission pay for two-storey houses, schools, an orphanage, a hospital, a post office, a dispensary and a corn mill, together with farm buildings and fields reclaimed from the mountains. The mission settlement on Achill was the centre for a bitter religious conflict between Nangle and Catholic Archbishop McHale of Tuam for almost twenty years. McHale made a number of highly charged visits to Achill and insisted on setting up Catholic schools adjacent to those of Nangle's mission. He also appointed a number of hostile parish priests to Achill in the hope of counteracting Nangle's activities. On Achill, converts to Protestantism were frequently ostracised, and indeed threatened with physical violence. In contrast, charges of 'souperism' were made against Nangle's mission, particularly in the years of the Great Famine when many Achill Catholics became Protestants in return for food and education for their children.

Throughout his time on Achill, Nangle appears to have had a deep compassion for its people. He travelled extensively to England to raise funds for his project. In spite of the Catholic opposition to his mission, Nangle's work continued to flourish. In 1835, the foundation stone was laid for a new church – the first ever Protestant church on Achill. In the same year he acquired a printing press funded by his supporters in London and York. This led to the publication of *The Achill Missionary Herald and Western* and at one stage its circulation reached 3,000. The press produced many volumes on Protestant doctrine and even an Irish language dictionary. Visitors to Achill during the nineteenth century such as Mr and Mrs Samuel Hall praised the promotion of the native tongue in their 1840s book *Ireland, its Scenery and Character*, though they were also critical of what they saw as 'souperism' – where 'starving children were fed during the Great Famine on the condition of receiving religious instruction in the Protestant faith'. However, it seems reasonable to suggest that without Nangle and his mission, thousands of the natives of Achill would probably have died of starvation during the Famine.

At its height the Achill mission consisted of five churches, schools, a hospital, an orphanage, a dispensary, a post office, an hotel and a mission press. The islanders benefited in particular from the presence of Nangle's friend and fellow missionary Dr Neason Adams, who resigned his medical practice in Dublin to come and look after the sick and the poor. It was mainly due to Nangle, too, that the economy of the island benefited from the presence of the mission. In 1847, Nangle reported that the mission was giving employment to more than 2,000 labourers and feeding 600 children every day in its schools. Visits by a number of nineteenth-century travellers such as the Halls and debates about the mission in the British press and in Parliament drew tourists to the island. This led to infrastructures being built, agricultural reform and the development of tourism.

It is interesting to recall that, although Nangle settled on Achill in 1834, he actually only served as rector for less than two years. It suited Nangle to work as a missionary rather than being the administrator of a parish. Finally, in 1852 he resigned and moved to Sligo, where he was appointed rector of Skreen. However, he continued to retain his interest in Achill and returned there for three months every year. Unfortunately, he did not retain good relations with the mission committee and trustees. In the early 1860s, there was a long, drawn-out legal battle with Joseph Napier, one of the trustees of the Achill mission committee. This became a major court case that lasted for years, thus draining the resources of the Achill estate. Nangle eventually won the case but it broke the mission.

Nangle continued as rector of Skreen for twenty-one years until he retired at the age of 74 in 1873, when he also resigned as a trustee of the Achill mission. He returned to live in Achill briefly in 1879. However, by the 1880s the mission was dead in all but name. The remains of the colony in the form of the mission buildings and church stand today as a legacy to the work of Nangle. The question remains was Nangle's aim to save the lives of the starving people of Achill or was his aim and ambition solely focused on converting them to Protestantism?

Nangle retired to Dublin with his second wife, Sarah, whom he had married shortly after arriving in Skreen. He had a large family with Sarah, with one son and three daughters surviving into adulthood. He died at his home, No. 23 Morehampton Road, Donnybrook, on 9 September 1883 at the age of 84 and is buried in Dean's Grange Cemetery. His first wife, Eliza, and a number of their children, are buried in the graveyard on the slopes of Slievemore mountain on Achill Island.

Further Reading

Byrne, Patricia, *The Preacher and the Prelate*, Merrion Press, Dublin, 2018.

Kelly, Tom and Lunney, Linda, 'Nangle, Edward Walter', in *Dictionary of Irish Biography*, edited by James McGuire and James Quinn, Cambridge University Press, Cambridge.

Seddall, Henry, *Edward Nangle, the Apostle of Achill*, Hodges Figgis, Dublin, 1884.

O'Connor, Batt (1870–1935)
Builder and Politician
1 Brendan Road, Donnybrook, Dublin 4

Born in Brosna, Co. Kerry, on 4 July 1870 to Daniel O'Connor and his wife Ellen O'Connor (*née* Curtain), Bartholomew O'Connor (known as Batt), grew up in Kerry. He attended the local national school and then trained as a stonemason with his father and elder brother. He left Kerry at the age of 17 and moved to New Hampshire, USA, where he worked as a builder for three years from 1893. He described participating in a St Patrick's Day parade on Rhode Island as a time when he became politically aware and he says he 'awoke to full consciousness of my love for my country'. When he returned to Ireland in 1898, he worked for a short time as a bricklayer in Cobh, Co. Cork. From there he moved to Dublin, and at the age of 28, established himself as a speculative builder. He built houses on Anglesea Road in Ballsbridge, Kilmainham, and Eglinton Road in Donnybrook. He was responsible for the development of Brendan Road. Some of the houses in Brendan Road have interconnecting doors so that the men on the run could escape easily if the house they were staying in was raided. O'Connor built twelve houses in Brendan Road and he retained possession of them, renting them to tenants.

O'Connor joined the Gaelic League in 1900 and there he met many of the future leaders of the Irish political movement, including Tom Clarke and Seán Mac Diarmada. In 1909, he became a member of the Irish Republican Brotherhood and was sworn in as a member. This organisation was a secret oath-bound fraternal organisation dedicated to the establishment of an independent democratic republic. In this organisation, Batt became friendly with a number of the revolutionary leaders. He also joined the Irish Volunteers in 1913 but was not actively involved in the 1916 Rising because he was in Kerry for the first week of it awaiting instructions about the Rising planned for his county. When he heard of the arrest of Sir Roger Casement and the loss of the arms from Germany, he returned to Dublin, where he was recognised and was put under arrest. He was court martialled and sentenced to be shot. In the event he was sent first to Kilmainham Gaol, then to Richmond Barracks, Wandsworth Prison, and then to Frongoch internment camp in North Wales along with other Irish prisoners. Frongoch has been described as the IRA

University where, as O'Connor is reputed to have said, 'many a lad came in a harmless gossoon and left with the seeds of Fenianism deep in his heart'. It is said that Frongoch laid the foundations for the politics of resistance in jails and internment camps, and that Collins left it with a great deal of experience under his belt. It was in Frongoch that O'Connor formed a close relationship with Collins and on their release in 1916 he helped him reorganise the IRB network, the Irish Volunteers and the Sinn Fein organisation.

On returning to Dublin, O'Connor re-established his building business and became very active in politics. For example, he canvassed for by-elections in Kilkenny and Armagh on behalf of two Sinn Fein candidates, W.T. Cosgrave and Patrick McCartan. Throughout the War of Independence, O'Connor was a very close ally of Collins. He handled money on his behalf and frequently hid documents for him in secret drawers, which he had built into a number of different houses. Back in Dublin, he used his building expertise to great effect, creating hiding places in houses throughout Dublin for those on the run. He also purchased No. 76 Harcourt Street on behalf of Collins after the Sinn Fein office at No. 6 Harcourt Street was raided. As a builder, he created hiding places for private papers and created means of escape by way of skylights. In another house, No. 5 Mespil Road, which was Collins's headquarters for more than fifteen years, O'Connor created a small cupboard in the woodwork beneath the kitchen stairs on the ground floor where Collins could hide material he was working on. Although this house was raided in April 1921, this secret cupboard was never discovered. O'Connor persuaded Collins to go to London to form part of the Anglo-Irish Treaty delegations.

O'Connor built No. 36 Ailesbury Road for Nell Humphreys, whose brother, Michael O'Rahilly, was one of the founders of the Irish volunteers and was killed near the GPO during the 1916 Rising. Her family in Kerry were wealthy supporters of Irish independence. This house was used as a safe house in the War of Independence, sheltering many Irishmen on the run. The house was also used for cabinet meetings of the underground Republican movement. In this house, O'Connor built a false wall, behind which Ernie O'Malley, Chief of Staff of the IRA, lived for several months. The house was raided by the Free State troops, who had become aware of the secret room, and O'Malley was sprung from his hideout in a gun battle that left one soldier dead and O'Malley injured.

O'Connor became involved in the National Loan raised by Collins in order to fund the fledgling Dail. According to O'Connor, the Dail Loan raised almost £400,000, of which £25,000 was held in gold. This loan had been declared illegal and it was lodged in individual bank accounts belonging to the trustees. The gold was buried beneath the concrete floor in O'Connor's house at No. 1 Brendan Road until 1922, when it was handed over to the Irish Government.

In 1920, O'Connor became a Sinn Fein councillor for Pembroke Urban Council and he very soon became Chairman of the Council, which swore allegiance to Dail Éireann. He supported the Anglo–Irish Treaty and was ousted as treasurer of Donnybrook Sinn Fein in March 1922. He remained a Councillor for Cumann na nGaedheal after 1922 and was a joint treasurer of the party. O'Connor was an unsuccessful candidate for Dublin county in the 1923 general election. However, he did become a Dail member in 1924, and remained a TD until he died in 1935. During his time in the Dail, he continued to run his building business. He was most concerned in the Dail with local government and issues such as unemployment, housing and trade. He was not a very frequent speaker in the Dail itself.

In 1899, O'Connor married Bridget Dennehy, who, like him, was a native of Brosna, Co. Kerry. They had five children, including the Irish architect Brendan O'Connor (1911–1986). They are both buried in Glasnevin Cemetery. O'Connor's book, *With Michael Collins in the Fight for Irish Independence*, was published in London in 1929. The Batt O'Connor papers are in UCD Archives Department.

Further Reading

Coleman, Marie, 'O'Connor, Bartholomew (Batt)', in *Dictionary of Irish Biography*, edited by James McGuire and James Quinn, Cambridge University Press, Cambridge, in progress.

O'Connor, Batt, *With Michael Collins in the Fight for Irish Independence*, Peter Davies, London, 1929.

O'Connor, Bertie, *Bartholomew O'Connor: An Account of his Life and Fight for Irish Independence*, Brosna, Co. Kerry, 2018.

O'Kelly, Seán T. (1882–1966)
President of Ireland
38 Anglesea Road, Ballsbridge, Dublin 4

Seán O'Kelly was born in Dublin at No. 4 Lower Wellington Street, Dublin, on 25 August 1882. His father was Samuel O'Kelly, a master boot and shoe maker, and his mother was Catherine O'Dea. The family consisted of four boys and three girls. Two of his brothers attended St Enda's School, founded by Patrick Pearse. He attended O'Connell schools for his secondary education, where he acquired his great love of the Irish language.

In 1898, O'Kelly became a junior assistant at the National Library of Ireland and that same year he joined the Gaelic League. The National Librarian, T.W. Lyster, took an interest in him, and advised him on continuing his self-education. While there he became a subscriber to the Celtic Literary Society, founded in Dublin in 1893, which was descended from the Leinster Literary Society, established in the late 1880s. Because he was a member of the Gaelic League founded in 1893, and since the National Library of Ireland was under the British Government, he decided that holding a job there was incompatible with his separatist views. Instead, O'Kelly became a business manager for the Gaelic League newspaper *An Claidheamh Soluis* (1899–1932). He also worked for newspapers including the *United Irishman* (1899–1906).

O'Kelly joined the Irish Republican Brotherhood (IRB) in 1901 and in 1905 he joined Sinn Fein as one of its founding members. The following year (1906) he was elected a Sinn Fein member of Dublin Corporation for the Inns Quay Ward. In 1908, O'Kelly presented an Irish language address to Pope Pius X on behalf of Dublin Corporation. O'Kelly was also involved in the founding of the Irish Volunteers in 1913. In 1915, O'Kelly was sent to New York on an IRB mission to secure funds from Clan na Gael, an Irish Republican organisation in the United States in the late nineteenth and twentieth centuries. He was sent to inform Clan na Gael of the plans for the forthcoming rising in Dublin.

Back in Dublin after his visit to the United States, O'Kelly was appointed by Padraig Pearse as his staff captain in preparation for the Rising. During Easter Week 1916, O'Kelly was involved in posting copies of the proclamation that

Ireland was a republic around the city centre in Dublin. It was during the Easter Rising in the General Post Office on O'Connell Street that O'Kelly met his first wife, Mary Kate Ryan. She lectured in French at University College Dublin and they were married in 1918.

O'Kelly was arrested after the Rising but his court martial was delayed through, it is said, the influence of Archbishop William Walsh (1841–1921), Archbishop of Dublin. He was eventually sent to Wandsworth Prison in London and then to Woking military prison. He also spent three weeks at Frongoch internment camp in Wales before being transferred to Reading Gaol. When he returned to Ireland, O'Kelly again became involved with the Irish Volunteers. This caused his re-arrest and detainment, first in Oxford, then in Fairford. He eventually returned home to Ireland without permission.

In the general election of 1918, O'Kelly became a Sinn Fein member of Parliament for Dublin, College Green. As the newly elected Sinn Fein members did not recognise the authority of the British Parliament, they assembled instead in the Mansion House, Dublin, to form the first Dail Éireann with Éamon de Valera as President. O'Kelly became Cean Comhairle, or Speaker of Dail Éireann. Shortly after this he was sent as the envoy of the Republican Government to peace conferences in Paris, Rome and Washington. During his stay in Rome, he fell ill with rheumatic fever and spent three months convalescing at the Irish College, where he became friendly with the Rectors. The Catholic Church contacts he made in Rome were later important for Fianna Fáil as he was a devout member both of the Church and the party.

O'Kelly opposed the Anglo–Irish Treaty of 6 December 1921, agreed by representatives of the British Government and those of the Irish Republic including Michael Collins and Arthur Griffith. This Treaty formally established the Irish Free State with Dominion status, and it incorporated an Oath of Allegiance to the King. The Treaty also involved the Free State in relinquishing control of the six counties in Northern Ireland, which remained part of Great Britain. De Valera denounced the Treaty and he resigned from the office of President. During the Civil War that followed, O'Kelly was detained in Kilmainham Prison and Gormanston internment camp until December 1923. In 1923, after the deaths of almost 800 people, de Valera finally issued a command to give up arms and the fight. Following the truce, O'Kelly too denounced the Anglo–Irish Treaty, and acted as chief whip to the anti-Treaty side during Dail debates. Between 1924 and 1927, O'Kelly was in the United States on behalf of de Valera, where he succeeded in securing support for Fianna Fáil after it ceded from Sinn Fein. He went on to become a founding vice president of Fianna Fáil and in 1927 he was made editor of *The Nation,* the party organ. He spent almost three years (1924–1927) as Irish envoy in the United States. When he returned to Ireland and Fianna Fáil came into power in 1932, O'Kelly became Vice President of the Executive Council (1932–1937) and Tanaiste (1938–1945).

In 1932, O'Kelly became Minister for Public Health and Local Government and it was during this period that a major slum clearance and house building programme was initiated. He became Minister for Finance in 1939, which brought him into conflict with Séan Lemass (1899–1971). However, he succeeded in passing the Central Bank Act in 1942, which was controversial at the time since there were only five deputies present in the Dail. O'Kelly became a candidate for the Presidency of Ireland in 1945 and defeated the other two candidates, Seán Mac Eoin (Fine Gael) and Patrick McCartan (Independent). His wife, Kate, had died in 1934, and he married her sister, Phyllis, in 1936. Both O'Kelly and Phyllis were very popular, and his presidency was a popular one, so he was re-elected unopposed in 1952.The Republic of Ireland Act of 1949 permitted the President of Ireland to be recognised as the head of state. He was therefore then in a position to make formal visits abroad, and diplomats were able to present their credentials to him at Áras An Uachtaráin. As President, he frequently called for reconciliation between those on opposite sides during the Civil war. He made many trips abroad as President of Ireland and received many orders and decorations from the Papacy, Spain, Italy, the Netherlands, France and Germany. He visited the United States in 1959 and addressed a joint session of both houses of Congress on 17 May that year.

When he retired as President of Ireland on 25 June 1959, he was succeeded by Eamon de Valera (1882–1975). The Presidency of O'Kelly was a most successful and popular one and on leaving it he and Phyllis retired to their home in Roundwood, Co. Wicklow. He died on 23 November 1966 aged 84 in the Mater Private Nursing Home and is buried in Glasnevin Cemetery, Dublin.

Further Reading

Kenna, Kevin, *The Lives and Times of the Presidents of Ireland*, Liffey Press, Dublin, 2010.

Lee, Joseph J., *Ireland 1912–1985: Politics and Society*, Cambridge University Press, Cambridge, 2006.

Maume, Patrick, 'O'Kelly, Sean Thomas', in *Dictionary of Irish Biography*, edited by James McGuire and James Quinn, Cambridge University Press, Cambridge, in progress.

O'Rahilly, Michael Joseph (The O'Rahilly) (1875–1916)

40 Herbert Park, Donnybrook, Dublin 4

Michael Joseph O'Rahilly was born in Ballylongford, Co. Kerry, on 22 April 1875 to Richard Rahilly, a grocer and businessman, who was also a magistrate. His mother was Ellen (*née* Mangan). Both his parents claimed distinguished forebears – his father claimed he was descended from Aogán Ó Rathaille (*c.*1670–1726), a poet, who wrote in the Irish language. His mother claimed she was descendant from James Clarence Mangan (1803–1849), a well-known Irish poet. Michael had two sisters who became very well known in Republican circles in Ireland: Nell Humphreys (*née* Rahilly) and Anno O'Rahilly. Michael was educated in the local national school, before going on to attend Clongowes Wood College

as a boarder. He registered to study medicine at the Catholic University, the forerunner of University College Dublin (1894–1896), but he became ill with tuberculosis and returned to Kerry to look after the family business after his father died. As an adult, he became a Republican and an enthusiast for the Irish language. He changed his name to O'Rahilly and later still (self-styled) The O'Rahilly.

A meeting with Nancy Browne, one of five wealthy American sisters who were touring Europe as part of their education, led to him to follow her to America. He sold his family business in Co. Kerry before moving. He and Nancy were married on 15 April 1899. O'Rahilly worked for Nancy's father's Brown Mills Company for a short time. They lived in New York until 1902, before moving back to Ireland. They moved to Bray originally, and lived at Wilfort Cottage on the Dublin Road. In 1904, they returned to Philadelphia, where they endeavoured to salvage his in-laws' (the Browns) family linen mills. In 1909, they were back in Dublin once again, and then they lived at No. 38

Upper Leeson Street before moving to No. 40 Herbert Park in 1912, where members of the family still lived until recently when the house was demolished to make way for a block of apartments.

From the sale of the family business in Kerry, O'Rahilly received a settlement that gave him £450 a year, on which one could live comfortably in those days. He joined the Gaelic League and became a member of its governing body. He subscribed £100 to the organisation and worked as a journalist for its daily newspaper, *An Claidheamh Soluis*. He revamped it and published regular contributions from Eóin MacNeill and Padraig Pearse. He was convinced that Britain would not relinquish its control on Ireland unless it was compelled to do so. O'Rahilly therefore became a founding member of the Irish Volunteers from 1913, and he played a key role in recruiting men and gathering arms for the organisation. He served as Director of Arms and was responsible for the first major arming of this organisation. He was involved in training the Volunteers and in the landing of the 900 Mauser rifles during the Howth gun running on 26 July 1914. He was also responsible for the orchestration of opposition to the Royal visit to Ireland by King George V in 1911.

O'Rahilly never became a member of the Irish Republican Brotherhood (IRB). This was a secret oath-bound organisation that was dedicated to a future independent democratic republic in Ireland. He was therefore ignorant of the plans for the 1916 Rising, until Good Friday. The organisers of the Rising did everything they could to prevent the leaders in the Volunteers, who opposed unprovoked unilateral action, from learning about the proposed insurrection. Included in this group were the Chief of Staff of the Volunteers, Eóin MacNeill, Bulmer Hobson and, of course, The O'Rahilly. Along with Roger Casement, The O'Rahilly did not want the Rising to take place at all. In fact, he did everything he could to prevent it! He favoured the view of MacNeill and Hobson, who opposed a pre-emptive rising and instead favoured a benign strategy. At the request of MacNeill, he travelled throughout the country informing members of the Volunteers in Cork, Kerry, Tipperary and Limerick, that they were not to mobilise their forces on Sunday, the original day planned for the Insurrection.

Learning that the Rising was due to take place on Easter Monday on his return to Dublin, The O'Rahilly decided that since he had failed in his wish to prevent the mobilisation of the Volunteers, he would join them in their fight for freedom from Britain. It is said that he felt it his duty to join the men he had trained. He therefore set out to join the leaders of the Rising, and he was in the GPO during Easter Week with Pearse and the other leaders. He used his car to fetch supplies during the siege, and later used it as a barrier, but unfortunately it did not survive the Rising as it was burned out. While in the GPO, he was in charge, along with Desmond Fitzgerald, his aide de camp, of the roof, the food stores and the prisoners. He is reputed to have treated the latter with great humanity. Despite requests for The O'Rahilly to return home to his pregnant wife and children, he remained in the GPO.

The GPO was on fire by Friday, 28 April 1916 and The O'Rahilly volunteered to lead a party of twelve men down Moore Street to a factory on Great Britain Street (Parnell Street), where he was hit by two bullets. He survived only for about nineteen hours after being severely wounded. He wrote a note to his wife on the back of a letter in his pocket, 'Darling Nancy, I was shot leading a rush up Moore Street. Took refuge in a doorway ... Tons and tons of love dearie to you and the boys ... It was a good fight anyhow.' This note was found in his breast pocket after he had been killed and it was delivered to Nancy by a nurse. He was the only leader of the 1916 Rising who was killed in action. He was 41 years of age.

The O'Rahilly family remained active in Republican politics after the death of The O'Rahilly. Nancy, known to her family and friends as Nannie, joined Cuman na mBan in 1914, and was elected to its founding Executive Committee. She went on to become a became a Vice President but resigned during the Civil War in 1922 when her son was fighting for the anti-Treaty side, which she also supported. The O'Rahilly is buried with Nannie in Glasnevin Cemetery.

Further Reading

Edwards, Ruth Dudley, *Patrick Pearse: The Triumph of Failure*, Irish Academic Press, Dublin, 2006.

Fitzgerald, Desmond, *Memoirs of Desmond Fitzgerald 1913–1916*, Routledge & Keegan Paul, London, 1968.

O'Rahilly, Aodogan, *Winding the Clock: O'Rahilly and the 1916 Rising*, Lilliput Press, Dublin, 1991.

Pearse, Margaret Mary (1878–1968)
Educator and Politician
5 George's Villas, Sandymount, Dublin 4

Margaret Mary Pearse was born on 24 August 1878 at the family home, No. 27 Great Brunswick Street in Dublin. She was the eldest of the family of James and Margaret Pearse (*née* Brady). Her father had been married before and had children from his first marriage who grew up with his second family. The father was a stonemason with his own business on Great Brunswick Street (now Pearse Street) and the family lived over the shop. They also sublet some of the rooms, so Margaret Mary grew up in quite cramped conditions. As the business improved, James Pearse moved his family to live in a house on Newbridge Avenue, Sandymount. Later again they moved to Sandymount Avenue. Margaret Mary received her primary education at a private school at No. 28 Wentworth Place, Dublin. She received her secondary education from the Holy Faith Sisters in Clarendon Street, Dublin. She was a very bright student and did exceptionally well in her final school examinations, receiving first place in all her subjects. She then trained in Domestic Economy at the Rathmines Technical Institute. She also obtained a certificate of competency from the Leinster College of Irish. Margaret Mary Pearse became very interested in the Irish language and insisted on signing her name in Irish and later she encouraged the teaching of the Irish language at St Enda's School.

Pearse did not seek paid employment immediately after receiving her third-level education, but always had a great interest in education. She accompanied her brother, Padraig, to Belgium to study their bilingual system of education, and to improve her knowledge of the French language. On her return from Brussels in 1907, she set up her own small preparatory school for girls and boys in their home, which was in Leeson Park, Dublin 4. This school was a success, and it eventually became the preparatory school for St Enda's, which began in Cullenswood House in Ranelagh. In 1910, St Enda's School moved to a 50-acre site at The Hermitage in Rathfarnham. Her two brothers, Padraig and Willie, had set up St Enda's in 1908. It was one of the most radical projects ever in the history of Irish education, being a bilingual school with Irish as its first language. Both Margaret Mary Pearse and her mother Margaret played an integral part in making the school a home from home for the students who boarded there. Margaret Mary focused mainly on the junior or preparatory school, where the school prospectus lists her as the Mistress of the Preparatory School between 1901 and 1910. As the fame of the school spread, the workload for Margaret and her mother became quite onerous. There was a regular series of guest lectures at the school, which made for a stimulating intellectual environment for the students.

After the 1916 Rising and the execution of her two brothers, Padraig and Willie, Margaret Mary Pearse, together with her mother, continued to run St Enda's, where she acted as both matron and housekeeper, while her mother was the headmistress. She also taught French and religion. Padraig died intestate and he left the school in serious debt. It did receive some bequests and donations, but there were constant quarrels between Margaret Mary and her mother as to how the funds should be spent. They ran into serious financial difficulties in relation to keeping the school open, and they endeavoured to fundraise both in Ireland and in the United States. The American St Enda's Committee did raise enough money to buy the school grounds and Pearse's lecture tour of the USA in 1926 raised additional funds. The death of Padraig was a major loss to St Enda's. The school missed his involvement and guidance as his mother and sister did not have the ability or the vision to keep it going.

Margaret Mary's sister, Mary Bridget, had been a delicate child, spending a good deal of her time in bed due to ill health. The two sisters differed considerably in their views of their brothers' revolutionary activity. Margaret Mary was fully supportive of the 1916 Rising, while Mary Bridget had visited the GPO in an attempt to persuade the brothers to return home and abandon the fight. Mary Bridget was a musician, teacher, actress and writer, and she taught music at St Enda's. Although Mary Bridget was in reality estranged from her mother and sister, she was still financially dependent on them. As a writer, she contributed children's stories to various magazines. In 1934, a popular magazine called *Our Boys* published several articles by her on the home life of her brothers. This led to quarrels between Mary Bridget and her sister in relation to the royalties from the brief autobiographical fragment of Padraig's that was included in the book. Mary Bridget died suddenly on 13 November 1947 at her home, No. 6 Beaufort Villas, Rathfarnham, Co. Dublin.

Margaret Mary had inherited St Enda's School on the death of her mother. She managed to keep the school open until 1935, when it became totally insolvent. She continued to live in The Hermitage after the school closed and allowed it to house a Red Cross Hospital during the Second World War. All her life, Margaret Mary carried the torch for her two brothers. To her, the Rising was 'tragic but glorious' and she liked to remember that her two brothers would spend eternity together. Over the years she attended all state and public ceremonies held to commemorate the 1916 Rising. Like her mother, Pearse opposed the Anglo–Irish Treaty and she supported the setting up of Fianna Fáil, which she joined in 1933 and became a TD in the constituency of County Dublin. However, she lost out when it became a five-seat constituency in 1937. She always had a close relationship with Éamon de Valera, she served on the Fianna Fáil National Executive and was the Hon. Treasurer of the party for many years. Both Margaret Mary and her mother were of the opinion that de Valera had always endeavoured to sustain Padraig's political vision. Margaret Mary was made a senator in 1938 and remained in the Senate, sometimes as the Taoiseach's nominee, until she died in 1968. It is interesting to note that Margaret Mary seldom spoke in either the Dail or Senate, but she did speak out strongly on some political, social and cultural issues in talks and speeches she gave throughout Ireland. When St Enda's closed, Margaret Mary became a founding member of the teaching staff of Ardscoil Eanna in Crumlin, Dublin, when it opened in 1939.

In 1966, Margaret Mary received an honorary D.Litt from the National University of Ireland along with other relatives of those executed in 1916. That same year she announced she would not leave The Hermitage to the state as per her mother's will but instead would leave it to a religious foundation. However, she was quickly persuaded to change her mind. It is now the Pearse Museum in Rathfarnham. The final years of her life were spent in Linden Convalescent Home in Blackrock, Co. Dublin. Ill health prevented her from attending the fiftieth anniversary commemoration of the 1916 Rising. The government of the day accorded her a state funeral when she died on 7 November 1968. She never married and is buried beside her parents and sister in Glasnevin Cemetery.

Further Reading

Edwards, Ruth Dudley, *Patrick Pearse: The Triumph of Failure*, 2nd edition, Irish Academic Press, Dublin, 2006.

Maye, Brian, 'Keeper of the Flame', *Irish Times*, 12 November 2018.

O'Donnell, Teresa and Louise, Marie, *Sisters of the Revolutionaries*, Merrion Press, Newbridge, 2017.

Pearse, Padraig (1879–1916)
Barrister, Writer and Revolutionary
5 George's Villas, Sandymount, Dublin 4

Patrick Henry Pearse was born in 1879 to James Pearse, an Englishman, who had a stone-carving business at No. 27 Great Brunswick Street (now Pearse Street) and his wife, Margaret (*née* Brady). In his childhood he is reputed to have been influenced greatly by his mother's aunt Margaret, who told him stories from Irish mythology and of patriotic revolutionaries such as Theobald Wolf Tone and Robert Emmett. His first school was Mrs Murphy's Private School, which he attended between 1887 and 1891. His secondary education was with the Christian Brothers in Westland Row, which he attended from 1891–1896. At this school, he developed a great interest in the Irish language, and joined the Gaelic League in 1896 when he was 17 years old.

Though not from a wealthy family, Pearse enrolled for a BA degree at the Royal University of Ireland, an examining body, where he studied Irish, English and French. At the same time, he attended Trinity College and the King's Inns to study law. He was called to the Bar in 1901 but did not practise, except for one case that he took and lost. He defended a poet and songwriter from Cresslough, Donegal, who received a fine for putting his name on a donkey cart in the Irish language, in what was described as illegible writing. Despite being commended by the judge for his defence, the ruling went against him. His next appearance in court was to defend himself at his court martial held after the 1916 Rising.

While still a student, Pearse was actively involved in the Gaelic League, where he worked on various committees. He wrote articles for *An Claidheamh Soluis* (The Sword of Light), an Irish nationalist weekly newspaper published by the League between 1899 and 1932. His articles were on a variety of topics, such as literature, history, education, emigration, politics and religion. He was the newspaper's salaried editor from 1903 to 1909. During his editorship, he continued to write poems and stories in both Irish and English. His best-known plays are perhaps *Iosagain* and *The Dearg-daol*. He firmly believed that language was an intrinsic part of a nation's identity. He usually spent his summer holidays in Rosmuc, Co. Galway, where, later in life, he had a summer cottage.

Workwise, Pearse taught Irish in a number of different schools in Dublin, including Alexandra College. He also lectured part time in Irish at University College Dublin. He had very strong views on the educational system in Ireland at the time, which, he believed, educated Irish men and women to become good Englishmen and women. He was also outspoken on the role of the Irish language in education and was active in the dispute that demanded that Irish be made compulsory in the matriculation for entry into the newly established National University of Ireland. Pearse had a great interest in bilingual pedagogy and he visited Belgium in 1905 to study bilingual teaching methods there.

Due to his visit to Belgium and his interest in bilingual education, he decided to open his own school, which he did in 1908. He named it St Enda's, in honour of a warrior-king of Oriel in Ulster, who became a priest and died about AD 530. The school began in Cullenswood House on Oakley Road, Ranelagh, in 1908. It provided a secondary education for Catholic boys that was 'distinctively Irish in complexion, bilingual in method, and of a high modern type generally'. Two years later, the school moved to The Hermitage in Rathfarnham. It attracted seventy pupils in its first year. It was a fee-paying school for both boarders and day pupils, but despite this, Pearse ran into financial difficulties, so it was not a great business success. The move to Rathfarnham proved to be ill judged, and Pearse very soon overstretched his limited financial resources. He had opened a girl's school called St Ita's in Cullenswood House in Ranelagh, which had similar education aims to St Enda's, but he was forced to close this in 1912 due to lack of funds.

St Enda's was a family business, with his younger brother Willie acting as one of the teachers, and his mother, Margaret, and his sisters, Margaret Mary and Mary Brigid, all involved. The range of subjects offered and the quality of the teaching was exceptional. Among the teachers were the poets Thomas MacDonagh and Padraic Colum. The students also received lectures and talks from some of the leading Irish cultural figures of the day, including Douglas Hyde, Maud Gonne and W.B. Yeats. Education-wise, St Enda's was a great success, but financially it was a disaster, despite the fact that Pearse made visits to the United States in 1914 to try and raise funds. With the Rising of 1916, the school closed. However, with his mother and sister, Margaret Mary, as well as with the help of well-wishers, it reopened later that year in Cullenswood House. In 1919, it moved back to The Hermitage, which was later bought with funds raised in the USA by the Save St Enda's Fund. Unfortunately, without the dynamism of Padraig the school did not survive and it finally closed in 1935.

Padraig appears to have been a moderate nationalist in the early twentieth century. He supported the Home Rule Bill in 1912, but the establishment of the Ulster Volunteers and their pledge to resist Home Rule changed his mind. In 1913, he became involved in the setting up of the Irish Volunteers, and later he became Director of Military operations on its behalf. There were two sections within the Irish Volunteers, one of which was the IRB (Irish Republican Brotherhood). The stated purpose of the Volunteers was not the establishment of a republic, but the IRB section on the other hand intended to do just that. They recruited people such as Joseph Plunkett, Thomas MacDonagh and Pearse too, became a member of the Supreme Council in 1915. Others recruited included Sean MacDermott, Éamonn Ceannt and James Connolly of the Irish Citizen Army. It was these men who planned the 1916 Rising. Padraig was very involved in organising the funeral of Jeremiah O'Donovan Rossa (1831–1915), an Irish Fenian leader and a prominent member of the Irish Republican brotherhood. He gave the graveside oration, which is one of the most famous speeches of the Irish independence movement and stirred his audience to a call to arms. He claimed that, 'Ireland unfree shall never be at peace.'

As Director of Military Operations for the Irish Volunteers in March 1915, Pearse became a pivotal figure in the planning process for a Rising. The background to the Rising was the great desire to end British rule in Ireland, and to establish an independent Irish Republic while the United Kingdom was involved in the First World War. The Military Council of the IRB planned for a rising to begin on Easter Sunday, 23 April 1916. Just before Easter, Pearse issued orders to all Volunteer units in Ireland for three days of manoeuvres to begin on Easter Sunday. These were to be the signal for a general rebellion. Some 20,000 rifles were expected from Germany but the boat, the *Aud*, carrying them was captured by the Royal Navy off the coast of Kerry on Good Friday.

The chief of staff of the Volunteers was Eóin MacNeill, who had been kept in the dark in relation to the proposed Rising. When he learned of it without the availability of promised arms from Germany, he countermanded the orders. Originally the plan was for the Rising to occur on the Sunday, but with the publication countermanding the manoeuvres in the *Sunday Independent*, the number of people throughout the country who turned out was quite small.

The Easter Rising took place on Easter Monday, 24 April 1916. Pearse was responsible for drafting the Proclamation of the Republic, and he was chosen as its President. He duly read the Proclamation after the rebels had seized the General Post Office in O'Connell Street. After the Rising, Pearse claimed that the rebels would have won out but for MacNeill countermanding the orders, but he also did not blame MacNeill as he understood he had acted in the best interests of Ireland.

Pearse's surrender to the British Army on 29 April 1916 appears to have been based on the hope of saving civilian lives as well as his followers. Pearse, his brother Willie, Thomas Clarke and Thomas MacDonagh were the first of the rebels to be executed, on 3 May 1916 at Kilmainham Gaol. He is buried in the Military Cemetery at Arbour Hill Prison along with thirteen of the executed leaders of the Rising. He was 37 years old.

Further Reading

Edwards, Ruth Dudley, *Patrick Pearse: The Triumph of Failure*, Irish Academic Press, Dublin, 2006.

Lee, Joseph J., 'Pearse, Patrick Henry', in *Dictionary of Irish Biography*, edited by James McGuire and James Quinn, Cambridge University Press, Cambridge, in progress.

O'Donnell, Ruan, *Patrick Pearse*, O'Brien Press, Dublin, 2016.

Plunkett, Joseph Mary (1887–1916)
Poet and Revolutionary
17 Marlborough Road, Donnybrook, Dublin 4

Joseph Mary Plunkett was born at No. 26 Upper Fitzwilliam Street, Dublin, to George Noble Plunkett (1851–1948), barrister, nationalist and Papal Count, and his wife, Mary Josephine Plunkett (*née* Cranny, 1858–1944). Both Joseph's paternal grandfather and his maternal grandfather, Patrick Plunkett and Patrick Cranny, were builders. They built houses in Rathmines, Donnybrook and Ballsbridge. As a result, the family owned substantial properties in Dublin and some are still in their ownership to this day.

Plunkett grew up in Dublin. His mother was a very strong personality, while his father, as was the norm at the time, seems to have been detached from domestic life and all its problems and tribulations. Joseph suffered ill health from the time he was a young child due to glandular tuberculosis. He also suffered from bouts of pleurisy and pneumonia throughout his entire life. He was sent to the Catholic University School (CUS) in Leeson Street for his primary education. He spent a year in Paris, too, attending a Marist College. On return to Dublin, he attended Belvedere College, and later still another Jesuit College: Stonyhurst, in Lancashire, England. It was in the latter that he acquired some second-hand military knowledge as he was not strong enough to be a member of the school's Officer Training Corps. Through his education and reading, Plunkett developed wide interests including history, politics, economics, scholastic philosophy, physics, chemistry, aeronautics, wireless telegraphy and photography. He also studied Esperanto and was a founding member of the Irish Esperanto League.

In an effort to cure his pulmonary tuberculosis, Plunkett travelled widely in Europe and North Africa. In 1911 when he was 23 years old, he travelled to Italy, Sicily and Malta with his mother. He spent the winter of 1912 in Algiers with his sister, Moya. There he studied the Arabic language and literature, and wrote some of his early poems. He is even reputed to have composed some poetry in Arabic. It was in Algiers that Plunkett found time to roller skate, which was very popular in Dublin during the 1900s. He became an expert, and at one time considered an offer to do it professionally!

Plunkett was very interested in his Irish heritage in particular, and in the Irish language. He formed a close friendship with his Irish language teacher, Thomas

MacDonagh (1878–1916). He went on to marry MacDonagh's sister-in-law, Grace Gifford. His initial interest in the Irish language was his wish to prepare for the matriculation examination as he hoped to study medicine or science at university. MacDonagh, too, was a poet, and he encouraged Plunkett's interest in poetry. He was responsible for the publication of Plunkett's first book of poetry, *The Circle and the Sword*, in 1911, while he was still in Algeria. It was through him, that Plunkett purchased the *Irish Review* from Padraic Colum, a well-known literary magazine. Plunkett became editor of this journal, and moved its focus to politics and literature, as well as promoting Arthur Griffith's Sinn Fein policies. Contributors to the *Irish Review* included P.H. Pearse, Thomas MacDonagh, James Connolly, Roger Casement, Alice Stopford Green, Mary Hayden, Eleanor Farjeon, Arthur Griffith and Francis and Hannah Sheehy Skeffington. These and many more were frequent callers at the house on Marlborough Road. The *Irish Review* supported the workers during the famous Dublin Lockout; a major industrial dispute between some 20,000 workers and 300 employers in Dublin in 1913. Plunkett and his brother-in-law, Thomas Dillon, were joint secretaries of Thomas Kettle's Peace Committee.

The Irish Volunteers was a military organisation established in 1913 in Dublin in response to the formation in 1912 of the Ulster Volunteers. The latter was a Unionist militia, founded to block Home Rule for Ireland. Plunkett attended the inaugural meeting of the Irish Volunteers in 1913, becoming a member of its Provisional Committee. During 1914, Plunkett joined the Irish Republican Brotherhood (IRB), a secret oath-bound fraternal organisation dedicated to the establishment of an Irish republic. Plunkett very quickly became Director of Military operations and a key person involved in the planning of the Rising. In 1915, Plunkett was appointed to the IRB's Military Council. A room in No. 17 Marlborough Road, Plunkett's home, was dedicated to H.G. Well's game Little Wars – good practice for a revolution! One of the Plunkett family homes at Larkfield in Kimmage was used to store weapons and the drilling and training of the Volunteers took place there, too. Early in 1915, Plunkett went to Germany on behalf of the IRB to buy guns and ammunition for the Rising. Roger Casement had gone there in 1914 with a similar idea, and he worked with Plunkett, introducing him to military and political men. They had produced a plan for the Rising, known as the Ireland Report, and Plunkett was its chief author. This plan described their proposed military strategy, which was centred on the seizure of major buildings in the city of Dublin. From the German Chancellor Theobald Bethmann-Hollweg (1856–1921), Plunkett and Casement received the promise of a cargo of arms to reach Ireland on Easter Sunday 1916. Plunkett also travelled to New York to brief Clan na Gael on the progress of their German negotiations, and he provided details of their plans for an Easter Rising.

Plunkett, together with Seán Mac Diarmada (1883–1916), were considered to have been responsible for the Castle Document. This suggested that the British were going to suppress the Irish Volunteers. Eóin MacNeill (1867–1945), a fellow member of the Irish Volunteers, was sceptical of the idea of holding a Rising in 1916, and he in fact countermanded the instructions for the Easter Sunday parades that were to become a Rising throughout the country. Despite his ill health, Plunkett left his sickbed and joined his comrades in the General Post Office (GPO) to fight on Easter Monday 1916. By then he had become a mentor to a young Volunteer called Michael Collins (1890–1922). Collins had returned to Ireland in 1915 and worked for the Plunkett family on their real estate holdings, which were extensive. Plunkett and Collins developed a close friendship, and he chose Collins as his aide-de-camp and bodyguard in the GPO during the Rising.

The Military Council of the IRB during the Rising became the Provisional Government of the Irish Republic and proclaimed Ireland's independence from England. The Proclamation was read by Patrick Pearse (1879–1916) outside the General Post Office. Plunkett was a Marconi enthusiast, and he had made his own radio set, so he was able to broadcast the true facts about the Rising and contradict the version from England, where it had been described as 'a small riot'.

All seven men who had signed the Proclamation were executed by the British after the Rising. Fourteen of those executed are buried in Arbour Hill Prison, including Plunkett, who was aged 28. Some seven hours before he was executed on 4 May 1916, Plunkett married Grace Gifford, his fiancée, in the prison chapel in Kilmainham Gaol. Plunkett's poetry continues to be well known. Waterford's main railway station is named for him and is known as Plunkett Station. A barracks in the Curragh, Co. Kildare, is also named for him: Plunkett Barracks.

Further Reading

Dillon, Geraldine, *Plunkett: All in the Blood: a Memoir*, edited by Honor O Brolchain, A. & A. Farmer, Dublin, 2012.

O Brolchain, Honor, *Joseph Plunkett*, O'Brien Press, Dublin, 2012.

White, Lawrence William, 'Plunkett, Joseph Mary', in *Dictionary of Irish Biography*, edited by James McGuire and James Quinn, Cambridge University Press, Cambridge, in progress.

Purser, Sarah (1848–1943)
Portrait Painter and Artist
Mespil House, Mespil Road, Dublin 4

Sarah Purser was born in Kingstown (Dun Laoghaire) on 22 March 1848 to Benjamin Purser, a grain merchant, and his wife, Anne (*née* Mallet) from Dungarvan, Co. Waterford. They had eight children and Sarah was the third daughter. The family was a wealthy Anglo–Irish family, but her father emigrated to America when his grain business failed. Two of her brothers became distinguished academics in Trinity College Dublin – Professor John Mallet Purser was a well-known medical scientist, and Professor Louis Claude Purser was an eminent classical scholar.

During her childhood, Purser and her sisters were sent to school in Switzerland (1861–1863), where they became fluent French speakers. Purser lived with her mother as her father remained in the United States. She studied at the College of Art in Dublin for a period, and on her mother's death she studied at the Académie Julian in Paris, where she met many of the distinguished painters of the day. Among the students was a Swiss Artist called Louise Breslau, who became Purser's lifelong friend. Every year, Purser visited Paris in order to keep up to date with trends in painting and the art world in general. In Ireland she first exhibited at the Royal Hibernian Academy in 1879 and her work received excellent reviews. By 1881, Purser was showing her portraits of well-known figures at the Academy to much acclaim.

One of Purser's most famous painting is that of Constance and Eva Gore Booth, which hung over the mantelpiece at their home in Lissadel in Sligo for many years and is now in the Merrion Hotel in Dublin. This beautiful painting led to Sarah acquiring commissions from numerous members of the British aristocracy to paint their portraits, too. In 1880, Purser received recognition from the Royal Hibernian Academy for her work by being elected to Honorary Academician status. This was the only recognition available to women at that time. For more than twenty years, Purser continued to be a highly paid portrait painter. She painted so many of the British aristocracy that she often claimed that she 'went through the British aristocracy like measles'.

Purser was always kind and generous to fellow artists who would not have been as wealthy as she. In 1901, for example, she organised a significant exhibition in Dublin of the work of Nathaniel Hone and John B. Yeats. One of the visitors to this exhibition was Hugh Lane, who became one of her close friends. For Lane's proposed collection of national portraits, Purser painted Douglas Hyde, Edward Martyn and Maud Gonne. Her generosity also extended to other artists, including Jack B. Yeats and Evie Hone, and she organised exhibitions for them in 1903. Also in that year, Purser and her friend, Edward Martyn, set up An Túr Gloine (The Tower of Glass), which was a workshop for stained glass artists based at No. 24 Upper Pembroke Street in Dublin, which Purser was involved in until her death in 1943. Martyn was advising on a new Catholic cathedral at Loughrea, Co. Galway, and was anxious to involve Irish artists. Leading Irish stained-glass artists who trained there included Michael Healy and Evie Hone, and with Purser, they were also involved in the decoration of Loughrea Cathedral. The Archive of An Túr Gloine is held at the Centre for the Study of Irish Art at the National Gallery of Ireland.

By the beginning of the twentieth century some of Purser's best-known Irish portraits included distinguished men of the day, for example, Stokes, Ferguson, Graves, Bergan, the Yeats brothers and AE, and these people became her friends. Due to her literary friends, she became involved with the Irish Literary Theatre, founded by W.B. Yeats, Lady Gregory and George Moore. Their aim was to produce plays by Irish authors. Throughout the twentieth century, Purser was very active in the art world and was involved in the setting up of the Hugh Lane Municipal Gallery. It was Purser who persuaded the Irish Government to provide Charlemont House on Parnell Square as a home for the gallery. In 1924, the Royal Hibernian Academy made her a member, the first woman to join this prestigious body. That year, too, she set up the Friends of the National Collections of Ireland, which held its first meeting at the Royal Irish Academy on Dawson Street. The stated purpose of the Friends was 'to secure works of art and objects of historic interest or importance for the national or public collections of Ireland by purchase, gift or bequest'. Among its distinguished members from the beginning were George Bernard Shaw, W.B. Yeats and Oliver St John Gogarty.

Shortly after its foundation, the Friends turned their focus towards the return of the Lane pictures to Dublin. When Hugh Lane died, in his will he bequeathed his entire art collection to London, but later an unwitnessed codicil bequeathed it to Dublin. Contact with the National Gallery in London has continued over the years and in 1959 it was agreed that half the Lane bequest would be lent and shown in Dublin every five years. In 1993, the agreement was changed so that thirty-one of the thirty-nine paintings would remain in Ireland. The paintings continued to be shared for purposes of exhibitions between the National Gallery, London, and Dublin.

Mespil House in Mespil Road became Purser's home in 1911, and she lived there with her brother, John, for thirty-four years. Mespil House dated from 1751 and it was built for a distinguished physician from Cork, Dr Edward Barry (later Sir Edward Barry) who was President of the Royal College of Physicians of Ireland (1749) and a member of Parliament for Charleville, Co. Cork. The house contained beautiful eighteenth-century stucco ceilings, some of which were transferred to Dublin Castle and Áras an Uachtaráin when it was demolished. Blocks of apartments (Mespil flats) were built on the site of the house and its grounds in the early 1950s.

Purser was famous for her salons or 'at homes' (held in Mespil House), which were a well-known feature of Irish society. These events were normally a forum for discussions on the literary, theatrical and artistic life in the city. Invitations were extended to the leading figures of the day, and Purser herself became a pivotal influence on cultural affairs in Ireland. She appears to have been a nationalist, while most of her friends were Unionists. The name An Túr Gloine suggests a sympathy with the Irish language. Learning Irish became a symbol of nationalism, and Purser made a number of attempts to learn it. She was appointed by the Lord Mayor of Dublin to the 1912 Mansion House Committee looking at forwarding plans for a modern art gallery in the city. The Viceroy also appointed Purser to the National Gallery of Ireland Board of Directors in 1912. In 1933, Purser and Sir John Griffin funded a series of lectures that bear their name to this very day – the Purser Griffith lectures at University College Dublin.

Purser continued to paint into her 80s, and she exhibited landscape and various portraits at exhibitions in Dublin and abroad. She continued to be active in An Túr Gloine until she died at the age of 95 on 7 August 1943 in Dublin. She is buried in Mount Jerome Cemetery beside two of her brothers.

Further Reading
O'Grady, John, *The Life and Work of Sarah Purser*, Four Courts Press, Dublin, 1996.

O'Grady, John, 'Purser, Sarah', in *Dictionary of Irish Biography*, edited by James McGuire and James Quinn, University Press, Cambridge.

Brennan-Holohan, Mary, *A Portrait of Sarah Purser*, P.C.D. & J. Publishing, Dublin, 1996.

Roe, Alderman George (1796–1863)
Distiller and Former Lord Mayor of Dublin
Nutley, Priesthouse, Donnybrook, Dublin 4

George Edward Roe was born in Booterstown, Co. Dublin, in 1796, to Peter Roe (*c*.1746–1826) and his wife, Margaret (*c*.1761–1841). He married Mary, daughter of the late Alexander Franklin and his wife Olivia, at St Peter's Church, Aungier Street, Dublin, in 1819. They had no recorded children.

The Roe family played a key role in the history of Dublin and particularly of the Liberties. During the early eighteenth and nineteenth centuries several members of the family operated a number of different distilleries in Dublin. George Roe was descended from this family, and he inherited the Thomas Street Distillery (1757) from his father. He took it over in 1820s and amalgamated it with another of his family's distilleries in Pimlico. He very quickly expanded by buying up premises and land in the area as the business grew. The combined distillery became known as George Roe & Co. It covered more than 17 acres and was located at Nos 157–159 Thomas Street, but it extended all the way to the River Liffey. At one stage it was the largest producer of whiskey in Europe, with a capacity of around 2 million gallons a year. Roe's Distillery was powered by a very large smock windmill, which was built in 1759 and it is still in existence. Today it is known as Saint Patrick's Tower and is located in the grounds of the Guinness Brewery.

By 1887, George Roe & Co. was considered to be one of the largest distilleries in Europe, exporting whiskey to the United States, Great Britain and Canada. When the distillery finally closed in 1926 most of its buildings were demolished but a few were incorporated into the Guinness Brewery and are still in existence. Diageo (formerly Guinness) has created a new whiskey known as

Roe & Co. in honour of George Roe, and it has turned the former Guinness Power House on Thomas Street into a new distillery called Roe & Co.

George Roe's brother, Henry (born *c.* 1794), had an address in Fitzwilliam Square, and also at Mount Anville Park in Dundrum, and is described as a merchant, and like George, was a member of the Royal Dublin Society, and a Director of a number of major Dublin companies. In the absence of any progeny from George and Mary, it was Henry's two sons also called George and Henry, who inherited Roe's Distillery along with their father. Henry junior gave £230,000 (€35million in today's money!) to pay for the restoration of Christ Church Cathedral and the construction of a new Synod Hall.

Roe was a member of the Church of Ireland and a liberal in politics. He was a member of the Central Relief Committee for all Ireland established by Joseph Bewley in 1846 for the relief of Famine victims. He was also active in the Friends of Reform. He was a Justice of the Peace and Deputy Lieutenant for Dublin City. He became Lord Mayor of Dublin on 1 November 1842, succeeding Daniel O'Connell. This was at the time when the City of Dublin administration was reformed. As a result, the date of the election of the Lord Mayor was changed to 1 December, and the date of assuming office was changed to 1 January. Roe therefore served as Lord Mayor for two years until 1 January 1844. During his term of office as Lord Mayor he was noted for 'his high-minded integrity and impartial administration of the functions and powers of the office'.

Roe was a friend of Daniel O'Connell, and though he was a Protestant and a Unionist, he was a supporter of Catholic emancipation. His civic career included being Chief Magistrate of the City of Dublin. He was described as having carried out his duties in an 'indefatigable, conciliatory, firm and impartial manner'. Roe was also a member of the Wide Streets Commission in 1841. He was High Sheriff of Dublin in 1847, a member of the Paving Lighting and Cleaning Committee of Dublin City Council (1854–1863), member of the Sewerage and Improvements Committee, member of the City Estate Committee (1854–1863) and the General Finance Committee (1854–1863). He was also Chairman of the Committee of the Great Industrial Exhibition of 1853 known as Dargan's Exhibition, which was financially supported by William Dargan (1799–1867), the well-known building contractor and railway entrepreneur, who built Ireland's first railway from Dublin to Dun Laoghaire.

Roe's other public roles in life included being a Council Member of the Horticultural Society of Ireland, Vice Patron of the Meath Street Savings Bank, a Governor of the Meath Hospital and a Trustee of the Sick and Indigent Roomkeepers Society and the South Dublin Penny Bank. He was a Director of the National Insurance Company, and of the Dublin and Kingstown Railway Company. He was a member of the Council of the Royal Agricultural Society and a life member of the Royal Dublin Society (RDS) from 1829. He was a prize winner for his flowers and livestock at many of the annual Spring Show and Horse Show. He was also a member of the RDS Botany Committee. The National Botanic Gardens were founded in 1795 by the Dublin Society (later the Royal Dublin Society) and it was Roe who, as a member of the Botany Committee of the RDS, proposed a motion that the Botanic Gardens should be open on a Sunday once a month to the public and that the RDS should employ a band so that people promenading in the gardens would have additional pleasure. Though not an academic by profession, Roe had the honour of being elected to membership of the Royal Irish Academy in January 1852. His nominators included Sir Robert Kane, First President of Queen's College Cork, and George Petrie, the distinguished antiquary.

Roe's main residence was at Nutley in Donnybrook (now Elm Park Golf and Sports Club), where he entertained many distinguished visitors whose visits were recorded in the daily newspapers. They included Queen Victoria when she was in Dublin for the Great Exhibition of 1853. He also entertained Daniel O'Connell. The Lord Lieutenant, the Earl of St Germans and the Countess St Germans appear to have visited Roe's demesne at Nutley on more than one occasion for lunch and dinner. One of the newspaper reports stated the Vice Regal party spent three hours at Nutley, inspecting the garden and farm operations 'with which they were much pleased'. This is hardly surprising as Roe's demesne at Nutley has been described as 'one of the finest demesnes in the county of Dublin – it was planted and kept with exquisite taste, surrounding a mansion furnished in a manner with which a duke might be satisfied'. Nutley House had its main entrance on the Stillorgan Road. Roe engaged Ninian Niven, Director of the Botanic Gardens, to design a garden, park, lake and tall belvedere at Nutley. The gardens on the south-east side of the house are still a delight. The semicircular wall with niches set at regular intervals still contain the statuary. A circular fountain representing a shell resting on a rustic base with herons perched on the edge of the shell was part of Ninian Niven's design for the lawn and it is still in situ on what is now the putting green. Today, the house and part of the grounds are owned by the Religious Sisters of Charity, and together with additional land are laid out as a golf course for Elm Park Golf and Sports Club.

Suffering from ill health in the early 1860s that forced him to retire from business and his public offices, Roe and his wife moved to milder climates in the south of England. They lived in Torquay, Devon, where he died on 20 July 1863 and his body was returned to Dublin for burial in Mount Jerome Cemetery. His funeral from his home in Nutley was the largest ever seen in Dublin with the exception of Daniel O'Connell's. Newspapers of the day reported there were about 400 carriages, most of them private, in the funeral procession, including the carriage of the Lord Lieutenant, the Lord Chancellor, the Lord Mayor and members of Dublin Corporation. In front of the procession walked 200 of the employees of Roe & Co., all wearing white scarves and headbands. Next came all the labourers employed at Nutley, also wearing scarves and headbands. As the cortège passed through Donnybrook, all the shops were closed and the local people stood in respect for their former benefactor.

Roe occupied a distinguished place in the social and business history of Dublin and his death left a great void. His obituaries state that he was known and esteemed more than any other citizen and as a tribute to his memory the flags on the Ballast Office, club house, yachts and shipping in the harbour of Kingstown (Dun Laoghaire) were hoisted at half-mast. After her husband's death, Mary Roe continued to live at Nutley until her death in 1877 and they are both buried in Mount Jerome Cemetery. Their tomb has been restored recently by Diageo.

Further Reading

Barnard, Alfred, *The Whisky Distilleries of the United Kingdom*, 1st ed., London, reprinted 1969.

Clark, Mary, *George Roe (d.1863) Lord Mayor of Dublin 1842–1843*, Dublin City Archives, Dublin, 2017.

Obituaries and funeral details, the *Irish Times*, 20 and 27 July 1863 and 22 August 1863.

Murphy, Sean, 'The Roe family & Roe's Distillery', *Dublin Historical Record*, 72 (1) pp.80–92. Includes family tree.

Salkeld, Blanaid (1880–1959)
Poet, Publisher and Actor
43 Morehampton Road, Donnybrook, Dublin 4

Blanaid Salkeld was born Florence Ffrench Mullen in Chittagong, now Bangladesh, where her father, Lieutenant Colonel Jarleth Ffrench Mullen from Galway, was a doctor in the Indian Medical service. As a young girl, she learned Bengali and Irish at her father's knee and was also familiar with the great Indian poet Rabindranath Tagore (1861–1941) who, in 1913, became the first non-European to win the Nobel Prize for Literature. Like many children born in colonial India, she was sent back to England and Ireland to be educated. She wrote regularly to her father and included poems she had written. He was so impressed with them that he had two volumes of these printed privately in Calcutta.

Salkeld met her husband Henry Lyde Salkeld in India, but he was from Cumbria, England. He was an Assistant Commissioner in Assam, and a member of the Indian Civil Service. They were married in 1902. Salkeld spent six years in India with him until his death in 1909 from typhoid fever. She lived for the rest of her life on his Civil Service pension. Widowed at the age of 28, Blanaid returned to Dublin with their two sons and rented a flat at No. 50 Marlborough Road from Count and Countess Plunkett, who owned several properties on this road.

Back in Dublin, Salkeld met Padraig Pearse, Padraic Colum and Thomas MacDonagh at a time that Ireland was striving for its independence from Britain. She joined the Abbey Theatre as an actor and began using the Irish form of her name (Blanaid) from then onwards. Salkeld began her acting life under the stage name of Nell Byrne and was in the Metropolitan Players' version of Ibsen's *Little Eyolf* in 1912. As a member of the Abbey's second company, she played Stella in a dramatisation of the life of Jonathan Swift by Sidney Paternoster in 1913. She was also involved with the Irish Theatre in Hardwick Street, and as an Irish language enthusiast acted in a number of Irish language productions. She had a number of friends in the Irish literary movement, including AE (George Russell) and W.B. Yeats, whose father John Yeats painted her portrait. She was also an early member of Sinn Fein and Cumann na mBan.

Salkeld was one of the early members of the Gaelic League (Conrad na Gaeilge) founded in 1893 by Eóin MacNeill and other enthusiasts of the Irish language and culture. Its first President was Douglas Hyde (1860–1949), who served as President of Ireland (1938–1945). She was a regular attender at AE's Sunday evening soirees, where she would have met the leading literati of the day, and indeed she hosted her own salon for Irish poets and writers at her home at No. 43 Morehampton Road, Donnybrook. Among the regular attenders at her at homes were Patrick Kavanagh and Flann O'Brien. During the 1920s, Salkeld became interested in translation and in the writing of original poetry, which appeared in *The Bell*, the *Dublin Magazine* and *Irish Writing*. Salkeld also contributed numerous book reviews to these magazines and focused in particular on contemporary poetry. She was always keen to promote poetry written by Irish women. Salkeld's first book of poems was published in 1933 (when she was 53 years old) and called *Hello Eternity*. This work was praised by the writer Samuel Beckett (1906–1989) and it was followed by others in 1935 and 1937. However, they were not as well received as her first collection. One of her verse plays, *Scarecrow over the Corn*, was produced some years ago at the Gate Theatre in Dublin. She also wrote for ballet and radio.

The importance of publishers in the dissemination of texts cannot be overemphasised. It has been suggested that the significant role of the individual as an agent of change in the history of books is often overlooked. This would seem to be true in the case of Salkeld and the Gayfield Press, which she founded with her son, the artist Cecil Ffrench Salkeld (1904–1969). Having her own publishing house gave her freedom, and her 1937 book *The Engine is Left Running* was illustrated by her son and published by their own Gayfield Press. There is very little documentation in existence regarding the Gayfield Press, which for many years was considered to be owned solely by her son Cecil French Salkeld. However, in fact, his mother Blanaid was the controlling owner and editor. As has been pointed out recently, 'the business ownership, and consequently financial and editorial power rested with (Blanaid) Salkeld'. It was registered under the name the Gayfield Press on 7 October 1937, and the registration was signed by Florence Salkeld with an address at No. 43 Morehampton Road, Donnybrook, Dublin. Having sole ownership of the Gayfield Press allowed Salkeld to create her own 'literary mark in the publishing industry and augment her reputation as a poet'.

Salkeld promoted her press as a publisher of deluxe editions of Irish writing. Her intention was to specialise in limited editions, fine art productions and handwritten manuscripts for the connoisseur, in addition to ordinary publications. In order to promote the Gayfield Press, Salkeld attended various book fairs to promote Irish writers and Irish books. She often gave talks at book fairs about the book trade and Irish publishing.

The Gayfield Press was successful in that it managed to publish quite a wide variety of texts. As a private press, it could challenge dominant cultures and provide a vital resource that could operate without interference from Church and State. From the Censorship of Publications Act of 1929, the Irish Free State became more conservative and more dominated by the Catholic Church. People such as Salkeld and her fellow writers formed part of a resistance to this act.

Salkeld's Gayfield Press published more books by women writers than any other publishers in Dublin. It published two of her own works, *The Engine is Left Running* (1937) and *Experiment in Error* (1955). Blanaid Salkeld was also the founder of the radical Women Writers Club (1933–1958), which was a literary club for women writers. In fact, out of eight publications from her press, five were by women who were members of her club. Salkeld seems to have had a great desire for her Gayfield Press to remain independent and impartial. On the cover of *Forty North, Fifty West* published in 1938 she states: 'The Gayfield Press published entirely at its own discretion – uninfluenced by fashionable tastes, cliques or coteries. It will continue to bring out limited and illustrated Editions (sic) of special interest.'

In 1956, Salkeld was elected to the Council of the Irish Academy of Letters, which had been founded by W.B. Yeats and George Bernard Shaw in 1932. Its aim was to 'reward publicly literary achievement and to organise writers to oppose literary censorship'. Apart from her writing, Salkeld was interested in ballet and going to art exhibitions. An obituary in the *Irish Times* of 22 December 1958 stated that 'in an age of obscurity and stultification, her excellent poems are well known to a great many people. She had a curious erudition all her own and an eternally fresh outlook on nearly everything. Her patience and friendliness were the talk of her neighbourhood.'

Her granddaughter, Beatrice Behan, wrote in her book *My Life with Brendan Behan* that her grandmother had been an invalid for the last ten years of her life and had thus been unable to attend her wedding. Salkeld died at her home, No. 43 Morehampton Road, Donnybrook on 18 December 1958 and is buried in Glasnevin Cemetery.

Further Reading

Allen, Nicholas, 'Salkeld, Blanaid', in *Dictionary of Irish Biography*, edited by James McGuire and James Quinn, Cambridge University Press, Cambridge.

Lynch, Deirdre, 'The Modernist Presses and the Gayfield Press', *Bibliologia*, www.torrossa.com, 2014.

Obituary, *Irish Times*, 15 October 1958, 22 December 1958.

Shackleton, Sir Ernest (1874–1922)
Antarctic Explorer
35 Marlborough Road, Donnybrook, Dublin 4

Ernest Shackleton was born into an Anglo-Irish family in Kilkea House, Kilkea, Co. Kildare, on 15 February 1874. His father, Henry, was a gentleman farmer, and his mother was Henrietta Letitia (*née* Gavan). When Ernest was 6, his father decided to give up farming and to study Medicine at Trinity College in Dublin. The family therefore moved to the city and lived at No. 35 Marlborough Road, Donnybrook. Shackleton never forgot he was Irish and was very proud of his roots. He was educated by governesses in Ireland until the family moved to London, where his father established a successful medical practice in Sydenham. He spent time in London at Fir Lodge Preparatory School in West Hill, Dulwich, before going on to complete his education at Dulwich College (now an independent day and boarding school) in 1887.

Shackleton was always a great reader from the time he was a child, and this seems to have sparked adventure in him. He left school at 16 to go to sea. He served his apprenticeship on a sailing vessel, and he spent the next four years at sea learning his trade. Over the next few years he took the various examinations and in 1898 became a Master Mariner. When the Boer War broke out in 1899, Shackleton worked on the troopship *Tintagel Castle*. There he met an Army lieutenant with whom he became friendly called Cedric Longstaff, whose father Llewellyn was the main financial backer of the National Antarctic Exhibition organised from London. As a result of this friendship, Shackleton obtained a recommendation to Sir Clements Markham, who was in charge of the expedition. On 17 February 1901, Shackleton received his appointment as a third officer on the expedition's ship *Discovery*.

The *Discovery* expedition of 1901–1903 was led by Robert Falcon Scott, a Royal Navy Commander, and its purpose was scientific and geographical discovery. Shackleton found it difficult to deal with Scott's manner, which was very authoritarian. The *Discovery* departed from London on 31 July 1901 and arrived in the Antarctic on 8 January 1902. Shackleton was chosen by Scott to accompany him and another on the expedition's southern journey, with the aim of attaining the highest possible altitude in the direction of the South Pole. Scott has described their feat as being 'a combination of success and failure'. It was a hazardous journey and the three men suffered from snow blindness, frostbite and scurvy. Shackleton in particular became quite ill, and Scott decided to send him home to recuperate. He spent time in New Zealand first, and then he returned to England via San Francisco and New York.

Back in London after his ordeal in Antarctica, Shackleton found he was in demand as a speaker and in addition he was consulted by the Government about proposals for future expeditions to Antarctica. In 1904, Shackleton became secretary of the Royal Scottish Geographical Society, and in the same year he had an unsuccessful foray into politics. He stood as a liberal Unionist candidate for Dundee, opposed to Irish Home Rule. That year too, he married Emily Dorman, and they had three children: Raymond, Cecily and Edward. In 1907, Shackleton announced he would again attempt to reach the South Pole, and he called his expedition the British Antarctic Expedition, 1907. He carried out great fund-raising for this next trip, and his ship the *Nimrod* left England in August 1907. Scott pressured him before he left England not to base himself in the McMurdo area of Antarctica, which Scott was claiming as his own area for his research. Shackleton tried to base himself and his ship elsewhere in Antarctica, but the icy conditions were unstable, and it was not possible despite his best efforts to set up his base elsewhere. So, he had to return to McMurdo Sound and set up base there in early in 1908.

Shackleton's expedition to reach the South Pole began on 29 October 1908. With his three companions, Frank Wild (1873–1939), Eric Marshall (1879–1963) and Jameson Adams (1880–1952), they set off from their base and reached within 12 miles of the Pole before weather conditions forced them to turn back. However, they discovered the Beardmore Glacier, which was named for Shackleton's patron, Sir William Beardmore (1856–1936), a Scottish industrialist and one of the sponsors of the expedition. The men were also the first to see and travel on the Polar Plateau. They managed to ascend Mount Erebus too, the second highest volcano in Antarctica. The group discovered the approximate location of the south magnetic pole. Their return journey to the McMurdo Sound was a nightmare and was a race against starvation.

Shackleton was greeted on his return to England in 1909 as a hero. He was knighted by King Edward VII and was awarded the gold medal of the Royal Geographical Society and the Livingstone gold medal of the Royal Scottish Geographical Society. The expedition had left Shackleton in great debt and he was unable to meet the financial guarantees he had given to his backers. However, Parliament in England voted him £20,000 to help defray the costs of the expedition, which was most welcome. After his return to London, Shackleton pursued a strenuous schedule of public lectures and social engagements. He published a book called *The Heart of the Antarctic* in London in 1909, to much acclaim. Shackleton was determined to return to Antarctica, however, the war broke out in 1914 and his proposed trip was therefore cancelled. Shackleton served in the Army as officer in charge of supplies for the British forces in the White Sea and Northern Russia until the end of the war.

Shackleton's final expedition was the Trans-Antarctic Expedition 1914–1917. Unfortunately, his ship, the *Endurance,* was beset by pack ice and the crew had to abandon it on 27 October 1915. Shackleton and some of his crew reached Elephant Island on 15 April 1916, but he realised that they were unlikely to be rescued. He set off with a small group of men and it was 10 May 1916 by the time they reached South Georgia. After a harrowing sea journey of seventeen days, they arrived on the west side of the island, and this required them to cross the mountainous interior of the island without specialised mountaineering equipment. They finally reached the whaling station at Storminess on 20 May 1916. The rescue of the men left behind on Elephant Island was foremost in Shackleton's mind, and after three failed attempts he managed to rescue his men. His book *South*, published in 1919, describes the hazards involved in this journey.

Shackleton's final expedition took place in 1922, when he set out again for Antarctica on the *Quest*. However, his health deteriorated on the voyage; he suffered from heart problems and asthma. As a result of a bout of influenza, he died from angina and is buried at the whaling station cemetery at Grytviken on South Georgia, at the request of his wife. A memorial service for Shackleton was held at St Paul's Cathedral on 2 March 1922, and this was attended by King George V and Queen Mary.

During his life, Shackleton received many honours, including an honorary LLD from the University of Glasgow in 1914. He also received a number of foreign orders and decorations. In the Antarctic, the Shackleton Inlet and the Shackleton Ice Shelf were named in his honour. In Canada, one of the Rockies is named Mount Shackleton, and there is another mountain called after him in Greenland.

Further Reading

Alexander, Caroline, *The Endurance: Shackleton's Legendary Antarctic Expedition*, Bloomsbury, London, 1998.

Morrell, Margot and Capparell, Stephanie, *Shackleton's Way: Leadership Lessons from the Great Antarctic Explorer*, Viking, New York, 2001.

Murphy, David, 'Shackleton, Sir Ernest Henry', in *Dictionary of Irish Biography,* edited by James McGuire and James Quinn, Cambridge University Press, Cambridge.

Smyllie, Robert M. (1893–1954)
Editor of the *Irish Times*
23 Pembroke Park, Donnybrook, Dublin 4

Robert 'Bertie' Marie Smyllie was a journalist and editor of the *Irish Times* from 1943–1954. He has been described as one of the most influential editors this newspaper has ever had. He was born on 20 March 1893 in Glasgow, the eldest of five children of Robert Smyllie, a Presbyterian, and Elizabeth Follis, who originally came from Cork. Bertie Smyllie was educated at Sligo Grammar School and spent only two years as an undergraduate at Trinity College. He left and became a tutor to a wealthy American family doing a tour of Europe. He was with them in Germany when the First World War broke out. They were able to return to the United States, but he was travelling on a British passport, so was interned in a German prisoner-of-war camp called Ruhleben, near Berlin. There he read widely and attended many of the organised camp lectures, where he learned about the history and politics of Central Europe. While interned in the camp he also improved his knowledge of German and French.

On applying for a job at the *Irish Times,* when he returned to Ireland, Smyllie's fluency in foreign languages and his knowledge of European affairs made him very employable. The editor of the *Irish Times* at this time was John Edward Healy (1872–1934), who was the longest-serving of its editors, from 1907 to 1934. The *Irish Times* had been founded in 1859 by a retired British Army Major, Laurence E. Knox. The staff reflected the origins of the paper, those being mainly Protestant and belonging to the upper middle classes. With such a background as Smyllie's, he was an obvious choice for the editor to send to Paris to cover the Paris Peace Conference. Among his scoops in Paris was an exclusive interview with the then British Prime Minister, David Lloyd George. On his return to Dublin, he was appointed assistant editor to Healy, who commissioned him to write both general feature articles and leading articles on European affairs.

During the 1920s, Smyllie quickly rose up through the newspaper's hierarchy. He was responsible for the creation in 1927 of the now famous Irishman's Diary, which still appears daily in the *Irish Times*. Smyllie signed this column Quidnunc, as did many of its later writers. Originally the column reflected the

Anglo–Irish view of the growth and development of Irish society in general. It also gently ridiculed some of the efforts of the Government to run the country.

On the death of Healy in 1934, Smyllie became editor. This title carried with it the post of Irish correspondent for *The Times* (London) and the additional salary was welcomed by the new editor since newspaper salaries were, in general, very low. On taking over, Smyllie shifted the emphasis of the paper from dwindling British links to publishing material on purely Irish affairs. He carried out a number of foreign assignments himself on behalf of the paper, and in the 1930s a series of articles about Nazi Germany appeared. Smyllie frequently wrote under the pseudonym Nichevo. His great contribution to this newspaper as editor was to transform this bastion of 'West Britonism' into one of Ireland's most progressive newspapers.

The first five years of Smyllie's editorship appear to have been the most successful. He was an extraordinary looking figure around Dublin, being grossly overweight, and he wore a green sombrero and an overcoat that looked more like a cape. He used his bicycle for getting to work from his home in Pembroke Park, Donnybrook, and carried a typewriter on the handlebars of his bicycle. He often had a half bottle of Scotch hanging out of his pocket as well! In the *Irish Times* office, he was known to sing parts of his editorials to operatic arias. He also grew the nail on his little finger into the shape of a pen nib, similar to John Keats, the poet. His flamboyant personality often obscured the seriousness with which he took responsibility for his job. He also gave a chance to a number of Irish writers, such as Brian O'Nolan, who wrote in both Irish and English, under the pseudonym of Myles na Gopaleen and Flann O'Brien.

Smyllie had no interest in the administrative side of the business but the success of the paper was hindered by its dangerously small circulation. The reduction of the numbers of Protestants in Ireland between 1911 and 1923 made it obvious that if the paper was to survive it would have to remove the idea that it was purely Protestant orientated. During his tenure as editor, Smyllie was responsible for appointing to the *Irish Times* well-known journalists such as Brian Inglis, Jack White, Tony Olden, Seamus Kelly, Cathal O'Shannon and Tony Gray.

Smyllie encountered a number of political challenges during his editorship. For example, during the Spanish Civil War (1936–1939) when Catholic Ireland was enthusiastically pro-Franco, he ensured that articles in his newspaper were balanced and fair. During the 1930s too, he was aware of the forthcoming European crisis and the paper carried a series of news reports and editorial warnings. During the Second World War, Smyllie found himself and the *Irish Times* the target of a new Censorship Board, which led him to have a specific dislike for Frank Aiken, Minister for the Co-ordination of Defensive Measures. During the war years, censorship was very strictly imposed, and that on the

Irish Times was more severe than that imposed on other newspapers, probably because it made no secret of which side of the war it was on.

In the 1940s and '50s The Palace Bar in Fleet Street, close to the old *Irish Times* office in D'Olier Street, became the social home of writers and newsmen, correspondents and compositors of Dublin's three daily papers, under the patronage of Smyllie. Smyllie's 'court' was held almost daily in the Palace Bar and later in the Pearl Bar in Dublin's Fleet Street.

Under Smyllie, the *Irish Times* became a paper that promoted cultural liberalism together with political independence. He was often critical of the Catholic Church, especially during the Dr Noel Browne controversy and the Mother and Child scheme. However, during all of this, he managed to maintain a good relationship with Dr John Charles McQuaid, Archbishop of Dublin, who invited him to dinner once a year to discuss matters of mutual concern.

Over the years, Smyllie's health deteriorated and this may have been the reason he decided to adopt a quieter lifestyle. He left his comfortable home in Pembroke Park and moved to live in Delgany, Co. Wicklow. Since he did not drive a car, he had to depend on public transport, so he was often absent from the *Irish Times* office in the centre of Dublin. Smyllie had married Kathlyn Reid (1895–1974) in 1925, the daughter of a landowner from Meath. They had no family. Smyllie died of heart failure in the Adelaide Hospital in Dublin on 11 September 1954 and was buried in Mount Jerome Cemetery. His widow survived until March 1974.

Further Reading

Gray, Tony, *Mr Smyllie, Sir*, Gill & Macmillan, Dublin, 1964.

Horgan, John, 'Smyllie, Robert Marie', in *Dictionary of Irish Biography*, edited by James McGuire and James Quinn, Cambridge University Press, Cambridge.

Richardson, Caleb Wood, *Smyllie's Ireland*, Indiana University Press, Bloomington, 2019.

Solomons, Estella Frances (1882–1968)
Artist and Portrait Painter
2 Morehampton Road, Donnybrook, Dublin 4

Estella Frances Solomons was born to Maurice E. Solomons and his wife Rosa Jane Solomons (*née* Jacobs) on 2 April 1882 at the family home, No. 32 Waterloo Road. The family were Jewish, and her father was an optician with a practice at No. 19 Nassau Street. Both her parents were involved in the establishment of the Progressive Jewish congregation in Dublin in 1946. Estella was one of four children, of whom Bethel, one of her brothers, became a distinguished obstetrician and Master of the Rotunda Hospital from 1926–1933. He was also a distinguished international rugby player. Estella's mother, Rosa, wrote poetry, and both parents were philanthropists and gave money to a number of good causes in Dublin.

Estella Solomons (known as Stella) was educated locally at Miss Wade's School on Morehampton Road in Donnybrook, and she spent a year in Hamburg before finishing her education at Alexandra College. When she was 16, she enrolled at the Dublin Metropolitan School of Art. She was a talented artist and won many prizes. There she studied under Walter Osborne (1859–1903) and was also taught by William Orpen (1878–1931), whose paintings of Dublin street life made a great impression on her. Among her classmates at the Metropolitan School of Art were other well-known artists such as Mary Swanzy (1882–1978), Eva Hamilton (1876–1960) and William Leach (1881–1968). She spent three years in London, and studied at the Chelsea School of Art. From there she went to Paris and studied at the Académie Collarossi, a highly thought of Paris art school dating from the nineteenth century.

Solomons' visit to the Rembrandt Tercentenary Exhibition in Amsterdam in 1906 made a great impact on her as an artist. About this time she bought an etching press and began contributing to the annual exhibitions of the Royal Hibernian Academy in Dublin, which she continued up to the 1950s. Like her brother, Bethel Solomons, she was a great supporter of the Gaelic and nationalist movement during the early twentieth century. She became active in politics before and during the Irish War of Independence. In 1915, she joined Cuman na mBan in Rathmines, along with her good friend, Kathleen Goodfellow (1891–1980). During their membership they were trained by Phyllis Ryan (1895–1983), later the wife of President Seán T. O'Kelly (1882–1966). In Cuman na mBan they were also taught how to shoot a revolver. Solomons supported the Republican side in the Irish Civil War, and her studio was used regularly as a safe house for volunteers. She began teaching at the Dublin Municipal Technical Schools in the early 1920s and resigned when she refused to take the oath of allegiance to the British Crown. During the 1920s, Solomons was active in her studio in distributing and concealing arms and ammunition for the Republican side. She was also known to hide Republican weapons in the garden of her parents' house in Waterloo Road. Solomons painted many of the members of the Irish Republican party who were on the run, and who stayed in her studio at No. 17 Great Brunswick Street (now Pearse Street). Unfortunately, some of her paintings of the rebels had to be destroyed for fear of the consequences, but a number of them have survived. Hilary Pyle, the distinguished art historian and writer, reproduced those that survived under the title *Estella Solomons: Portraits of Patriots* (1966). Among Solomons' portraits are those of Austin Clarke (1896–1974), Frank Aiken (1898–1983) when he was the IRA Chief of Staff, and Padraic Colum (1881–1972). She also painted Arthur Griffith (1871–1922), Jack B. Yeats (1871–1957), Count Plunkett (1851–1948) and Daryll Figgis (1882–1925). James Stephens (1880–1950), who had a flat just below her studio in Great Brunswick Street, was another person whom she painted. Solomons knew the IRA Commander Ernie O'Malley (1897–1957) and they corresponded while he was recovering from hunger strike in Kilmainham Gaol in 1923.

Solomons exhibited at a number of different venues during her lifetime including the Leinster Gallery, Molesworth Street, at the Dublin Painters Gallery at Mills Hall, and at the Arlington Gallery in London. She also held an exhibition at her Great Brunswick Street Studio in 1926. Many of her exhibitions were dominated by her landscapes. Her prints are also of particular interest as they show the alleyways, byways and parks of Dublin. *The Glamour of Dublin* by D.L. Kelleher has illustrations by Solomons. This book was published originally after the Rising of 1916, but the later edition features eight views of places in Dublin such as the Merchant's Arch and the King's Inns. She also illustrated a book by Padraic Colum called *The Road Round Ireland* (1926). A book called *Leabhar Ultain* was published in 1920, and it featured illustrations by several well-known Irish artists including Solomons, who contributed an etching of 'A Georgian Doorway'. This book, by Katherine McCormack, was a fund-raiser for the St Ultan's Children's Hospital in Charlemont Street founded by two fellow members of Cuman na mBan, Kathleen Lynn and Madeleine Ffrench-Mullen.

After the Treaty, Solomons, who took the Republican side, gave shelter to those on the run and the Free State troops raided her studio frequently. Solomons withdrew from political activities after the Civil War and was elected an Associate Member of the Royal Hibernian Academy in 1925. However, it was not until 1966 that she was elected as an Honorary Member.

From about 1911, Seumas O'Sullivan became part of Solomons life, and in 1926 they married. He was a poet, also known as James Starkey. He was a Methodist, and her family were against her marrying outside her Jewish faith. Out of respect for her parents, they delayed their marriage until after her parents had died. Seumas and Stella appear to have had a very happy marriage. Their Sunday afternoon salons, held at their home in Rathfarnham, were a popular venue for the Dublin literati, which also included artists and critics. A regular attender was George Russell (AE), and Stella frequently accompanied him on his painting trips to Donegal.

Solomon's great friend was Kathleen Goodfellow (1891–1980), who owned a number of properties in Dublin including houses on the Morehampton Road in Donnybrook. The O'Sullivans had a large library of 10,000 volumes but the house in Rathfarnham was damp and they were afraid for the future of their books. Goodfellow, who lived at No. 4 Morehampton Road, needed a tenant for the house next door to her at No. 2. She offered the house to Stella and Seumas at a nominal rent, and so they moved to Donnybrook, where they continued with their literary salons and where Stella frequently painted in the Grove, an area of natural and wild beauty that belonged to Goodfellow. The Grove is now in the care of An Taisce and the Upper Leeson Street Residents Association also contribute to its upkeep.

From 1923, Solomons worked almost full time for her husband and his magazine, the *Dublin Magazine,* of which he was the editor for thirty-five years. This was a monthly Irish literary journal that existed from August 1923 to August 1925 until it ceased publication on O'Sullivan's death in 1958. This magazine played major role in encouraging Irish art and literature from the 1920s. Together with Goodfellow, Solomons worked tirelessly in acquiring advertising revenue for the *Dublin Magazine.* Goodfellow played a substantial and editorial role in this magazine, too, and contributed many articles to the magazine under the pseudonym Michael Scot. Goodfellow was also the primary patron of this publication, with her income coming largely from family property. For more than fifty years, Solomons and Goodfellow were close friends, so it is hardly surprising that Solomons painted her on numerous occasions. One of these portraits is in the National Gallery of Ireland and the other is in the Model and Niland Collection in Sligo – both were bequeathed to these institutions by Goodfellow.

Solomons was one of the outstanding artists of her generation and some of her work can be seen in the Hugh Lane Gallery in Dublin, in the National Gallery of Ireland, in the Irish Jewish Museum in Dublin, the Limerick City Gallery of Art, the Crawford Municipal Art Gallery in Cork and in the Ulster Museum in Belfast. Solomons appears to have been a strong nationalist like her brother, Bethel, and a feminist. Like many artists of her generation, she was proud to be Irish. She hosted many literary evenings at her homes in Rathfarnham and in Morehampton Road in Donnybrook, and was at the centre of Irish cultural life for some fifty years. A number of self-portraits and photographs indicate that she was a woman of outstanding beauty and was also a member of a generation of extraordinary independent Irish women.

Seumas died in 1958, and Solomons painted her last painting, 'The Estuary', in 1962. She died on 2 November 1968 at the age of 86 in her home at No. 2 Morehampton Road, and chose to be buried in Woodtown Cemetery, Rathfarnham, with her Jewish ancestors.

Further Reading

Miller, Liam, *Retrospect: The Work of Seumas O'Sullivan (1879–1958) and Stella Solomons, (1882–1968)*, Dolmen Press, Dublin, 1973.

Pyle, Hilary, *Portraits of Patriots*, Allen Figgis, Dublin, 1966.

Pyle. Hilary, 'Estella Solomons 1882–1968', in *Works from an Artists' Studio*, Crawford Gallery, Cork, 1986.

Starkie, Enid Mary (1897–1970)
Academic and Writer
Melfort, Shrewsbury Road, Ballsbridge, Dublin 4

Enid Mary Starkie was born in 1897 in Killiney, Co. Dublin, into an academic Anglo–Irish family. Her father was the Rt Hon. William Joseph Myles Starkey (1860–1920), a classical scholar and translator of Aristophanes, and her mother was May Caroline Walsh (1871–1961). She was one of six children – four girls and two boys – but one of the boys died as a baby. Her father became President of Queen's College Galway (1897–1899) and for two years the family lived in Galway. In 1899, Enid's father was offered the post of Resident Commissioner of National Education for Ireland under British rule. In her autobiography, Enid recalled the houses in which the family lived during her childhood: Undercliffe (Killiney), Somerset (Blackrock) and Melfort (Shrewsbury Road).

Together with her sisters and brother, Starkie was educated first by governesses, one of whom, Leonie Cora, imbued the children with a great love of music and of everything French. Starkie was then sent to Alexandra School and College in Dublin, along with her three sisters. She was also a pupil at the Royal Irish Academy of Music, and, with her sister Muriel, was one of the winners of the Coulson Exhibitions in 1913. Starkie became an accomplished pianist and at one time considered a musical career. In 1916 she was winning prizes at the Dublin Feis Ceoil along with her sisters, who were also highly talented musicians. One of her sisters, Ida (Chou Chou), became Professor of Cello at the Royal Irish Academy of Music. Her brother was the academic Walter Starkie. He too was a very talented violinist who at one stage led the life of a wandering minstrel. He became Professor of Spanish and Italian at Trinity College Dublin, and an authority on gypsy life. He retired from Trinity to become Head of the British Council in Madrid and a visiting professor at a number of American universities.

In 1916, Starkie won a Scholarship to Somerville College in Oxford, where she studied Modern Languages. She graduated from Oxford with a first-class honours degree in 1921. Her first appointment as a teacher was at a girls school called Lingholt School in Surrey, where she spent two terms, after which she moved to Paris. She won a Gilchrist studentship to the Sorbonne, which allowed her to study for a doctorate on Émile Verhaeren (1855–1916), a Belgium poet who wrote in French. She was awarded a prize by the French Academy for her thesis. Starkie spent two years as an assistant lecturer at the University College of the South West, in Exeter, before being appointed in 1929 to the first Sarah Smithson Lectureship in French literature, at Somerville College, Oxford University. She proved to be an excellent lecturer, popular with undergraduates and as a supervisor of research students. In 1935, she was elected a Fellow and was awarded the first D.Litt. by the Modern Languages Faculty in 1939. In 1946, the university appointed her Reader in French Literature

Starkie quickly established herself as a distinguished scholar in the study of French literature, writing important biographies of Charles Pierre Baudelaire (1933) and Arthur Rimbaud (1938). She wrote more than fifteen books and specialised in French authors of the nineteenth century. Included among her books were a brief study of André Gide, whom she knew personally, which she published in 1954, and another called *Flaubert: The Making of the Master* (published in two volumes), the first volume of which was published in 1967, and the second volume posthumously in 1971. Enid became a great French scholar, well known and highly rated in France as an academic, writer and critic. In 1948, she was created Chevalier of the Légion d'Honneur and in 1958, she became Officer of the Légion d'Honneur. During her life, Starkie also acquired a number of other honours. She was elected to membership of the Irish Academy of Letters (founded by W.B. Yeats and George Bernard Shaw in 1932), and she became a Fellow of the Royal Society of Literature. She received a number of Honorary Doctorates: from Exeter (1960), Trinity College Dublin (1960) and Aix-en-Provence (1967). She was made a CBE (Commander of the Most Excellent Order of the British Empire) in England, in 1965.

In 1941, while she was still young, Starkie published her autobiography, titled *A Lady's Child*. This book describes her childhood and early youth in Dublin where her family was part of the 'Castle Catholics', the Catholic upper middle class, in Edwardian Dublin. The book caused quite a sensation when it was published and was described in a review in the *Irish Times* as 'an unpardonable piece of disloyalty'. Her family was outraged with this book and sought to remove it from the shelves of the main booksellers in Dublin. It was an extraordinarily candid and not very accurate account of her living relatives, and she does not appear to have realised she was hurting her close family members. For a period of time, she became estranged from them as a result of this book. However, she seems to have always retained her love for Ireland and was a frequent visitor to Dublin over the years, to see her family and friends, especially during university holidays.

To many people, Starkie was an eccentric. Her biographer, Joanna Richardson, a former student, described her as 'a small electric figure in scarlet and royal blue, a voluble, flamboyant hummingbird'. Starkie seems to have had a great personality, and was very kind to her undergraduate and postgraduate students. She had great vigour and versatility throughout her life, and a great capacity for her academic work. She travelled widely and was a well-known figure at national and international conferences as a speaker and presenter. She spent time in the United States between 1951 and 1968 as a visiting professor to the Universities of Berkeley, Seattle, Columbia and Virginia. Starkie was very happy in the USA and loved her time at Hollins College in Virginia. This college became the main benefactor of her will, and as a result there is a building there named after her. Starkie loved socialising and meeting people. She was often to be found in the senior common room. She became the Chair of the college wine cellar and had a great knowledge of wines. She attended at all the main formal and informal events at Somerville College and in the university.

At Oxford, Starkie became active in university politics and acquired a reputation as being a kingmaker. She secured an honorary doctorate for André Gide in 1947. She campaigned to have the elected Professor of Poetry in the University to be a practising poet rather than a critic. In the election that followed, Cecil Day-Lewis defeated C.S. Lewis. Starkie also campaigned successfully for the Chair of Poetry for W.H. Auden in 1956 and for Robert Graves (1961) and Edmund Blunden (1966). She applied for this Chair herself in 1968 and finished second to R.B. Fuller (1912–1991).

Starkie had an outstanding career as an academic at Somerville College and Oxford University. However, her one regret was that she was not successful in obtaining a University Professorship at Oxford. In the last few decades of her life, cancer of the lungs was diagnosed. As a result, she resigned from her post as Reader at the university in 1965, and in the same year she was elected an Honorary Fellow. In her last years she suffered much ill health. As a lecturer, researcher, critic and writer, Starkie led a remarkable academic and personal life at the University of Oxford for more than forty years. She died at her home in Walton Street, Oxford, on 20 April 1970 and is buried in Wolvercote Cemetery, Oxford.

Further Reading
Richardson, Johanna, *Enid Starkie*, Macmillan, London, 1973.

Starkie, Enid, *A Lady's Child*, Faber & Faber, London, 1941.

Starkie, Enid, 'Nostalgie de Paris d'une irlandaise', *Aguedal*, May 1943.

Starkie, Walter Fitzwilliam (1894–1976)
Hispanic Scholar and Travel Writer
Melfort, Shrewsbury Road, Ballsbridge, Dublin 4

Walter Starkie was born in Killiney, Co. Dublin, in 1894 to William Joseph Myles Starkie (1860–1920) and his wife, May Caroline Starkie (*née* Walsh, 1871–1961). His father was a distinguished classical scholar, Fellow of Trinity College and translator of Aristophanes. W.J.M. Starkie also held posts as President of Queens College Galway and was the last Resident Commissioner of National Education for Ireland under British rule. Walter's sister was the well-known Cambridge academic Enid Starkie (1897–1970). His family were 'Castle Catholics' and Unionists, and members of the Edwardian Dublin elite.

Like his siblings, Walter was originally educated by German and French governesses, of whom one, Leonie Cora, imbued him and his sisters with a love of music and everything French. He attended Avravon School in Wicklow before going on to Strangeways School, a private school at Nos 74–75 St Stephen's Green, where he remained briefly. Starkie developed asthma as a child, which affected his attendance at school. His father had been a pupil at Shrewsbury in Shropshire, so it was hardly surprising when he decided to send his son to the same public school. Starkie studied the violin at the Royal Irish Academy of Music, winning prizes at the Dublin Feis Ceoil in 1913. He also won a Vandelaer Academy violin scholarship in 1913. He would have liked to pursue a career in music, but his father wanted him to study classics and become a classical scholar like himself. Starkie was an extremely talented violinist and he continued to play all his life. He entered Trinity College Dublin in 1913 where he studied the Classics, History and Political Science. He proved to be an excellent student, becoming a Scholar of Trinity in 1913. He graduated with first-class honours in 1917.

With the advent of the First World War, Starkie endeavoured to enlist as a volunteer but was rejected due to his chronic asthmatic condition. He worked briefly in London as a civil servant in the Colonial Office, moving on from there to work as a volunteer with the YMCA in Italy from 1917–1919 and carrying out humanitarian work. It was in Italy that he met his future wife, Italia Augusta Porchietti, an Italian Red Cross nurse and amateur opera singer, whom he married in 1921. They had two children, Landi and Alma, and the family spent their summer in holidays in Italy. It was while he was in Italy in 1929 that he decided to travel with his violin in central Europe and this resulted in his book *Raggle Taggle*, published in 1933. He also travelled all around Spain as a type of wandering minstrel and an account of his travels there were recorded in *Spanish Raggle-Taggle* (1934), *The Road to Santiago* (1957) and *Don Gypsy* (1936). Starkie was also an active translator and editor of the major Spanish authors.

In 1920, Starkie was appointed lecturer in Romance Languages at Trinity College. He carried out an extensive range of lectures in Trinity and began publishing in academic journals. In 1923, he applied for membership of the Royal Irish Academy and was accepted. Starkie became a Fellow of Trinity College in 1924 and Professor of Spanish and Lecturer in Italian from 1926–1947. During his period in Trinity, one of his students was the distinguished writer Samuel Beckett (1906–1989). Starkie joined the board of the Abbey Theatre in 1927 at the request of Lady Gregory and W.B. Yeats, and remained a Director until 1942. Starkie was a Catholic, so his presence brought ecumenical balance to the board. He voted in favour of the theatre producing *The Silver Tassie* by Seán O'Casey in 1927, which was rejected. As a member of the board, he was tasked to inform Denis Johnston that his play Shadowdance had been rejected. Starkie wrote on the title page of this play 'The Old Lady Says No' (referring to Lady Gregory) and in time Johnston gave the play this title and the Gate Theatre staged it under its new name! Starkie went on to join the board of the Gate Theatre and served there for a number of years.

At the beginning of the Second World War, the British Council decided to send a Catholic to Spain as its first representative there and Starkie was chosen to fill this post because of his religion. During his time in Spain he became familiar with all the major Spanish and political figures of the 1930s and '40s. From 1940 to 1954, Starkie was Director of the British Institute in Madrid and acted as the British Council representative in Spain. The Institute was founded with the objective of strengthening cultural ties between Great Britain and Spain. Walter became actively involved in the day-to-day running of the Institute. As well as founding the British Institute in Madrid, Starkie also opened branches in Barcelona, Bilbao, Seville and Valencia. With support from the British Council, the Institute offered classes in English, together with lectures and exhibitions. As a result, Starkie became a leading figure in the arts and cultural life in Madrid. During his time in Spain he became familiar with all the major Spanish and British political figures of the 1930s and '40s. He was a *bon viveur* and as a result he had a wide circle of friends and acquaintances. On any evening, distinguished writers, poets and actors (including Leslie Howard) were to be found giving lectures at the British Institute in Madrid. Starkie had resigned his Chair in Trinity College and his Fellowship in 1947, which meant that his pension when he came to retire was very limited. While in Madrid, from 1947–1956 he was also Professor of Comparative Literature at the University of Madrid.

During his time in Madrid, Starkie was an invited lecturer at American universities such as the University of Texas (Austin), New York University, the University of Kansas and the University of Colorado. When he retired from the British Institute in Madrid, he became Professor in Residence in Los Angeles at the University of California (UCLA) for almost ten years between 1961 and 1970. In 1974, the Board of Trinity College gave Starkie a visiting professorship for a term. Starkie and Italia retired to Madrid in 1970. Throughout his life he was acknowledged as a literary scholar of some note and a wonderful musician. He received many honours, including his Fellowship from Trinity College, his DLitt, Fellow of the Royal Society of Arts, Fellow of the Royal Society of Literature and corresponding member of the Spanish Academy. In Spain he became a Knight of the Order of King Alfonso XII, and Commander of the Order of Isabel the Catholic, and from England he received a CBE (Commander of the British Empire). He died in Madrid in November 1976 aged 82 and is buried there. Italia died six months later.

Further Reading

Hurtley, Jacqueline, *Walter Starkie: An Odyssey,* Four Courts Press, Dublin, 2013.

Segara, Eda, 'Starkie, Walter', in *Dictionary of Irish Biography*, edited by James McGuire and James Quinn, Cambridge University Press, Cambridge.

Whiston, James, 'Walter Fitzwilliam Starkie', in *Oxford Dictionary of National Biography*, Oxford University Press, Oxford.

Travers, Pamela L. (1899–1996) Writer

69 Upper Leeson Street, Dublin 4

Helen Lyndon Goff Born was born in Maryborough, Queensland, to Travers Goff and his wife, Margaret, on 9 August 1899. Later, she changed her name to Pamela Lyndon Travers, and she wrote under the name P.L. Travers. Her father was of Irish descent and he worked as a bank manager before he was demoted to a clerk due to chronic alcoholism. He died in his early 40s, leaving the family more or less destitute, as her mother had also lost most of her inheritance when the Queensland National Bank became insolvent. Margaret was of Irish and Scottish descent and was a sister of a former premier of Queensland. Fortunately, her mother had a great aunt, Helen

Morehead, who was wealthy and looked after the family. She lived in Woollahara, Sydney, and the Goff family moved there. In childhood, Helen loved fairy tales and animals. At the age of 10, she appeared on the stage in a professional production of *A Midsummer Night's Dream*. She read widely as a child, including such advanced works as Gibbon's *The Decline and Fall of the Roman Empire*. She began writing as a teenager and published with some degree of success. On leaving school, she worked for a short time as a secretary in a cashier's office, which she eventually left, and she became an actress and toured New South Wales with a Shakespearian company.

By 1924, Helen had some of her poetry published and she also worked as a journalist. In that same year she sailed to England to visit relatives. She remained on in London and started working as a correspondent for some of the Australian newspapers. For example, she turned the voyage from Australia to England into several travel articles that sold to Australian publications. She also sent articles about the arts back to Australia and New Zealand. In England she became very conscious of her Irish background, and in 1925 she contacted the Irish poet AE (George Russell, 1867–1935) in Dublin, whose work she was familiar with. He was the editor of a leading literary journal, the *Irish Statesman*, the paper of the Irish Dominion League. She sent one of her poems to AE and included a stamped self-addressed envelope for his approval – he published it straight away and sent her back £2 in her self-addressed envelope! AE also extended an invitation to Travers in London to visit him either in his office, or at his home in Rathgar in Dublin, where his Sunday evening soirees with leading writers and artists were a notable feature of Dublin literary life. AE was also a mystic and a founder member of the Theosophical Society of Ireland. He became a close friend of Travers, a friendship that lasted until his death in 1935. When she travelled to Dublin in 1925 to meet him, he introduced her to William Butler Yeats, the Irish poet and winner of the Nobel Prize in Literature. AE also introduced Travers to the study of spiritualism, theosophy and other types of mysticism, which continued to be great interest to her throughout her life. She later became a disciple of the famed spiritual guru, George Gurdjieff (1877–1949).

It was AE who introduced Travers to Madge Burnand, the daughter of one of his friends, Sir Francis Burnand (1836–1917), a playwright and a former editor of *Punch* magazine. The two women became very close friends, sharing flats in London and then a thatched cottage near Mayfield in East Sussex. It was in 1933 that Pamela Lyndon Travers first adopted the pen name P.L. Travers and she began the first of her eight *Mary Poppins* books while living in Sussex. This was her first great literary success. *Mary Poppins* was based on her formidable aunt, Helen Morehead, who had looked after the children and their mother when their father died. Like Mary Poppins, her aunt was 'bossy and stern'. Her first book was called simply *Mary Poppins* and was about a governess with magic powers who used a parrot-head umbrella as her means of transport. She is blown by the wind to No. 17 Cherry Tree Lane, London, and into the Banks' household to look after their children. The books describe the fraught relationships between the children and their parents through 'a combination of mythological allusion and biting social critique'. This book was an immediate international success. More books followed with *Mary Poppins Comes Back* (1935), *Mary Poppins Opens the Door* (1943), *Mary Poppins in the Park* (1952), *Mary Poppins in Cherry Tree Lane* (1982) and *Mary Poppins and the House Next door* (1988). There were two additional books: *Mary Poppins from A to Z* (1962), which was later translated into Latin, and *Mary Poppins in the Kitchen* (1975).

The first Mary Poppins book was the basis for a musical film called *Mary Poppins* (1964). The film starred Julie Andrews as Mary Poppins and Dick van Dyke as her best friend, Bert. Travers had a very difficult business relationship with Walt Disney, who had purchased the rights from her in 1960. It took

Disney almost fifteen years to acquire the rights, and she was not happy with this first screen version of *Mary Poppins*, although the Disney adaptation did make her quite wealthy. In 1965, the film won five Oscars, including Best Actress for Julie Andrews, Best Music and Best Song for the catchy tune *Chim Chim Cher-ee*. Travers had made every effort to ensure that her work was faithfully translated to the screen, and a fictionalised version of this became a film called *Saving Mr Banks* in 2013, starring Emma Thompson as Travers. She eventually sanctioned a stage musical version of *Mary Poppins* written by Julian Fellows, which debuted in Bristol in 2004, after her death. A follow-up to the original film called *Mary Poppins Returns* was released in 2018 with Emily Blunt as *Mary Poppins*. This version was fifty-four years after *Mary Poppins* and it set a record as the longest gap between a live action movie and its sequel.

Due to her years of friendship with AE, and about ten years after she first visited Dublin, Travers decided to adopt a young Irish boy called Camillus, whom she brought up as her own. He was a grandchild of Joseph Hone (1882–1959), one of W.B. Yeats's biographers, who was bringing up his seven grandchildren with his wife. Camillus was a twin, but Travers refused to take his brother, so the boys were separated. Camillus was brought up by Travers in London as her own, and they also spent time in the United States when she was a writer in residence at Smith and Radcliffe Colleges. Many years later, when he was 17, Camillus learned he was adopted when his twin, Anthony Hone, came to London and knocked on the door of the Travers family home in Chelsea. Travers refused to allow them to meet, and following an argument with her, Camillus went looking for his twin and found him.

In the late 1960s, Travers decided to relocate to Dublin, and she lived at No. 69 Upper Leeson Street, which had once been her father's home. She continued to write for both children and adults. The house is still in existence and has a plaque commemorating Travers on the wall outside the hall door. After spending a good deal of time in the United States and also owning a house in London, Travers decided to sell the Dublin house and spend the rest of her life in London. She never married, though she is known to have had close relationships with both men and women. In 1977, Travers received an OBE in the New Year's Honours List. She lived out her life in London, where she died on 23 April 1996 aged 96 and is buried in St Mary's Churchyard, Twickenham.

Further Reading

Guppy, Shusha and Vallance, Tom, obituary P.L. Travers, *Independent*, 25 April 1996.

Lawson, Valerie, *Mary Poppins, She Wrote*, Simon & Schuster, New York, 2013.

Travers, P.L., Illustrated by Mary Shepherd, *Mary Poppins*, Harcourt Brace, New York, 1962.

Trollope, Anthony (1815–1882)
Writer and Novelist

5 Seaview Terrace, Donnybrook, Dublin 4

Anthony Trollope was born on 24 April 1815 at No. 16 Keppel Street, Russell Square, London, to Thomas Anthony Trollope (1774–1835) and his wife, Frances (Fanny) *née* Milton (1779–1863). His father was a practising barrister in London but bought a farm in Harrow to augment his salary and to enable his sons to attend Harrow School. His father planned ultimately for his sons to attend Winchester College, his own alma mater. Anthony was unhappy at Harrow and then spent time at a private school at Sunbury, which was not a success either. In 1827 he became a pupil at Winchester College, where again he was very unhappy. His father had major financial problems and failed to pay his son's fees at Winchester and in 1830 he withdrew him from the school. During this time, his mother, Fanny, spent four years in America and in 1832 she published a book called *Domestic Manners of the Americans*, which provided additional income for the family. Unfortunately, by 1834 the family's finances had worsened and his father fled to Brussels to avoid being arrested for outstanding debts. The family followed soon afterwards, and they settled in Bruges, where they remained for some time.

Through his mother's family connections, Trollope secured a clerkship in the office of the secretary at the London postal headquarters. The beginning of Trollope's working life was not a success – he was never on time for work and the quality of his work was unsatisfactory. His pay was sometimes docked, and there was talk of dismissing him. Like his father, he ran into financial problems and even fell into the hands of a money lender. It is hardly surprising that when he began to write money and indebtedness played a prominent role in his early fiction. In 1841, after working for seven years in the English Post Office, he decided to apply for the post of assistant or clerk to a surveyor in Ireland. His application was successful, and he always claimed that moving to Ireland changed his life.

Like many Englishmen, Trollope did not know much about Ireland when he accepted the Post Office appointment. He accepted the post on offer with alacrity, and his superiors in London were delighted to have it filled. His initial posting was to Banagher, then in King's County (now Offaly). This post meant that he had to travel around the country, inspecting the accounts of the various postmasters throughout Ireland. This new post in Ireland gave him a higher social standing than if he had remained in England. He very quickly moved through provincial society, and he took up fox hunting and joined the order of Freemasons. He loved hunting, and it became a great passion for him until he was forced to give it up by old age. Living in Ireland, he found it difficult to understand that he could socialise with Protestants and Catholics, but not with both, something he ignored.

Trollope had hardly been in Ireland a year when he met Rose Heseltine (1820–1917), daughter of Edward Heseltine, a Yorkshire banker. They were married in Yorkshire on 11 June 1844. Very little is known about Rose, who actually outlived her husband by thirty-five years. Initially the Trollopes lived at Clonmel, Co. Tipperary, and then in Mallow, Co. Cork. Their two sons were born in Clonmel. It was while living in Ireland that his literary talent began to emerge. His early writings were Irish, and over the years he returned to Irish subjects from time to time. During his engagement in 1843, he began his first novel, *The Macdermots of Ballycloran* (1847), which is a tale of seduction, conspiracy and murder. It was published in London when Trollope was almost 32 years old. His second novel, *The Kellys and the O'Kellys* (1848) was also set in Ireland. This was a major portrait of pre-famine Ireland. Trollope lived in Ireland for twenty years, and his Irish novels introduced Irish characters and issues into his political novels. His interest in Ireland never seems to have waned, and it was the setting for his last, unfinished, novel, *The Landleaguers*.

In 1851, Trollope was recalled to England on loan to help expand the rural postal service in the west of England. He also visited the Channel Islands, and he took the idea of roadside letter boxes from France. He was responsible therefore, for introducing roadside letter boxes (pillar boxes) to England. The first post boxes were erected in 1852, and very shortly afterwards they spread throughout Britain. Shortly afterwards, Trollope was recalled to Ireland as an acting surveyor and in 1854 he became surveyor for the north of Ireland. It was there that he completed his first Barchester novel, *The Warden* (1855). Six of his novels that constitute *The Chronicles of Barsestshire* are set in a fictitious

English county and its cathedral town of Barchester. The novels are about the interactions of the clergy and the gentry of the area, together with the political and social manoeuvrings that take place between them. Of the six novels, the second in the series, *Barchester Towers,* is probably the best known. Trollope is also well known for his *Palliser* novels. *Can You Forgive Her?, Phineas Finn, Phineas Redux* and *The Prime Minister* are considered by Trollope to be the four novels that constitute the Palliser series.

Trollope sought permission to live in Dublin rather than in the country and he took a house at No. 5 Seaview Terrace, in Donnybrook, in 1855. Designed by the Irish architect John Semple (1801–1882), this small terrace of Georgian townhouses dates to 1830. All of the six houses on the terrace were built to the same design. It was in this house that he wrote *Barchester Towers* (1858) and his breakthrough novel, *Doctor Thorne* (1858). Soon after this, the Trollopes returned to live in England permanently. He held the post of Post Office surveyor of the eastern district, and the family moved to live at Waltham Cross, 12 miles north of London.

Trollope's novel *Framley Parsonage* (1860–1861) was published in monthly instalments in the *Cornhill Magazine* edited by William Makepeace Thackeray (1811–1863). It proved enormously popular and helped to establish Trollope's reputation as a well-known novelist. His connection with this magazine served also to introduce him to the literary world in England. The magazine's publisher was George Murray Smith (1824–1921), at whose dinner parties Trollope attended. As an indication of his increased social status, Trollope became a member of the Cosmopolitan Club in London in 1861, and the following year a member of the Garrick Club. Then, in 1864, he was elected to membership of the Athenaeum Club. Trollope resigned from his post in the Post Office in 1867 and lived from then onwards on his investments. He decided to go into politics and contested the East Yorkshire borough of Beverley as a conservative liberal in 1868, but was defeated. Beverley was notorious for rigged elections and after this particular one the borough was disenfranchised.

Trollope was always proud of his Barchester and Palliser novels. His output as a novelist was startling – he wrote forty-seven novels and five volumes of collected short stories, together with a number of other stories. He wrote travel books as he was an indefatigable traveller. In 1873, after travelling for two years to Australia and New Zealand, he moved back to London to No. 39 Montagu Square. In 1880, Trollope, who was always fond of rural life, moved with his wife, Rose, to South Harting in Sussex on the border of Hampshire.

Trollope had a wonderful work ethic and rose at 5 a.m. every morning to write. During his time in Ireland he used the many train journeys to write en route. The novels are in great contrast to the writer himself, who was described as 'bluff, loud, stormy and contentious, neither a brilliant talker not a good speaker'. Trollope's health deteriorated in the 1880s and he had a stroke on 3 November 1882. This left his right side paralysed and his speech was greatly affected. He died in a nursing home in London on 6 December 1882 and is buried in All Souls Cemetery, Kensal Green.

Further Reading

Glendinning, Victoria, *Trollope*, Pimlico, London, 2002.

Snow, C.P., *Trollope*, House of Stratus, London, 2001.

Trollope, Anthony, et al., *Autobiography*, OUP, new edition, Oxford, 2008.

Whitaker, Thomas Kenneth (Ken) (1916–2017) Economist and Civil Servant
148 Stillorgan Road, Donnybrook, Dublin 4

Thomas Kenneth (Ken) Whitaker was born in Rostrevor, Co. Down, on 8 December 1916, the son of Edward Whitaker, assistant manager of a linen mill called Forestbrook. His father was a member of the Church of Ireland, and his mother was Jane O'Connor, a Catholic who came from Coolmeen, Co. Clare. In 1922, the family moved to Drogheda, Co. Louth, where his father took up a position with the Greenmount and Boyne Mill. Ken Whitaker was educated at the local Christian Brothers School in Drogheda, and he obtained top marks in his leaving certificate examination.

Limited family resources meant that Ken did not attend university immediately after leaving school. He applied for the Irish Civil Service and took the examination for clerical officer. He obtained first place in this examination and was posted initially to the Civil Service Commission, where he continued to study part time. After four years, he became a junior administrative officer in the Department of Finance.

Whitaker had a keen interest in economics and maths as a civil servant, and he studied part time for a degree in Maths, Celtic Studies and Latin from London University. He obtained an Honours BA in Economics in 1941, followed by an MSc in 1952. He excelled at his work in the civil service, and was very quickly identified by a number of different Government Ministers as a high flyer. In 1956, at the early age of 39, Whitaker was appointed Secretary of the Department of Finance, over the heads of more senior civil servants. From 1932, a Fianna Fáil Government led by Éamon de Valera introduced a protectionist policy for this country, with tariffs introduced for a wide range of imported goods, most of which came from Britain. The Government considered this to be necessary to develop native industries, so the country would no longer be dependent on Britain. Ireland in the 1950s was in economic decline, with the scale of emigration at an all-time high. Between 1951 and 1956, almost 200,000 people left the country. The decision to abandon protectionism and move to a more open economy was one of the most strategic and important developments in modern Irish history. This was spearheaded by Whitaker as Secretary to the Department of Finance. It came about against the backdrop of a decade of profound crisis, which led many to question the viability of the Irish state.

Whitaker, as Secretary to the Department of Finance, firmly believed that free trade with increased competition was the way forward for Ireland. He also believed that Ireland needed to change from being an agricultural country to one of industry and services. He placed a note on the desk of the then Minister for Finance pointing out to him the very poor state of the economy. He told the Government that unless Ireland opened up to foreign investment and industrial development and ended its dependence on agriculture, the country might be reapplying for admission to the United Kingdom! Whitaker believed that the Government should borrow abroad to finance productive investment.

Whitaker worked with a team within the Department of Finance to produce a paper called *The Irish Economy*, setting out the challenges for the Government of the day. As a result of this paper, the Government gave the go ahead to join the International Monetary Fund and the World Bank. His team within the Department of Finance then began working on a white paper called 'Programme for Economic Expansion', which was accepted as Government policy going forward. An earlier version was known as the Grey Book from its cover, and it named Whitaker as the author – it was very unusual to have a civil servant named as the author of a Government report.

The immediate target of the Whitaker Report was the abolition of a policy of protectionism. Instead, the country began moving towards competition and an increasingly outward export focus. In 1961, Ireland applied to join what was then the new European Economic Community (EEC). Whitaker led a group from the Irish Government to visit the six member states. He reported back to the Government that Irish neutrality and the economic state of Ireland at that time could provide obstacles to full membership of the EEC. He advised the Government of the day to wait awhile before applying for membership again. This delay in obtaining membership was offset in 1965 with a bilateral trade agreement with the United Kingdom known as the first Anglo–Irish Free Trade Agreement. Again, Whitaker led the team of civil servants who negotiated with the UK over a six-month period of hard bargaining. The importance of this first Anglo–Irish Trade agreement for Irish exports cannot be overemphasised, especially during the years prior to Ireland's membership of the EEC. On 1 January 1973, the Republic of Ireland joined the EEC, now known as the European Union (EU). This had a tremendous impact on the growth and development of the country. For example, Irish farmers were able to establish their own markets and to decide prices for their own products. The improvements in Irish roads and the development of communication technologies are due to finance made available by the EU.

Whitaker always retained a tremendous interest in the north of Ireland where he was born. As Secretary of a Government department, he continued to maintain high level contacts with the Government of Northern Ireland. He was responsible for arranging visits by Séan Lemass and Jack Lynch to Stormont. He also maintained an interest in the civil rights movement in the North and urged more co-operation in cross-border projects. Whitaker was one of the founders of the British Irish Association, which annually brings together major speakers from both Ireland and the United Kingdom.

Outside the Department of Finance, Whitaker also had great impact on the various other developments taking place in Ireland in the 1970s. He resigned from the Department of Finance to take up the role of Governor of the Central Bank of Ireland in 1969, a post he held until 1977. Although no longer in the Department of Finance, Whitaker remained a policy advisor to Jack Lynch on Northern Ireland. He also worked with the Ford Foundation to acquire funding to create the Economic and Social Research Institute in 1960, and he was President of this organisation for more than fifteen years. He also served as President of the Statistical and Social Inquiry Society from 1969–1971, having already been secretary to this society. When Jack Lynch took over as Taoiseach again in 1977, he appointed Whitaker to the Irish Seanad, where he sat as an independent. He was appointed for a second term to the Seanad by Garret FitzGerald in 1981. Fitzgerald also appointed him to chair a Committee of Inquiry into the Irish penal system. He also chaired a parole board or sentence review for a number of years.

Whittaker was as busy as ever during his retirement. He served as Chancellor of the National University of Ireland between 1976 and 1996 and he promoted many reforms that led to the autonomy of the three constituent colleges and St Patrick's College, Maynooth. He was elected President of the Royal Irish Academy and served there in 1985–1987. President Mary Robinson appointed Whitaker to the Council of State in 1991. He always had a great love for the Irish language and his family spoke it at home. A seminal collection of Irish poetry edited by Professor Seán Ó Tuama and Thomas Kinsella, *An Duanaire: Poems of the Dispossessed 1600–1900*, was dedicated to Whitaker in 1981.

Whitaker served as the first Chairman of the Scholarship Board of the O'Reilly Foundation, and was the first Chairman of the Agency for Personal Service Overseas (APSO). He was the first Irish person to receive the Order of Commandeur de la Légion d'Honneur, the highest French Order of Merit. Honorary doctorates were conferred on Whitaker by the National University of Ireland, Trinity College, Queen's University, University of Ulster, Dublin City University and London University.

Whittaker was married twice. His first wife, Nora Fogarty, was a fellow civil servant, with whom he had six children. She pre-deceased him in 1994 and he married Mary Moore in 2005, who also pre-deceased him in 2008. In 2002, Whitaker had been voted Irishman of the Twentieth Century by RTÉ viewers and a year later received the ESB/Rehab Greatest Living Irish Person award. Dundalk Institute of Technology named a building in his honour in 2001, and in 2005 Whitaker Square, a development in the docklands, was also named in his honour. He was conferred with an Honorary Fellowship of the Institute of Banking in 2014, and the institute created an annual T.K. Whitaker Scholarship in his name. On 8 December 2016, Whitaker celebrated his 100th birthday and a month later, on 9 January 2017, he died. He is buried in Shanganagh Cemetery, Shankhill, Co. Dublin.

Further Reading

Boland, Vincent, 'Thomas Kenneth Whitaker, Irish Civil Servant 1916–2017', *Financial Times*, 10 January 2017.

Chambers, Anne, *T.K. Whitaker: Portrait of a Patriot*, Doubleday, Dublin, 2015.

Obituary, 'The architect of modern Ireland: Ken Whitaker', *Irish Times*, 11 January 2017.

Woods, Mary (Mollie) Flannery (1875–1954) Republican Activist

St Enda's, 131 Morehampton Road, Donnybrook, Dublin 4

Mary (or Mollie) was born in 1875 to James Flannery and his wife, Bridget (*née* Gallagher), in Co. Sligo. She grew up about 5 miles from Ballaghadarreen, where she attended primary school. Her family was very nationalistic, and Mary remained a nationalist and Republican all her life. As a child, she attended Land League meetings with her family and friends. Her brothers were active politically, and she recalls them returning home from political meetings with kettledrums and gold sashes. She also says she witnessed a number of evictions when she was a child. When she finished school, she worked as a monitor in her old primary school, and later, she spent three years teaching the children of the family of a Mr P.J. Murray in Galway. Then she moved to a medical family in Dublin in Fitzwilliam Square. She travelled with the family of Surgeon-General Thomas O'Farrell (1843–1917) to Malta, where he held a senior medical appointment.

Mary Flannery remained in Malta for a year, and then came home in 1901 to marry Andrew Woods of Donnybrook, whom she had known previously. From a young age, Mary had been writing stories and poems, which were published in the columns of *The Freeman's Journal*. During her time in Malta, Mary and Andrew had kept up regular correspondence and he came to Liverpool to meet her on her return. Andrew was twenty years her junior, but despite this age gap, they were married in February 1901. Her sister, Bridget, also joined the Woods family by marrying Andrew's brother, Bernard.

Andrew Woods' father was a dairyman and builder, who had built a number of houses in Eglington Terrace in Donnybrook. He was also the owner of the grounds where the Ever Ready Garage was later built. Mary and Andrew began their married life in No. 9 Eglinton Terrace, which was owned by his father. In 1918, Andrew purchased No. 131 Morehampton Road. The house was named St Enda's, in honour of Padraig Pearse's school. The Woods family were always great admirers of Pearse. The family home became a hotbed of Republican activity for many years. Mary Woods was a lifelong Republican, and was responsible for hiding men and arms in the family home, as well as holding official meetings of members of the movement there.

Early in their married life, Andrew and Mary Woods joined the Dublin branch of the Irish Literary Society, which had been established in London in 1892. This society is still in existence. From time to time members of the society read papers or gave talks to other members. Woods read a paper to the Society on 'Vanishing Connacht', which was also published in the *Sligo Champion* on 10 May 1919. She later became a Council member of this Society. Both Woods were also members of the Ancient Order of Hibernians, an Irish Catholic fraternal organisation. Mary became a member of the Ladies Auxiliary section of the AOH and worked with this group in helping the poor in Dublin by buying them materials and clothing.

The Woods family was staunchly Republican, and both Mary and Andrew took part in anti-recruiting demonstrations in Woodenbridge in Wicklow in 1914, where John Redmond, leader of the Irish Parliamentary Party, called on members of the Irish Volunteers to join the British Army. Mary became friendly with Mrs Batt O'Connor (whose husband was a well-known builder and politician). It was through Mrs. O'Connor's influence, that Mary joined Cumann na mBan in 1916. Mary always regretted that she was not active in the 1916 Rising. As a Republican activist, she was a friend of Michael Collins, Cathal Brugha and Liam Mellows. She was also a close friend of Countess Markievicz, Maud Gonne McBride and Charlotte Despard. She also joined the Volunteers and was active in both organisations, helping with bill posting, finding safe houses for those on the run and feeding, clothing and housing them. She also looked after Irish prisoners returning to Dublin from English jails.

Woods and her husband had five children; three boys and two girls. They were all brought up to be very nationalistic. She sent her daughters to Louise Gavan Duffy's all-Irish school, and one of her sons, Tony, attended Pearse's school St Enda's, which began in Oakley Road in Ranelagh. The entire Woods family were involved in the fight for Irish freedom. Tony was imprisoned in Kilmainham at the age of 16, and their daughters were also involved in the struggle. Tony was in the Four Courts during the Civil War.

The Woods house on Morehampton Road was the headquarters for two years for Liam Mellows (1892–1922), Irish Republican and Sinn Fein politician. Mary was his assistant when he was Director of Purchases for the IRA, and she was actively involved in acquiring arms. The Woods home was therefore a major centre of Irish nationalistic activities in the early part of the twentieth century. Andrew Woods was more of a parliamentarian, but he supported his wife in her Republican activities. In fact, it was Andrew who helped Éamon de Valera to escape across the border to Northern Ireland in 1919. There was always a cache of arms hidden in their home and the house was raided frequently by British forces in the War of Independence, and during the Civil War by pro-Treaty forces.

Prior to the Civil War, Woods was very friendly with Michael Collins, and she was involved in buying several safe houses for him including No. 17 Harcourt Terrace, which he used regularly when he was on the run. According to her own testimony for the Bureau of Military History, Woods opposed the 1921 Anglo–Irish Treaty. She continued to be politically active after the Treaty, and during the Civil War she spent her time moving guns around Dublin, driving IRA men around the city, carrying dispatches, or acting as a centre of communication.

Anti-imperialism was a central part of Irish nationalism in the 1920s and '30s. Irish anti-imperialistic views focused on similarities between England's activities in its colonies and their activities in Ireland. Woods, along with Maude Gonne McBride and Charlotte Despard, became a founding member of the Indian–Ireland Independence League and was heavily involved in it. It supported the Indian cause for Home Rule. Woods used her nationalistic connections and anti-imperialist leanings to make contact with and host nationalistic Indian men.

Eileen Woods, a daughter of Andrew and Mary, met and later married an Indian TCD medical student, Tripura Dey. The two families met up in the early 1930s, but the couple did not marry until 1936. This close association may be why Woods became active politically with the Indian nationalist movement. In 1931, Woods met Mahatma Gandhi in London and invited him to visit her in Dublin, and he agreed to do so. In the event, the visit did not take place as he had to return to India unexpectedly.

The boycott of British goods campaign was a joint venture by people in both Ireland and India. This boycott coincided with targeting of British goods organised by Cumann na mBan and other Republican organisations.

The Woods family was so highly thought of that when Andrew Woods died in 1929, de Valera was one of the pallbearers at his funeral from the Church of the Sacred Heart, Donnybrook. Mary lived on until 1954. Full military honours were accorded to her at her funeral from the Church of the Sacred Heart, Donnybrook. She is buried in Glencullen Cemetery.

Further Reading

Bureau of Military History, *Memories of the Period 1895–1924*, witness statement by Mrs Mary Flannery Woods.

Joy, Marie Therese, *A History of a House: 131 Morehampton Road*, Private Printing, Dublin.

O'Malley, Kate, 'Irish Women Activists and the Struggle for Indian Independence', *History Ireland* 26 (2), 2018, pp.46–49.

Boston College, Flannery Woods's Papers 1897–1952.

Yeats, Jack B. (1871–1957) Artist

61 Marlborough Road, Donnybrook, Dublin 4

Jack B. Yeats was born in London on 29 August 1871 at 23 Fitzroy Road to the artist John Butler Yeats (1839–1922) and his wife, Susan Yeats (*née* Pollexfen). He was their fifth child and their youngest son. He was the brother of the well-known poet, William Butler Yeats (1865–1939). Theirs was a Church of Ireland family, who originally owned land in Thomastown, Co. Kilkenny. The family settled in Dublin in the middle of the nineteenth century. His mother's family, on the other hand, were a wealthy merchant family in Sligo in the milling and shipping business. Jack B. Yeats has been described as the most important Irish artist of the twentieth century.

Jack B. Yeats spent a great deal of his childhood in Sligo. His father John Butler Yeats was trained as a barrister but decided to become an artist, and as a result there was very little money in the family. Due to the family's financial situation, his wife Susan and their children spent a good deal of time with her family in Sligo. As a child, Jack B. Yeats loved Sligo and often travelled on his grandfather's ships between Liverpool and Sligo. Sligo was to be his home until he went to art school in 1886. It was a very comfortable home; a large house with servants and grooms. It was from his grandfather, William Pollexfen, that he developed his love of the sea, which was to appear in so many of his paintings. Of his many paintings, quite a large number of them drew their inspiration and subject matter from his youth in Sligo.

In 1887, Jack B. Yeats returned to London and enrolled firstly at the South Kensington Art School. He later moved to the Chiswick School of Art in Bedford Park. He attended two other schools of art, the West London School of Art and the Westminster School of Art. As soon as he began earning money from his paintings and drawings, like his siblings, Jack B. Yeats was required to contribute to the family income. He worked as an illustrator for magazines including *The Boy's Own Paper* and *Judy* for many years. He also illustrated more than 500 cartoons for *Punch* between 1910 and 1948 under the pseudonym W. Bird.

Jack B. Yeats met Mary Cottenham (Cottie) White (1869–1947), who was a fellow art student in London, and they married in 1894. After their marriage, they moved to a house in Chertsey, Surrey. By now they were both accomplished artists, Jack B. Yeats worked in watercolour and Cottie was also a fine watercolourist. Initially they lived frugally, but then Cottie received a family financial settlement for her lifetime. This enabled them to move to Strete in Devon. It was there that Jack B. Yeats worked on his collection for his first exhibition, which took place in 1897 at the Clifford Galleries in London. The exhibition consisted of his drawings and watercolours with scenes of racing, boxing, fairgrounds, children and animals. This showing was a great success and it was widely publicised in newspapers of the day. Augusta, Lady Gregory (1852–1932), who was involved in the artistic revival of the late nineteenth century in Ireland, noted this new talent. She was keen for Jack B. Yeats to become involved in the artistic revival in Ireland. He and his wife were regular visitors to Ireland, and both contributed designs to the Dun Emer Guild established in Dundrum, Dublin, by Evelyn Gleeson and the Yeats sisters in 1902. It was a hive of traditional Irish industry and was inspired by the arts and crafts movement, which was linked to the burgeoning Celtic revival.

Jack B. Yeats and Cottie seem to have had a very happy marriage, and though they had no recorded children, they appear to have had a very close relationship, which lasted until her death in Dublin in 1947. On their return to Ireland at the beginning of the twentieth century, they lived in Greystones, Co. Wicklow, but they were regular visitors to the west of Ireland, where they both continued to paint. Jack B. Yeats began to work in oils when they returned to Ireland, and his early paintings emulate the realist approach of his graphic work and concentrate on scenes of rural and urban life. He painted scenes that included Irish landscapes, horses, travelling players, fights, disputes, parades, circus giants and dwarfs, as well as scenes at race meetings and fairs. Later on, he experimented more with colour, and used larger canvases. Dr Vivien Igoe has pointed out in her *Literary Guide to Dublin*: 'In the autumn of 1917, the couple moved to 61 Marlborough Road, in Donnybrook, Dublin, which was in a less lonely area (than their previous house in Greystones) and more convenient for meeting friends.' Unlike his brother, W.B. Yeats, Jack B. became a nationalist sympathiser. He supported Éamon de Valera in the Civil War, and was sympathetic to his political views and the views of those against the 1921 Anglo–Irish Treaty between Ireland and Britain

In 1914, Jack B. Yeats was made an Associate of the Royal Hibernian Academy, and the following year he became a full academician. In 1915 he had a nervous breakdown, which lasted for two years. His paintings from this time include crowds attending sporting events at Croke Park, women singing in the street, in bars or on trains, and theatrical subjects such as men of the streets including newspaper sellers and pavement artists. At the Irish Race Congress held in Paris in 1922, Yeats gave his only lecture, 'Modern Aspects of Irish Art', which he seems to have done without naming a single artist! His brother, W.B. Yeats, gave a lecture on Anglo–Irish literature at the same conference. Delegates attending this congress were from all parts of the world where Irish people or their descendants were to be found.

Despite being a painter, Jack B. Yeats had a significant interest in the theatre and in literature. He and Samuel Beckett (1906–1989) were close friends. Yeats illustrated J.M. Synge's book, *The Aran Islands*, published in 1907, and he also wrote a number of plays for miniature theatre, a collection of short stories for children and several plays and novels that were published throughout the 1930s and '40s. His literary output includes fantasy and the colourful haphazard expressions that appear in his painting. John Masefield (1878–1967) and J.M. Synge (1871–1909) were also his close friends. His novels and plays won the admiration of James Joyce and Samuel Beckett. Three of his plays were produced at the Abbey Theatre. They were *Harlequin's Position* (1939), *La La Noo* (1942) and *In Sand* (1949). His literary output included *The Careless Flower, The Amaranthers, Ah Well, A Romance in Perpetuity, And to you Also* and *The Charmed Life*.

In 1941, through the intervention of John Betjeman (1906–1984), Jack B. Yeats held an exhibition at the National Gallery in London with William Nicholson (1872–1949). The exhibition was critically acclaimed, and it helped increase his stature in Ireland. He had a retrospective exhibition in Dublin, which saw him become a revered artistic figure. Most of the 1,100 works he painted in the latter part of his life were oil paintings. He never took in art students into his studio in Dublin, but he welcomed callers. His paintings continue to come up at art auctions from time to time, and are to be found in the Yeats Museum and in the Model Art Gallery in Sligo. There is also a Yeats collection in the National Gallery of Ireland. His works can be found in many international institutions, including the Musée d'Art Moderne, Paris, and the Museum of Art, Washington DC. When his wife died, Jack B. Yeats moved into Portobello Nursing Home, Dublin, where he died aged 86, in 1957. He is buried with his wife in Mount Jerome Cemetery, Dublin.

Further Reading

Arnold, Bruce, *Jack Yeats*, Yale University Press, New Haven, C.T., 1998.

Kennedy, Brian, *Jack Butler Yeats 1871–1957*, Town House in association with the National Gallery of Ireland, Dublin, 1991.

Pyle, Hilary, *Jack B. Yeats: A Biography*, Andre Deutch, London, 1989.

Yeats, William Butler (1865–1939)
Poet and Nobel Prize Winner
5 Sandymount Avenue, Sandymount, Dublin 4

William Butler Yeats was born on 13 June 1865 at No. 5 Sandymount Avenue, Dublin 4. He was the eldest of the family of John Butler Yeats (1839–1922) and Susan Mary Yeats (*née* Pollexfen, 1841–1900). His father was a barrister, but moved the family to London, where he became a portrait painter. Yeats spend most of his childhood in Sligo with his mother and her family, the wealthy Pollexfen merchant family. Yeats loved Sligo, and it became an integral part of his poetry all his life. W.B. was the brother of the distinguished Irish artist Jack B. Yeats. He also had two  sisters, Susan 'Lily' Yeats (1866–1949) and Elizabeth 'Lolly' Yeats (1868–1940). The two Yeats girls were involved with the Dun Emer Guild, which pioneered Irish Arts and Crafts at the turn of the century. In 1908, the sisters decided to take their part of the business and formed the Cuala Industries in nearby Churchtown. They were publishers too, founding the Cuala Press. This was unusual in that it was the only Arts and Crafts press to be run and staffed by women.

Between 1879 and 1881, the Yeats family lived in an artists' colony in Bedford Park, London. They then moved back to Dublin in 1881. Yeats's education took place in both London and Dublin, where he attended the Godolphin School in Hammersmith, and The High School, then located in Harcourt Street, Dublin. In 1883, Yeats became a student at the Metropolitan School of Art in Dublin, later the National College of Art, where he met other artists and poets. He became a friend of George Russell (AE) (1837–1935) the poet, painter and critic. AE was involved in the Dublin branch of the Theosophical Society founded by Madame Helena Petrovna Blavatsky (1831–1891), and Yeats joined it, too.

The year 1885 was a significant one in Yeats's life. He had started writing poetry and plays in 1884, and his poetry was first published in the *Dublin*

University Review in 1885. It was about this time, too, that he became interested in occultism. He had been initiated in London into the Hermetic Order of the Golden Dawn, a secret society specialising in the occult. Back in Ireland, Yeats met John O'Leary, the famous Irish patriot who was a great enthusiast for Irish literature, music and ballads, and he encouraged potential writers to write about Irish subjects. Yeats accepted his advice, and wrote many poems based on Irish legends, folklore and the country's ballads and songs.

When the Yeats family returned to London in 1887, W.B. became part of the city's literary scene. He wrote poems, plays, novels and short stories with Irish characters and Irish scenes. It was in London that Yeats met Maud Gonne (1866–1953), a beautiful young English heiress passionately devoted to Irish nationalism, with whom Yeats fell madly in love. He courted her for almost three decades and proposed marriage to her five times. Each time he was rejected, although they remained good friends. Gonne encouraged Yeats to redouble his dedication to Irish nationalism, and as a result he wrote nationalistic plays such as *Countess Kathleen* (1892), dedicated to her, and *Cathleen Ní Houlihan* (1902), which was performed on the Abbey Stage with Gonne in the title role. Like Yeats, Gonne was interested in occultism and spiritualism.

While living in London, in 1890 Yeats and Ernest Rhys founded the Rhymers Club, which met in Fleet Street. His *Wanderings of Oisin and Other Poems*, was published in 1889, and it included the well-known Irish songs 'Down by the Sally Gardens' and 'The Stolen Child'. It was in London too that Yeats met Oscar Wilde and George Bernard Shaw. Yeats was frequently homesick for Ireland, and his poem 'The Lake Isle of Innisfree' is a reflection of this.

The 1916 Easter Rising in Dublin contributed to Yeats's decision to return to Ireland. There Yeats met his friend and patron Lady Augusta Gregory (1852–1932) Irish dramatist, folklorist and theatre manager. This was the beginning of his involvement with the Irish Literary Theatre, which was founded in Dublin in 1899. One of the first productions was a play by Yeats called *On Baile's Strand*. The Irish Literary Theatre became the Abbey Theatre in 1904, and it has been a flagship for Irish plays and actors to this very day. The Abbey produced a number of Yeats's plays over the years, including *The Land of Heart's Desire* and *The King's Threshold*. Lady Gregory's home was at Coole Park near Gort, Co. Galway, and Yeats spent a great deal of time there during the summers. He loved it there, and he wrote five poems about Coole Park, including 'The Wild Swans at Coole', 'I Walked Among the Seven Woods of Coole', 'In the Seven Woods', 'Coole Park, 1929', and 'Coole Park and Ballylee, 1931'. He eventually bought a ruined Norman castle called Thoor Ballylee, near Coole Park, in about 1916, for the nominal sum of £35. Yeats and his family lived there between 1921 and 1929.

Yeats was 51 years old when he married a wealthy English lady, Georgie Hyde-Lees (1892–1968) in 1916. Earlier that year he had asked Maud Gonne's daughter, Iseult, to marry him, and she too refused. Georgie was English and was the daughter of William Gilbert Hyde, an Army officer, and Edith Ellen Woodmass. Yeats and George were married on 20 October 1917 in a registry office. Their daughter, Anne Butler Yeats, was born in 1919, and they had a son, William Michael Yeats, in 1921. Anne became a well-known painter and stage designer, and she died in Dublin in 2001. Michael Yeats was an Irish barrister and Fianna Fáil politician. He also served two periods as a member of the Irish Seanad, and he died in 2007.

In the early days of their marriage, Yeats's wife (whom he insisted on calling George instead of Georgie) discovered a capacity for automatic writing. Yeats was fascinated by this. Yeats and George held more than 400 sessions of automatic writing, which Yeats studied and organised. It was from these sessions that Yeats formulated his theories about life and history. George remained a devoted wife all her life, even though he had romantic liaisons with other women including the poet and actress Margot Ruddock (1907–1951) and the novelist and journalist Ethel Mannin (1900–1984).

When the Irish State was founded in 1922, Yeats accepted an invitation from the Government of the day to become a member of the new Irish Senate, where he served for six years. His poems during this time are 'local, general, personal and public, Irish and universal'. He retired due to ill health in 1928. He contributed from time to time on social and cultural matters in the Senate. His speech on divorce reflected his belief in personal liberty, and it aroused a great deal of controversy. Yeats was invited to chair a coinage committee charged with the selection of a set of designs for the first currency of the Irish Free State.

In 1922, Yeats was awarded the Nobel Prize in Literature 'for his always inspired poetry, which in a highly artistic form gives expression to the spirit of a whole nation'. He was now an internationally celebrated figure, and he was one of the world's most modern poets. This prize led to a big increase in the sales of his books, and this enabled him to pay off his debts and those of his father. That same year (1922) he received an honorary D.Litt from Trinity College Dublin and honorary degrees from the universities of Aberdeen (1924) and Oxford (1931). Yeats edited the *Oxford Book of Modern Verse 1892–1935*, and it was published in 1936. It consisted of all the major poems he loved. His own last two verse collections *New Poems* and *Last Poems and Two Plays* were published in 1938 and 1939.

November 1927 saw Yeats and George visit Spain and the south of France. He suffered from congestion of the lungs while on the Continent, and he convalesced at Cannes in early 1928. When Yeats recovered, he and his wife moved to Rapallo in northern Italy, where they rented an apartment, and they intended to spend the winters there in future years. In 1933, Yeats became involved in the quasi-fascist Blueshirts movement in Ireland, to which he gave his support. This was a paramilitary movement in the Irish Free State in the early 1930s.

Suffering from increasing ill health, Yeats died at the Hôtel Idéal Séjour, Cap Martin, on 28 January 1939. He was buried initially in Roquebrune-Cap-Martin, in the south of France, but he was later reinterred in Drumcliff churchyard, Sligo, in 1948. George survived him and died on 23 August 1968. She is also buried with her husband of twenty-two years at Drumcliff churchyard. Yeats's papers are in several libraries in Ireland, Britain and the United States, and there are statues in Sligo town and in St Stephen's Green, Dublin. Several Irish and English artists painted his portrait, including Augustus John, John Singer Sargent and his father, John Butler Yeats.

Further Reading

Donoghue, Denis, *Yeats*, Fontaine, London, 1971.

Foster, R.F., *W.B. Yeats: A Life*, Oxford University Press, Oxford, 1997–2003.

Yeats, W.B., *The Autobiography of William Butler Yeats*, Macmillan, New York, 1987.

Select Bibliography

Archer, Joseph, *Statistical Survey of the County of Dublin*, Dublin Society, Dublin, 1801.

Arnold, Bruce, *Jack Yeats*, Yale University Press, Yale, 1998.

Ball, F.E., *A History of County Dublin*, Alex Thom, Dublin, 1903.

Ball, F.E., *Historical Sketch of Pembroke Township*, Alex Thom, Dublin, 1907.

Behan, Beatrice, *My life with Brendan*, Frewin, London, 1973.

Behan, Brendan, *Hold Your Hour and Have Another*, Hutchinson, London, 1963.

Bennett, D., *Encyclopaedia of Dublin*, Gill & Macmillan, Dublin, 1991.

Blacker, Rev. Beaver H., *Brief Sketches of the Parishes of Booterstown & Donnybrook in the County of Dublin*, Herbert, Dublin, 1874.

Boyd, G., *Dublin 1745–1922*, Four Courts Press, Dublin, 2006.

Boylan, Henry, *Dictionary of Irish Biography*, Barnes & Noble, New York, 1998.

Boylan, Patricia, *All Cultivated People*, Colin Smythe, Dublin, 1988.

Brady, J. and Simms, A., *Dublin through Space and Time*, Four Courts Press, Dublin, 2007.

Broderick, Marian, *Bold, Brilliant and Bad*, O'Brien Press, Dublin, 2018.

Broderick, Marian, *Wild Irish Women*, O'Brien Press, Dublin, 2016.

Burke, Sir Bernard, *A Genealogical and Heraldic History of the Landed Gentry in Ireland*, Harrison, Pall Mall, London, 1871.

Burke, Sir Bernard, *Burke's Landed Gentry of Ireland*, Burke's Peerage, London, 1899.

Burke, Helen, *The People and the Poor Law in Nineteenth Century Ireland*, Women's Education Bureau, Dublin, 1987.

Byrne, P.E., 'Anthony Trollope in Ireland', *Dublin Historical Record* (2), 1992, pp.126–128.

City of Dublin VEC, *The Old Township of Pembroke*, VEC, Dublin, 2011.

Clark, Mary, *Eminent Images; The Dublin Civic Portrait Collection*, Dublin City Council, Dublin, 2009.

Clark, Mary, 'The Municipal Archives of Dublin'. *Irish Archives Bulletin*, ii, 1981, pp.12–17.

Clarke, Desmond, *Dublin*, Batsford, London, 1977.

Cooke, J., 'John Boyd Dunlop 1840–1921', *Dublin Historical Record*, 49 (1), 1966, pp.16–31.

Colum, Mary, *Life and the Dream*, Macmillan, London, 1947.

Corkery, Tom, *Dublin*, Anvil Books, Dublin, 1980.

Cosgrove, Art, *Dublin through the Ages*, College Press, Dublin, 1988.

Costello, Peter, *The Dublin Literary Pub Crawl*, A & A Farmer, Dublin, 1966.

Costello, Peter, *T he Irish 100*, Citadel Press, New York, 2001.

Cowell, John, *Where they Lived in Dublin*, O'Brien Press, Dublin, 1980.

Craig, Maurice, *Dublin 1660–1860*, Allen Figgis, Dublin, 1980.

Crean, Cyril P., *Parish of the Sacred Heart, Donnybrook*, Drought, Dublin, 1966.

Crone, J., *Concise Dictionary of Irish Biography*, Talbot Press, Dublin, 1937.

Curtis, J., *Times, Chimes and Charms of Dublin*, Verge Books, Dublin, 1992.

Curtis, J., *Ringsend*, The History Press, Dublin, 2012.

Curtis, J., *Mount Merrion*, The History Press, Dublin, 2017.

D'Alton, J., *The History of County Dublin*, Dublin Hodges, 1838.

Daly, Mary E., *Dublin: the Deposed Capital*, Cork University Press, Cork, 1984.

De Burca, Seamus, *Brendan Behan: a memoir*, Proscenium Press, Newark, 1971

Dickson, David, *The Gorgeous Mask. Dublin 1700–1850*, Dublin History Workshop, Dublin, 1987.

Doran, Beatrice, *Donnybrook: A History*, The History Press, Dublin, 2013.

Doran, Beatrice, *Donnybrook Then & Now*, The History Press, Dublin, 2014.

Fagan, P., *Dublin: The Second City*, Branar, Dublin, 1986.

Farmer, Tony, *Privileged Lives: A Social History of Middle-Class Ireland 1882–1989*, A & A Farmer, Dublin, 2010.

Farmer, Tony, *Ordinary Lives*, 2nd edition, A & A Farmer, Dublin, 1999.

Fallis, Richard, *The Irish Renaissance*, Gill & Macmillan, Dublin, 1978.

Fleischman, Aloys ed., *Music in Ireland*, Cork University Press, Cork, 1952.

Finlay, K., *Dublin Day by Day*, Nonesuch Publications, Dublin, 2005.

Finlay, K., *Dublin 4*, Cottage Publications, Donaghadee, 2006.

Foster, R.F., *W.B. Yeats: A Life*, Oxford University Press, Oxford, 1997.

Gilbert, Sir J.T., *A History of the City of Dublin*, McGlashan, Dublin, 1854.

Gogarty, Oliver St J., *As I Was Going Down Sackville Street*, Sphere, London, 1988.

Gonne, Maud, *A Servant of the Queen*, Gollanz, London, 1974.

Gray, Tony, *Mr Smyllie, Sir*, Gill & Macmillan, Dublin, 1991.

Harvey, John, *Dublin: A Study in Environment*, Batsford, London, 1949.

Healy, Elizabeth, *Literary Tour of Ireland*, Wolfhound Press, Dublin, 1995.

Hill, Jacqueline, *From Patriots to Unionists*, Oxford University Press, Oxford, 1997.

Hoppen, K. Theodore, *Ireland since 1800*, Longman, London, 1989.

Horton, Charles, *Sir Alfred Chester Beatty*, Town House, Dublin, 2003.

Hughes, Andrew, *Lives Less Ordinary*, Liffey Press, Dublin, 2011.

Igoe, Vivien, *A Literary Guide to Dublin*, Methuen, London, 1994.

Igoe, Vivien, *Dublin Burial Grounds & Graveyards*, Wolfhound Press, Dublin, 2001.

Igoe, Vivien, *The Real People in James Joyce's Ulysses*, UCD Press, Dublin, 2016.

Irish Civil Registration Indexes 1845–1958.

James, Dermot, *From the Margins to the Centre: A History of The Irish Times*, The Woodfield Press, Dublin, 2008.

Jeffares, A., Norman, *A Short History of Irish Writers*, O'Brien Press, Dublin, 2014.

Jeffs, Rae, *Brendan Behan: Man and Showman*, Hutchinson, London, 1966.

Joyce, W. St John, *The Neighbourhood of Dublin*, Gill, Dublin, 1939.

Kain, Richard M., *Susan L. Mitchell*, Bucknell University Press, Lewisburg, 1972.

Kavanagh, Patrick, *The Green Fool*, Martin Brian & O'Keeffe, London, 1971.

Kavanagh, Patrick, *Self-Portrait*, Dolmen Press, Dublin, 1964.

Kavanagh, Peter, *Sacred Keeper*, Goldsmith Press, Curragh, 1979.

Kearney, Colbert, *The Writings of Brendan Behan*, Gill & Macmillan, Dublin, 1977.

Kelly, Deirdre, *Four Roads to Dublin*, O'Brien Press, Dublin, 1995.

Kennard, Nina H., *Lafcadio Hearn*, Appleton, New York, 1912.

Kennedy, Tom (ed.), *Victorian Dublin*, Albertine Kennedy with the Dublin Arts Festival, Dublin, 1980.

Kiely, Benedict, *The Waves Behind Us*, Methuen, London, 1999.

Kullmann, Kurt, *The Four Sisters: Ringsend, Irishtown, Sandymount, & Merrion*, The History Press, Dublin, 2017.

Kullmann, Kurt, *The Little Book of Sandymount*, The History Press, Dublin, 2016.

Lee, J.J., *The Modernisation of Irish Society*, Gill & Macmillan, Dublin, 1973.

Lalor, Brian ed., *The Encyclopaedia of Ireland*, Gill and Macmillan, Dublin, 2003.

Lennon, Sean, *Dublin Writers and their Haunts*, Fingal, Dublin, 2003.

Levenson, Leah, *The Four Seasons of Mary Lavin*, Marino Books, Dublin, 1998.

Lewis, Samuel, *A Topographical Dictionary of Ireland*, 2 vols, S. Lewis & Co., London, 1837.

Lynch, Brendan, *Parson's Bookshop*, Liffey Press, Dublin, 2006.

Lynch, Brendan, *Prodigals and Geniuses*, Liffey Press, Dublin, 2011.

Lyons, J.B., *The Enigma of Tom Kettle*, Glendale Press, Dublin, 1983.

Lyons, J.B., *An Assembly of Irish Surgeons*, Glendale Press, Dublin, 1984.

Lysaght, Charles, *Great Irish Lives*, Times Books, London, 2016.

MacCurtain, Margaret, *Ariadne's Thread: Writing Women into Irish History*, Arlen House, Galway, 2009.

MacDona, Anne, *From Newman to New Women*, New Island, Dublin, 2001.

McCoole. Sinéad, *No Ordinary Women*, O'Brien Press, Dublin, 2015.

McGuire, James and Quinn, James, eds, *Dictionary of Irish Biography*, Cambridge University Press and Royal Irish Academy, in progress.

McManus, Ruth, *Crampton Built*, G & T. Crampton, Dublin, 2008.

McManus, Ruth, *Dublin 1910–1940: Shaping the City & Suburbs*, Four Courts Press, Dublin, 2002.

Martin, F.X. and Byrne, F.J., *The Scholar Revolutionary: Eóin MacNeill, 1867–1945*, Barnes & Noble, New York, 1973.

Maxwell, Constantia, *Dublin Under the Georges*, Harrap, London, 1946.

Miller, Liam, *Retrospect: The Work of Seumas O'Sullivan and Estela F. Solomons*, Dolmen Press, Dublin, 1973.

Mollan, Charles et al., *Irish Innovators in Science and Technology*, Royal Irish Academy, Dublin, 2002.

Murphy, W.M., *Prodigal Father: Life of John Butler Yeats*, Cornell U.P., Ithaca, 1978.

O'Cleirigh, Nellie, *Hardship and High Living: Irish Women's Lives 1808–1923*, Portobello Press, Dublin, 2003.

O Ceirin, Kit and O Ceirin, Cyril, *Women of Ireland: A Biographical Dictionary*, Tir Eolas, Kinvara, 1996.

O'Connor, Ulick, *Brendan Behan*, Hamish Hamilton, London, 1970.

O Maitiu, Seamus, *Dublin's Suburban Towns 1834–1930*, Four Courts Press, Dublin, 2003.

Oram, Hugh, *Dublin: The Complete Guide*, Appletree Press, Belfast, 1995.

Oram, Hugh, *Leeson Street Upper & Lower*, Trafford Publishing, Dublin, 2018.

Oram, Hugh, *The Little Book of Ballsbridge*, The History Press, Dublin, 2014.

Oram Hugh, *The Little Book of Merrion and Booterstown*, The History Press, Dublin, 2018.

Oram, Hugh, *Sandymount*, The History Press, Dublin, 2016.

Oxford Dictionary of National Biography, Oxford University Press, Oxford, in progress.

Parkinson, Danny, *Donnybrook Graveyard*, Family History Society, Dublin, 1988.

Pearson, Peter, *Between the Mountains and the Sea*, O'Brien Press, Dublin, 1999.

Pearson, Peter, *The Heart of Dublin*, O'Brien Press, Dublin, 2000.

Pyle, H. and Solomons, E., *Portraits of Patriots*, Allen Figgis, Dublin, 1966.

Ryan, Louise and Ward, Margaret eds, *Irish Women and Nationalism*, Irish Academic Press, Dublin, 2004.

Share, Bernard and Bolger, William, *Irish Lives*, Allen & Figgis, Dublin, 1974.

Slevin, Fiona ed., *Cherishing our Heritage, Preserving Community*, Upper Leeson Street Residents Association, Dublin, 2018.

Somerville Large, Peter, *Dublin*, Hamish Hamilton, London, 1979.

Starkie, Enid, *A Lady's Child*, Faber & Faber, London, 1941.

Starkie, Walter, *Scholars and Gypsies*, Univ. of California Press, Berkeley, 1963.

Strickland, Walter G., *A Dictionary of Irish Artists*, Maunsel, Dublin, 1913.

Thom's Official Directory of the United Kingdom of Gt. Britain & Ireland, Alex. Thom & Co., Dublin, Published annually.

Vaughan, W.F. ed., *The A New History of Ireland*, vol. vi. *Ireland under the Union*, Oxford University Press, Oxford, 2010.

Walsh, Ged, *On the Banks of the Dodder*, O'Brien Press, Dublin, 2019.

Webb, Alfred, *A Compendium of Irish Biography*, Gill & Son, Dublin, 1878.

Weston Joyce, John, *The Neighbourhood of Dublin*, Gill & Macmillan, Dublin, 1976.

Wright G., *An Historical Guide to the City of Dublin*, Baldwin et al., London, 1825.

Newspapers
Dublin Builder
Dublin Penny Journal
The Freeman's Journal
Irish Builder
Irish Independent Irish Newspaper Archive
Irish Press
Irish Times Digital Archive

Journals
Dublin Historical Record
History Ireland
Irish Historical Studies
Journal of the Cork Historical and Archaeological Society
Journal of the Royal Society of Antiquaries of Ireland
Local History Review
Obelisk
Royal Irish Academy Proceedings
Royal Dublin Society Proceedings
Saothar

Websites
British Newspaper Archive
Bureau of Military History
Dictionary of Irish Architects
Dublin Forums
Irish Newspaper Archive
Irish Volunteers
National Archives
National Library of Ireland
Sources Database.

Index

Abbey Theatre 68, 122, 147, 162, 193, 210, 229, 231
Academie Collarossi, Paris 210, 229
Academie Julien, Paris 231
Achill Island 164–5
Adelaide Road 143
AE see Russell, George
Aer Lingus 185–6, 106
Aikenhead, Mother Mary 14–6
Alexandra College 59, 94, 202, 206
Ailesbury Road 29, 49, 82, 111
Ancient Order of Hibernians 224
An Claideamh Soluis 157,170,174,179
An Taisce 96
An Tur Gloine 187–8
Anglesea Road 167
Anglo Irish Treaty 77, 108, 151, 158, 168, 171, 177, 225, 228
Aosdana 136, 145
Apothecaries Hall, Dublin 55, 116–7
Arbour Hill Military Cemetery 34, 185
Armstrong, Reginald (Reg) 17–20
Architectural Association of Ireland 92
Ashford, William 21
Association of Women's Voluntary Groups 51

BBC 148
Barry Spranger 24–6
Beatty, Sir Alfred Chester 27–30
Beckett, Samuel 194, 210, 228–9
Behan, Blanaid 32, 35
Behan, Beatrice 31–3, 35, 195
Behan, Brendan 31–3, 34–6, 142,147
Behan, Brian 34
Behan, Dominic 34
Behan, Kathleen 34
Behan, Paudge 32
Behan, Stephen 34
Bell, The 121,141, 194
Belleek Porcelain 57
Bellaghy, Co. Derry 99–100
Belmont Avenue, Donnybrook 66
Benedict Kiely Literary Weekend 136
Bernelle, Agnes 37–9
Best, Richard Irvine 40–2
Blackrock College 75–6, 80, 83,152
Blavatsky, Madame Helena Petrovna 230
Blythe, Ernest 80
Boland, Harry 76
Bord Na gCapall 129
Boundary Commission 158
Batt O'Connor 167–8
Breslau, Louise 186
Brookvale Road, Donnybrook 52–4

Briscoe, Ben 43
Briscoe, Robert 43–5
Browne, Garech 148
Browne, Dr. Noel 50, 72–3, 201
Bryant, Sophie 46–8
Bryant, Dr William Hicks 45
Burnand, Madge 213
Buss, Frances Mary 46
Butler, Eleanor, Lady Wicklow
    49–51
Byrne, Frankie 52–4

Cameron, Sir Charles 55–8
Casement, Sir Roger 66, 107,
    167,174, 184
Catholic Truth Society 141
Censorship of Publications 135, 141,
    142, 195
Centre for Peace and Reconciliation
    50
Central Bank of Ireland 221
Chester Beatty Library 27–9
Cheshire Homes 50–1
Church of Ireland (RCB) 92
Civil War 77, 108, 111–2, 158, 171,
    175, 203–4, 224–5, 228
Clan na Gael 170, 184
Clann na Poblachta 112, 142
Clarke, Kathleen 150
Clarke, Thomas 150, 157, 167,
    181–2
Clongowes Wood College 131
Clyde Road 144
Coghill, Rhoda 59–61
Colgan, Pat 139
Collisson Dr. Houston 89
Confederation of Irish Industry 153
Coole Park 231
Colles, Abraham 62–4
Collins, Michael 44, 76–7, 80, 158,
    167–8 171, 185, 224
Colum, Mary Catherine 65–7,
    69–70

Colum, Padraic 66–70, 131, 161–2,
    180, 184, 193, 203
Confederation of Irish Industries
    153
Conradh na Gaeilge 157
Co-operation North 50–1
Cora, Leonie 206, Coras Trachtala
    72, 153
Cork 14, 15
Cosgrave Liam 86
Cosgrave, W.T. 72, 112, 168
Costello, John A 50, 71, 74, 77–8,
    121
Craig, Dr. Maurice 39
Crow Street Theatre 25–6
Cuala Press 161, 230
Cumann Na mBan 65, 80, 95,
    110–1, 112, 175, 193, 203, 224,
    225
Cumann na nGaedheal 72, 168–9
Curragh 34, 149

Dail Eireann 76–7, 169, 171
Daly, Emily 90
Despard, Charlotte 151, 224–5
De Valera, Eamon 43–4, 45, 72–3,
    75–8, 80–1, 171–2, 177–8, 219,
    225, 228
De Valera, Sinead 76, 78–81
Diageo 189–90, 192
Doctor Steevens Hospital 62, 64
Drumcliff Churchyard 233
Dublin Air Ferries Ltd 106
Dublin Corporation 56–7, 44, 96,
    168, 170
Dublin Institute for Advanced
    Studies 41
Dublin Lockout 132, 138, 184
Dublin Magazine 95, 120, 143, 194,
    204–5
Dublin Metropolitan School of Art
    113, 203
Dublin United Tramways 138, 152

Du Cros, Harvey 83
Dublin United Tramways 138, 152
Duffy, Louise Gavan 110, 224
Dun Emer Guild 228, 230
Dunlop, John Boyd 82–4
Dunlop Tyres 82–3
Dunsany Lord 143–4

Easter Rising 1916 80, 85, 108, 110,
   132, 150, 157–8, 161, 170–1,
   174–75, 177, 181–2, 185
Eblana Bookshop 129
Economic & Social Research
   Institute 221
Edinburgh University 63
Edward VII, Ki 206–7
Eglinton Road 87, 91, 93, 149, 167
Eglinton Terrace 223
Emergency 141, 151
Endurance, The 198
Envoy 121
European Union 87, 220–1
External Relations Act (1935) 72, 77

Father Mathew Record 134
Federation of Irish Manufacturers
   153
Feis Ceol 42, 60, 146
Fianna Eireann 44
Fianna Fail 44, 72–3, 77–8, 86–7,
   171–2, 177–8, 219–20
Finance, Department of 219–221
Fine Gael 72–3, 77–8
First World War 132–3, 190
Fitzgerald, Garret 73, 85–7, 221
Fleishmann, Prof. Aloys 147
Foyle, Derry 40
French, William Percy 88–90
Freemasons 57, 216
Freemans Journal, The 107–9, 161,
   223
Friends of the National Collections
   187

Fuller, James Franklin 91–3

Gaelic League 68, 79–81, 157, 167,
   170, 174, 179, 194
Gate Theatre 141, 194, 210
Gaiety Theatre, 38
Gandon, James 22–3
Garrick, David 24, 25
Gayfield Press 194–5
George's Villas, Sandymount 176
Gifford, Grace 184–5
Gilford Place 145
Glasnevin Cemetery 36
Goodfellow, Kathleen 94–6, 203–4
Good Friday Agreement 87
Goulding, Cathal 32
Gray, Sir John 107
Great Famine 117, 164–5, 190
Great Industrial Exhibition (1853)
   190
Gregory, Lady 65, 160, 187, 210,
   231
Griffith, Arthur 68, 77, 150, 153,
   171, 184, 203
Grove, The 96, 204
Gilford Place, Sandymount 143, 145
Guinness Brewery 189–190
Guinness Peat Aviation 87
Gurdjieff, George 213

Harmony Cottage 152
Harvard University 99
Haughey, Charles J. 85–6, 129, 145
Heaney, Marie 97–8
Heaney, Seamus 97–100
Hearn, Lafcadio 101–3
Heath, Sir James 105–6
Heath, Mary, Lady 104–6
Hempel, Dr. Eduard 151
Herbert Park 43, 71, 159, 173
Hobson Bulmer 174
Hollins College, West Virginia 135,
   208

Home Rule 47, 131, 132
Hooper, Patrick Joseph 107–9
Houston, David 66, 69
Hugh Lane Municipal Gallery 187
Hughes Hall, Cambridge 47
Humphreys, Nell 173
Humphreys, Sighle 110–2
Hyde, Dr. Douglas 95–6, 159, 162, 180, 194
Hyde–Lees, George 232

Igoe, Dr Vivien 228
Indian-Ireland Independence League 225
Industrial Development Authority 72, 153
Inghinidhe Na hEireann 65, 79–80, 150
Irish Academy of Letters 136, 145, 195, 207
Irish Agricultural Society 161
Irish Architectural Records Society 49
Irish Countrywomen's Association 51, 161
Irish Ecclesiastical Commissioners 92
Irish Distillers 154
Irish Ecclesiastical Record 157
Irish Flying Club 106
Irish Historical Society 159
Irish Homestead 161
Irish Independent 108, 121, 125, 134
Irish Jewish Museum 205
Irish Journal of Medical Science 116
Irish Literary Review 61, 65, 162
Irish Literary Society 48, 224
Irish Literary Theatre 187, 231
Irish Manuscripts Commission 41, 59
Irish Parliamentary Party 131–2, 224
Irish Peace Park (Messines) 133
Irish Press 121, 135

Irish Rugby Football Union 124
Irish Republican Army (IRA) 68, 73, 76–7, 111, 224–5
Irish Republican Brotherhood 167, 170, 174, 181, 184–5
Irish Review 66, 184
Irish Statesman 120, 161, 213
Irish Times 121, 136, 140, 195, 199–20, 208
Irish Transport & General Workers Union 137, 139
Irish Volunteers 76, 110, 132, 157–8, 167, 171–2, 174–5, 181, 184, 224
Irish Women Workers Union 137

Jabotinsky, Vladimir 44
Jacobs Biscuit Factory 38
Jacob's TV & Radio Awards 53
Japan 102–3
Jones, Sir Thomas Alfred 113–115
Joyce, James 42, 65–9, 70, 109, 131

Kane, Sir Robert 116–9, 191
Kaolin 57
Kavanagh, Patrick 35, 73–4, 97, 120–2, 136 194
Kavanagh, Peter 121
Kearney, Peadar 34
Kelleher, Kevin D. 123–6
Kennedy, John F. 52
Kettle, Thomas 131–3, 184
Kellett, Iris 128–130
Kildonan Aerodrome, Finglas 106
Kiely, Benedict 34–6

Labour Party 50
Lad Lane, Upper 144
Lane, Sir Hugh 161, 187–8
Larchet, Prof. John 147
Larkin, Denis 50
Larkin, James 137–8, 139
Laverty, Maura 140–2
Lavin, Mary 143–5

Leeson Park 152
Leeson Street, Upper 96, 101, 103, 131, 159
Leinster School of Music 59
Lemass, Sean 77, 154, 221
Leslie, Desmond 38–9
Liberty Hall 137–8, 139
Linden Home 78, 81, 178
London University 46–7
Loreto Abbey Rathfarnham 52
Lynch, Jack 221

McBride, Major John 150–1
McBride, Maud Gonne, 149–151, 180, 187, 224–5, 231
McBride, Sean 142, 150–1
McClintock, Jean 84
McCourt, Kevin 152–5
MacDermott, Sean 157, 167, 181, 185
MacDonagh, Thomas 65–6, 69, 180–2 183–4, 193–4
McHale, Archbishop John 164
McLoughlin, Valerie 54
MacNeill, Eoin 41, 156–9, 181, 185
McQuaid, Archbishop J.C .72, 80, 121, 152, 201
Magan, Croine 112
Marlborough Road 39, 59, 61, 100, 146, 183
Martyn, Edward 187
May, Frederick (Freddie) 146–8
Meade, Colin 124–5
Meath Hospital 36, 63, 116, 190
Melfort, Shrewsbury Road 206, 209
Mellows, Liam 224–5
Mespil Road 127, 129, 168, 188
Millevoye, Lucien 149–150
Military Museum, Curragh Camp 29
Mitchell, Susan Langstaff 160–2
Moneylenders Act (1933) 44
Moore, George 166, 187
Moral Rearmament 50

Morehampton Road 94, 109, 113, 119, 134, 202, 204, 223
Morehampton Terrace 75
Motor Cycle racing *see* Reg Armstrong
Mount Anville School 110
Mount Jerome 64, 93, 115, 130, 148, 188, 192
Mountjoy Gaol 34
Mulcahy, General Richard 73
Murphy, William Martin 108
Music Association of Ireland 148

Nangle, Edward 163–166
National Antarctic Exhibition 196
National College of Art & Design 113, 230
National Gallery London 229
National Gallery of Ireland 29, 94, 188, 205, 229
National Library of Ireland 40–1, 100, 136, 144, 161, 170
National Literary Society 161
National Museum of Ireland 31
National University of Ireland 136, 158, 221
Nobel Prize Winners 99, 232
North London Collegiate School 46, 48
Northern Ireland 12, 73, 77, 98, 221
Nutley House 191

O'Connell, Daniel 190–1
O'Connor, Batt 110–1, 167–9, 224
O'Donoghue, Donal 112
O'Dowda, Brendan 90
O'Duffy General Eoin 73
Old Time Fellowship of Cyclists 84
Oldham, Edith 42
Olympic Games 104, 128 170–2, 203
O'Malley, Ernie 111, 168, 203
O'Rahilly Anno 110, 173

O'Rahilly, Michael J. 110, 173–5
O'Rahilly, Nancy 175
Osborne, Walter 202
O'Sullivan, Seumas 61, 94, 95, 136,
    204, 205
Oxford University 99. 206–8

Palace Bar 136
Parson's Bookshop 121
Pearse, Mary Bridget 177, 180
Pearse, Margaret Mary 176–7, 180
Pearse, Padraig 131, 157–8, 170,
    174, 176–7, 179–82, 184–5,
    193
Peirce-Evans, Sophie see Mary, Lady
    Heath
Pembroke Park 200
Pembroke Road 142
Philosophical Magazine 117
Pyle, Hilary 203
Plunkett, George Noble, Count 193,
    203
Plunkett, Joseph M. 181, 183
Purser, Sarah 149, 160, 186–8

Quakers *see* Society of Friends
Queen's College Cork 118
Queen's University, Belfast 85, 97–8,
    99

Radio Eireann 52–35, 59–60, 13
Raglan Road 57
Religious Sisters of Charity 15
Ringsend Road 19
Roe, Alderman George 189–192
Roselyn Park, Sandymount 23
Royal College of Music, London 146
Royal College of Physicians of
    Ireland 55, 117
Royal College of Science in Ireland
    17, 118
Royal College of Surgeons in Ireland

55–6, 62
Royal Dublin Society 116, 117,
    127–9, 147, 190, 191
Royal Geographical Society 197
Royal Hibernian Academy 31, 88,
    112–14, 186–7, 204, 228
Royal Institute of Architects in
    Ireland 49
Royal Irish Academy 41, 116, 118,
    159, 221
Royal Irish Academy of Music 115,
    146–7, 206, 209
Royal Scottish Geographical Society
    197
Royal Society, London 117
Royal Society of Antiquaries of
    Ireland 93, 159
Royal University of Ireland 47
RTE Radio & Television 148–154
Russell, George (*AE*) 42, 65, 69,
    120, 150, 161–2, 193–4, 204,
    213–4, 230
Ryan, John 95, 121

St Conleth's College, Dublin 123–6
St Enda's College 110, 170, 176–9,
    180
St Ita's School, Ranelagh 65–6
St Vincent's Hospital 16
Salkeld, Blanaid 31, 35, 193–5
Saor Eire 111
Scott, Michael McDonald 143, 145
Scott, Robert Falcon 196–7
Seaview Terrace 215–7
Second Reformation 163–4
Semple, John 217
Shackleton, Sir Ernest 196–8
Shaw, George Bernard 136, 187,
    195, 207
Shepherd, Ann 124, 125
Shepherd, Bernard 124, 125
Shrewsbury Road 29

Sinn Fein 45, 76, 108, 112, 158, 168–9, 170, 184, 193
Sisters of Charity 15
Smyllie, Robert M. 199–201
Society of Friends 61, 63
Solomons, Estella 94–95, 96, 202–5
South Pole, The 196–8
Standard, The 162, 203
Starkie, Enid 206–8
Starkie Walter 206, 209–11
Stephens, James 162, 203
Stone, Edith 25, 29
Strickland, Walter 115
Stuart Iseult 150–1, 232
Suffragism 47
Synge, J.M. 42, 65–6, 229
Synod of Thurles (1850) 118

Taisce, An 96, 204
Theatre Royal, Cork 25
Theatre Royal, Dublin 24
Thomas Street Distillery 189
Travers, P.L. (Pamela Lyndon) 212–4
Trinity College Dublin 32, 62, 63, 86, 88, 113, 116, 118, 146, 160, 163, 206, 209–10, 211
Trollope, Anthony 215–6
Tynan, Katharine 90, 160

United Distillers of Ireland 154
United Irish League 131–2
University College Dublin 65, 68, 70–1 85–6, 104, 122–3, 131–3, 143, 145, 156, 159, 173, 180, 188
Archives Department 112, 122, 133
University of Limerick 129

Victoria, Queen 150, 1913, 144

Walsh, Archbishop William 138, 171
War of Independence 76–7, 111, 151, 203, 225
Waterloo Road 122, 203
Weil, Kurt 38
Wellington Road 41, 118, 137, 160
Whitaker, Thomas Kenneth 219–222
Wicklow, Lady see Butler, Eleanor
Woods, Andrew 223–5
Woods, Mary (Molly) 223–6
Women's Amateur Athletic Association 104
Workers Union of Ireland (WUI) *139*

Yeats, Anne Butler 232
Yeats, Elizabeth 230
Yeats, Jack Butler 187, 203, 227–9
Yeats, John Butler 160, 161, 187, 193, 227, 230, 233
Yeats, Lily (Susan) 160, 230
Yeats, Michael 86, 23
Yeats, William Butler 65, 66, 68, 70, 136, 149, 150, 161, 180, 187, 193, 195, 207, 210, 230–3